RECORDS OF WOMAN
WITH OTHER POEMS

RECORDS OF WOMAN
WITH OTHER POEMS

Felicia Hemans

‹   ›

Edited by
Paula R. Feldman

THE UNIVERSITY PRESS OF KENTUCKY

Publication of this volume was made possible
in part by a grant from the National Endowment for the Humanities.

Scholarly publisher for the Commonwealth,
serving Bellarmine College, Berea College, Centre
College of Kentucky, Eastern Kentucky University,
The Filson Club Historical Society, Georgetown College,
Kentucky Historical Society, Kentucky State University,
Morehead State University, Murray State University,
Northern Kentucky University, Transylvania University,
University of Kentucky, University of Louisville,
and Western Kentucky University.
All rights reserved.

Editorial and Sales Offices: The University Press of Kentucky
663 South Limestone Street, Lexington, Kentucky 40508–4008

03 02 01 00 99   5 4 3 2 1

Library of Congress Cataloging-in-Publication Data

Hemans, Felicia Dorothea Browne, 1793-1835
    Records of woman, with other poems / by Felicia Hemans ; edited
by Paula R. Feldman.
        p.   cm.
    ISBN 0-8131-0964-7 (paper : alk. paper)
    1. Women—Poetry. I. Feldman, Paula R. II. Title.
PR4780.R43   1999
821'.7—dc21   99-18327

This book is printed on acid-free recycled paper
meeting the requirements of the American National Standard
for Permanence of Paper for Printed Library Materials.

Manufactured in the United States of America

CONTENTS

ILLUSTRATIONS

Acknowledgments

I am deeply grateful to Stuart Curran and Susan Wolfson, who generously offered valuable insights and made important suggestions for revision.

My warm thanks also go to scholars and friends whose correspondence, advice, conversation, and support have been invaluable: Dan Albergotti, Catherine Castner, Glen T. Dibert-Himes, Sandra Gilbert, Kurt Goblirsch, Jim Hardin, Nicholas Jones, Gerda Jordan, Gary Kelly, Jerome McGann, Anne Mellor, Lucille Mould, Robert Newman, Tonya Wertz-Orbaugh, Faust Paluzzi, Margit Resch, Laurence Rhu, Daniel Riess, Daniel Robinson, Christa Sammons, John Shawcross, Judy Sullivan, W. Strehl, Nanora Sweet, and Duncan Wu. For research assistance, I am grateful to Thomas Anessi, Brian Cooney, Beth Diehls, Sharice Fair, Anne Goebel, Matt Hanley, Lee Anna Maynard, Lucy Morrison, Amanda Pettit, Todd Richardson, Staci Stone, C.S. Tucker, and Claire Wilson. The reference and interlibrary loan staffs of the Thomas Cooper Library at the University of South Carolina helped me to obtain necessary research materials; the Department of English provided clerical assistance, postage, and supplies. Finally, I would like to thank my students, whose enthusiasm for the poetry of Felicia Hemans led me to see the need for a complete, paperback edition of *Records of Woman: With Other Poems*.

*This book is edited
in memory of Maggie Adams.*

INTRODUCTION

Felicia Hemans was one of the most influential and widely read poets of the nineteenth century. *Records of Woman*, published in 1828, was her best-known book. It is of special interest to readers today not only for its remarkable lyricism and exploration of psychological states but also for the way in which it both engages and paradoxically defies stereotypical nineteenth-century views about the character, history, and emotional resources of women. The most personal of Hemans's books also struck a particularly responsive chord with the reading public of her time, both in Britain and in America. Hemans sold more copies of *Records of Woman* than any of her other books. When she died in 1835, many of her poems had already acquired the stature of standard English lyrics, including "The Homes of England" and "The Graves of a Household" from this volume.[1]

Hemans's poetry was admired by Lord Byron, Percy Bysshe Shelley, Marian Evans (George Eliot), Matthew Arnold, Lady Morgan, and countless other writers and literary critics of discerning taste. While Walter Scott, William Wordsworth, and Francis Jeffrey expressed some reservations about her style, each regarded her as a major poet. Her work was reviewed in some of the leading journals of her day, and she influenced authors as diverse as Elizabeth Barrett Browning, Henry Wadsworth Longfellow, and Alfred, Lord Tennyson.[2] Many aspiring writers imitated her style, including Lydia Sigourney, who came to be known as "The American Hemans." Of Hemans's contemporaries who are well-known today, only Lord Byron and Walter Scott sold more books than she in their lifetimes, and she was as respected, influential, and popular in the United States as in Britain.[3] Newspaper, magazine, and book publishers throughout the English-speaking world reprinted

Hemans's work for a clamoring public, often without permission. After her poetry went out of copyright in England in the 1870s, dozens more publishers brought out collected editions, sometimes in multivolume sets. Hemans's poetry was even more widely read in the Victorian era than in the Romantic. For nearly a century after it was first written, her work continued to be widely reprinted, anthologized, illustrated, quoted, sung, and memorized by countless school children. In 1914 Oxford University Press published a volume of her collected works in its Standard Authors series, just as in 1912 Ward, Lock and Company included her writing in its Great Poets book series.

Not until World War I did Hemans's work go out of print. Even then, "Casabianca" (best known by its first line, "The boy stood on the burning deck") continued for decades to be a school recitation piece and thus a favorite subject for tasteless parody. The sensibility of most romantic-era poems came to be seen as naive, melodramatic, old-fashioned, and embarrassingly sentimental. In the 1940s and 1950s, however, literary critics and academics began to rediscover and to revive much work by British romantic writers, though only the reputations of selected male poets were restored. By the 1960s, five writers constituted the poetic canon of the romantic era: William Wordsworth, Samuel Taylor Coleridge, Lord Byron, Percy Bysshe Shelley, and John Keats. The women poets of the era and their rich artistic legacy continued to be ignored, in literary histories as well as in anthologies and textbooks. Neglect rather than conspiracy kept Hemans and her female contemporaries out of view. No one stepped forward to advance their cause—as Newman Ivey White did for Percy Bysshe Shelley in the 1940s and Geoffrey Keynes did for William Blake in the 1960s. In the absence of sufficient curiosity and advocacy in the academy, the silence remained unbroken.

But in the 1990s, Hemans has garnered increasing interest from such respected scholars as Norma Clarke, Anthony Harding, Tricia Lootens, Jerome McGann, Nanora Sweet, Peter Trinder, Susan Wolfson, and others. Selections of her works have appeared in anthologies by Isobel Armstrong and Joseph Bristow, Andrew Ashfield, Jennifer Breen, Paula Feldman, Anne Mellor and Richard Matlak, and Duncan Wu. The *Norton Anthology of English Literature* now includes selections from her work, and Hemans is mentioned more than any other poet in Stephen C. Behrendt and Harriet Kramer Linkin's *Approaches to Teaching British Women Poets of the Romantic Period* (1997). Clearly, Hemans's star is rising.

Even so, Hemans is now at the center of controversy, the focus of current critical debate about romantic-era poets, the canon, and aesthetic value. As Jerome McGann explains in *The Poetics of Sensibility*,

> Both romanticism and modernism organized themselves in relation to the traditions of sensibility and sentiment. So far as high culture is concerned, however, these traditions remain something of an embarrassment—at best a topic of academic interest, at worst a perceived threat to the practice of art. . . . The internal conflicts of modernism . . . call us to return to the eighteenth century, and in particular to reconsider carefully the poetry of the 'feeling heart,' the *coeur sensible*. . . . I . . . assume that adequate reading begins (though it will not end) by entering into those conventions, by reading in the same spirit that the author writ.[4]

While many readers today enter enthusiastically into the aesthetic embraced by Hemans (and by Lord Byron in such poems as "Fare Thee Well"), others energetically reject it; diverse opinions have inspired strong debate. A query about the value of Hemans's writing was posted in July 1997 on the NASSR-L discussion list (a group of more than five hundred university professors and graduate students interested in romantic-era writing), provoking heated discussion for a full two weeks and generating sixty-four pages of text.[5] Some participants saw Hemans as an author of verse rather than of poetry and expressed fears about the debasement of literary studies. Others celebrated her work for its power, virtuosity, experimentation, and beauty. Some welcomed its inclusion as essential to understanding the diversity of poetic expression of the age. Various commentators suggested reading Hemans in light of popular culture, adventure, the gothic, horror, opera, performance, rhetoric, costumery, feminism, super-heroes, Orientalism, and more.

Who was Felicia Hemans in her own time? Born in the bustling, commercial city of Liverpool on 25 September 1793, she was the daughter of Felicity Dorothea Wagner and George Browne. Her father was an Irish merchant and banker and her mother the daughter of an Italian diplomat. The future poet was a precocious child and a voracious reader, with an extensive family library to explore. When she was seven, financial difficulties forced the family to leave Liverpool for North Wales, where they could live more economically. They took an old, isolated mansion called Gwrych, near Abergele, which was poised against rocky hills and with a view of the Irish Sea. The sights and sounds of this lonely and beautiful landscape appear frequently in Hemans's poetry. The castles that dot the countryside came to inhabit Hemans's literary imagination, along with shipwrecks, a not infrequent occurrence on the North Welsh coast. Hemans's mother taught her English grammar, several modern languages, piano, harp, and drawing. A local clergyman gave her instruction in Latin, ruing "that she was not a man to have borne away the highest honors at college!"[6] Her strong linguistic abilities led her eventually to learn French, German, Portuguese, Italian, and Spanish. She visited London in the winter of 1804 and 1805 but did not like it and never returned. Her mother considered her a genius, trumpeted her abilities, pushed her to publish her verse, and helped secure her a patron.

In 1808, with the financial backing of an elderly family friend, Matthew Nicholson, Hemans published a handsome quarto volume with the London firm of Cadell and Davies; it was embellished with copper-plate engravings and entitled simply *Poems*. The fourteen-year-old poet's name, Felicia Dorothea Browne, appears proudly on the title page. Much of the content is imitative and occasional, but the verse is technically skilled. Hemans was only temporarily discouraged by a review suggesting that *Poems* was premature and recommending more study and meditation, for her family apparently needed the funds her work might generate. Among the 978 subscribers were Captain Alfred Hemans and Thomas Medwin, first cousin of Percy Bysshe Shelley. Shelley later wrote to initiate a friendship, but Hemans's mother was put off by his atheism. The correspondence ceased, perhaps sparing Hemans the fate of the unhappy Harriet Shelley.

In *England and Spain; or, Valour and Patriotism* (1808), also a subsidized volume, Hemans expressed her support for the Peninsular War in which her brothers served as members of the 23rd Royal

Welsh Fusiliers. Over six hundred lines long and written in heroic couplets, this poem celebrates liberty as "Queen of the lofty thought, the generous deed" and "sovereign of the noble soul" while it blasts Napoleon as "Despot of France! destroyer of mankind." Although the meter becomes somewhat monotonous, the work shows vitality as well as virtuosity. Nevertheless, the work did not generate the hoped-for revenues; in 1809, with Hemans's father absent on a business venture and having failed for months to provide financial support, the family was evicted from Gwrych for not paying rent. They moved inland to a cheaper, less commodious house called Bronwylfa, near St. Asaph in Flintshire. Nearby was Conway Castle, then a romantic ruin, where Hemans first read one of Joanna Baillie's verse dramas.

Captain Alfred Hemans, considerably her senior, had declared his love before leaving for the Spanish front in 1809. Although her family initially had resisted the match, the couple married after his return three years later, on 30 July 1812. Shortly thereafter, and with the financial backing of Matthew Nicholson, she brought out the last of her privately printed volumes, *The Domestic Affections, and other Poems*, which was ignored by reviewers. Despite having published three books, Hemans was still virtually unknown to the literary world. Even so, she showed sufficient talent that when she sent Walter Scott a poem inspired by *Waverley*, he published it in the *Edinburgh Annual Register* for 1815. Captain Hemans was appointed adjutant to the Northamptonshire Local Militia, and the couple moved to Daventry, where they took a fine Georgian house on the High Street. Their first son, Arthur, was born there.

Soon afterwards, however, the size of the Northamptonshire Militia was reduced and Captain Hemans's services were no longer needed. The young family went to live with her mother at Bronwylfa. Three more sons were born in quick succession—George Willoughby, Claude Lewis, and Henry William. By 1817, Captain Hemans had retired on half pay. The marriage foundered just before the birth of their fifth son, Charles Lloyd (later known as Charles Isidore), in September 1818, when Alfred Hemans departed for Italy, never to see his wife again. Although the two corresponded about their children, they seem to have come to a mutual decision to live apart. Still, the loss of her marriage remained an intensely humiliating experience for the poet throughout her life, and she never spoke of it except indirectly in her imaginative work.

Hemans's writing career, however, began to take off once she landed John Murray as her publisher. Lord Byron considered *The Restoration of the Works of Art to Italy* (1816), her ambitious poem about the return of artistic treasures to Rome, Florence, and Venice after the Napoleonic war, "a good poem—very" even though he dismissed her lament about the passing of the classical age, *Modern Greece* (1817), as "Good for nothing—written by some one who had never been there."[7] Indeed, like Ann Radcliffe, Hemans rarely saw the places she wrote about, knowing them mostly through travel literature. *Blackwood's Magazine* published Hemans's "Stanzas on the Death of the Princess Charlotte" in April 1818, and soon afterward John Murray brought out a small edition of *Translations from Camoëns, and Other Poets, with Original Poetry*, containing translations from Metastasio, Lope de Vega, Tasso, and Petrarch as well as Camoëns. The essayist, poet, and fiction-writer, Maria Jane Jewsbury, later identified this period in Hemans's career as transitional and remarked, "her poetry was correct, classical and highly polished; but it wanted warmth: it partook more of the nature of statuary than of painting. She fettered her mind with facts and authorities, and drew upon her memory when she might have relied upon her imagination. She was diffident of herself, and, to quote her own admission, 'loved to repose under the shadow of mighty names.'"[8]

In 1819, Hemans's narrative poem "The Meeting of Wallace and Bruce on the Banks of the Carron" won a fifty-pound prize and was published in the September issue of *Blackwood's Edinburgh Magazine*, accompanied by John Wilson's comment that "Scotland has her Baillie—Ireland her Tighe—England her Hemans." One of Hemans's rivals in the competition—James Hogg, popularly known as "the Ettrick Shepherd"—admitted that her entry was "greatly superior both in elegance of thought and composition. Had I been constituted the judge myself, I would have given hers the preference by many degrees."[9]

Hemans brought out *Tales and Historic Scenes* in 1819. The reviews were good, and the book sold out; Murray later published a second edition. The *Quarterly Review* for October 1820 carried an appreciative four-year retrospective review of Hemans's work, aiding sales of her latest volume, *The Sceptic* (1820), a poem Hemans described as "a picture of the dangers resulting to public and private virtue and happiness, from the doctrines of Infidelity."[10] In June 1821 the Royal Society of Literature gave her a fifty-guinea prize for the best poem on the subject of Dartmoor. That same year she composed *Welsh Melodies*, recreations of Welsh history and translations of Welsh poems set to music.

In the spring of 1820 Hemans met Bishop Reginald Heber, who became her mentor and encouraged her to write plays. At his urging, London's Covent Garden produced her five-act tragedy, *The Vespers of Palermo*, on 12 December 1823, with Charles Kemble playing the tortured hero, Procida. Based on a historical incident, this play concerning the struggle for freedom contains two strong female heroes in a plot of love and violence. It closed after only one night; at Joanna Baillie's urging, however, Walter Scott persuaded Sarah Siddons to stage the play in Edinburgh the following April, where, with Siddons delivering an epilogue by Scott, it played successfully. The previous summer, John Murray had brought out *The Siege of Valencia; A Dramatic Poem* bound with *The Last Constantine: with other Poems* (1823) containing "The Voice of Spring," a poem soon set to music and widely sung.

Hemans's poems began appearing in 1823 in the *New Monthly Magazine,* where the public first read her "Lays of Many Lands." Hemans was gaining an appreciative audience in America in the mid-1820s. One of her staunchest champions was Professor Andrews Norton of Harvard University, who in 1825 began superintending the authorized publication of four Hemans volumes, including the first edition of *Hymns on the Works of Nature, for the Use of Children* (1827). Many pirated American editions appeared as well.

The literary annuals, especially the *Winter's Wreath*, the *Amulet, Friendship's Offering,* and the *Literary Souvenir,* brought Hemans's poetry before a larger reading public and considerably augmented her income. In 1827 she became a regular contributor to *Blackwood's Edinburgh Magazine,* which increased her readership even more. *The Forest Sanctuary, and other Poems,* which George Eliot called "exquisite," came out in 1825.[11] Written in a variation of the Spenserian stanza, the poem tells the story of a sixteenth-century Spanish hero who flees religious persecution and finds refuge in a North American forest. The second edition included "Casabianca," a poem recited by generations of school children over the following century. Ironically, it calls into question what it most seems to extoll: obedience to patriarchal authority.

In 1825, after her eldest brother married, Hemans moved with her sons, her mother, and her sister Harriet to Rhyllon, a house just across the River Clwyd. These next three years were the happiest of her life. But the forces that were to dissolve the household inspired many of the poems in Hemans's most successful book, *Records of Woman*, published in May 1828 by William Blackwood and dedicated to Joanna Baillie.[12] Hemans noted, "I have put my heart and individual feelings into it more than any thing else I have written."[13] The book was deeply colored by the last illness and death on 11 January 1827 of her mother and the impending marriage of her sister Harriet. Written mostly at Rhyllon, with her children at play around her, the poems document the courage, nobility, and tragedy of women's lives; embedded in their painful situations lies a critique of the domestic ideal. In six years, *Records of Woman* went through four British and several American editions, bringing the poet at least three hundred pounds, more than she had earned for any other single work and enough to support her family for several years. Although there were not many reviews of *Records of Woman*, Hemans's poetic career was at its height.[14] The distinguished critic Francis Jeffrey wrote a long, favorable review article for the October 1829 *Edinburgh Review*.

In the autumn of 1828, W.E. West painted Hemans's portrait at the request of Alaric Watts, editor of the *Literary Souvenir*, who was putting together a gallery of the living British poets. West stayed at Rhyllon and produced three portraits altogether, one of which was exhibited at Somerset House.[15] Not long after West's stay, Hemans left Wales for Wavertree, a town outside Liverpool, where she had friends and hoped to find better schools for her sons. She grew depressed and ill; the whole household, including the poet, contracted whooping cough. Even so, it was during her three years here that she got to know Henry Fothergill Chorley, Caroline Hamilton, and Rose D'Aguilar Lawrence, all of whom would write early biographies of her. Hemans's proximity to Liverpool and her growing reputation caused her to be besieged by admirers and autograph seekers from England and America.

In the summer of 1829, on a trip to Scotland, she visited Walter Scott. He had once told Joanna Baillie that Hemans "is somewhat too poetical for my taste—too many flowers I mean and too little fruit, but that may be the cynical criticism of an elderly gentleman."[16] Scott liked Hemans personally, however, and invited her to be his houseguest at Abbotsford, a visit she later regarded as one of the high points of her life. Scott told her at parting, "There are some whom we meet, and should like ever after to claim as kith and kin; and you are one of these."[17] On the same trip she stopped at Edinburgh, met Ann Grant of Laggan, dined with Francis Jeffrey, visited Henry Mackenzie, and sat for a bust by Angus Fletcher. In June 1830, she was William Wordsworth's guest for more than two weeks at Rydal Mount, then moved nearby to a little cottage

Felicia Hemans. Engraving (1849) by Edward Scrivens of the bust (1829) by Angus Fletcher. From the 1852 edition of Hemans's *Poems* published by William Blackwood and Sons, Edinburgh.

called Dove Nest on the banks of Lake Windermere, where she stayed until mid-August. She and Wordsworth became good friends, though the women in the household were far less enthusiastic. Later Hemans dedicated *Scenes and Hymns of Life* (1834) to Wordsworth. She published *Songs of the Affections* early in the summer of 1830. After sending her two oldest boys to join their father in Italy, she left Wavertree in April 1831 for Dublin, by way of Bronwylfa.

She took a house in Upper Pembroke Street in Dublin and began in the autumn of 1831 to compose melodies for her poems, including her influential *Hymns for Childhood* and *National Lyrics, and Songs for Music*.[18] Many of her poems would eventually be set to music by others. In 1834 she contracted scarlet fever, followed by a cold which turned to ague. Despite declining strength and health, she composed "Thoughts During Sickness," a series of seven sonnets. Eventually she lost the use of her limbs and barely had energy to read. Amid fever and delirium, on Sunday, 26 April 1835, she dictated the "Sabbath Sonnet," her last poem. She died at 20 Dawson Street in Dublin on 16 May, at the age of forty-one, and was buried nearby within the vaults of St. Anne's Church. Her brothers erected a tablet in the cathedral of St. Asaph which reads, "in memory of Felicia Hemans, whose character is best portrayed in her writings."[19]

RECORDS OF WOMAN

The "Records of Woman" series of nineteen poems forms the kernel of this book of fifty-seven poems and gives the larger collection its title. This powerful, elegiac opening section is a cohesive tour de force marking the height of Hemans's poetic achievement. Although Hemans marketed herself as a poet who celebrated the "domestic affections," as a defender of hearth and home, "Records of Woman" undercuts, even while it reinforces, conventional views of women. Placed in intensely trying situations, her heroines evince uncommon strength of character, courage, and nobility of spirit. They are determined, proud, and gutsy, not servile or helpless. Several, such as Joan of Arc, are leaders of men.

Many poems, such as "The Switzer's Wife," draw on the revisionist tradition of early feminist histories such as Mary Hays's *Female Biography* (1803) and Matilda Betham's *Biographical Dic-*

tionary (1804), which brought accounts of the lives of significant female figures to the reading public. Hemans's "The Switzer's Wife," for example, takes a legendary tale about the origin of modern Switzerland and imaginatively reconstructs a gap in the patriarchal account—the important role and perspective of a woman nearly erased from the record. Hemans dramatizes the force that can alter nations in Werner Stauffacher's nameless wife who gives *him* strength to act: "her clear glance kindling into sudden power." She is the catalyst for subsequent events, although it is his name that patriarchal history chooses to remember.[20] Hemans's project is akin to that of Lucy Aikin's *Epistles on Women* (1810), which foregrounds and vindicates woman's role in history.

Actual historical events are the basis for most of the poems in the series. But Hemans sees history as the recording not so much of grand occurrences but of human emotion and its implications. The monument in "The Memorial Pillar," for example, is a historical marker not of a public event but of a private moment—the final parting of a daughter and her mother. Hemans's history is personalized, feminized.

Contrary to expectations, woman's space, the domestic sphere in "Records," is far from being a safe, peaceful, and insulated place. At any moment, it threatens to succumb to violence and dissolution. For example, in "The Bride of the Greek Isle," a poem based on an actual 1822 incident at Scio, a wedding celebration transmutes itself into a massacre. Yet, the bride, Eudora, responds to wanton male destruction with cleansing violence of her own. The inferno she sets, a trope for her outrage, destroys her captors but also causes her own suttee-like self-immolation.

Death, as Hemans sees it, may be at times a woman's most forceful adversary but can also be her salvation. Each poem in the "Records of Woman" series protests death's inevitable wrenching of the bonds of human love, its violent severing of what affection most cherishes. But despite death's horrors, several of Hemans's heroines are led to embrace it (by fire in "Pauline," by water in "Indian Woman's Death Song," and by poison in "Imelda"). Some women even become killers. In "The Indian City," for instance, the distraught mother of a civilian war casualty achieves vengeance. Her voice and the power of her story "kindle that lightening flame" of indignation that cause others to burn the offending city, setting her child's murderers afire. The memorial she creates for herself, her record, is a ruin, mirroring her grief. Yet this bittersweet victory and "sad renown" does nothing to relieve "the yearning left by a broken tie."

The broken tie in Hemans's own life directly informs the emotional landscape of "Records." A little more than a year before the book's May 1828 publication, Hemans's mother died, shattering the poet's world. "Records of Woman" is, among other things, implicitly an extended elegy for Felicity Dorothea Wagner Browne. From the beginning, Browne had encouraged her daughter's literary career. And she also made possible Hemans's way of life after the poet's separation from her husband—managing the children, the household, and the finances as well as giving her crucial emotional support. Around the time *Records* was published, Hemans told Joanna Baillie that "the last winter deprived me of my truest and tenderest friend—the mother by whose unwearied spirit of love and hope I was encouraged to bear on through all the obstacles which beset my onward path."[21]

"Records of Woman" projects Hemans's own attendance by her mother's deathbed, as the poet obsessively reenacts the traumatic deathbed scene in various imagined times, places, and circumstances.[22] While some works, such as "The American Forest Girl," express a wish-fulfillment—the rescue of the one about to die—nearly every poem in the series describes a corpse or the anticipation of one. Hemans paints the deathbed from multiple perspectives, including the point of view of the dying as well as that of the bereaved. The central character in "Gertrude" is unable to stop the slow death by torture of the one she loves, but she musters strength to attend the dreadful event and heroically provides comfort while she herself is comfortless. Paradoxically, love in "Records" seems to require death or the threat of death for its most intense expression.

Reinforcing the sense of loss that informs the volume's contents was the anticipated separation of Hemans and her sister, Harriet, as a result of the latter's impending marriage. In a letter of 12 April 1828, when *Records of Woman* was in press, Hemans told Baillie, "I am to lose this, my only sister,—indeed I may almost say, my only companion,—very shortly; she is about to change her name and home, and remove very far from me. O how many deaths

there are in the world for the affections!"[23] These family separa-
tions were apparently so painful that in a 317–page memoir of the
poet published more than a decade after these events, Hemans's
sister devotes only two sentences to *Records of Woman*, the book
that evokes the partings. In addition to the emotional toll, Browne's
death had important practical implications for Hemans, for it forced
her to take over certain household responsibilities for the first time
in her life. In fact, Hemans experienced her mother's death as a
kind of widowhood. "I am now," she wrote, "for the first time in
my life holding the reins of government, independently managing a
household myself, and I never liked any thing less than *ce triste
empire de soi-même*."[24]

Hemans dramatizes "this sad empire of oneself" in the opening
poem of *Records*. The historical figure Arabella Stuart, who is in
solitary confinement, chafes against her bonds. She has dared to
love without the permission of King James I, the patriarchal au-
thority who fears her unsanctioned marriage may produce heirs to
the throne. In Hemans's revision of the tale, Arabella Stuart is not
mad, as conventional histories assert, but broken by yearning and
despair, by the betrayal of her trust, and by the crushing of her
hope. The poem is an extraordinary imaginative reconstruction of
the human psyche under almost unbearable stress. If love is all,
then for Stuart all hope is lost. She is a woman with great emo-
tional and, by implication, sexual hunger, who is slowly being
starved to death. As a monologue, the poem highlights not only
Stuart's words but the silence of her husband, Edward Seymour, as
well. Stuart's longing for a reunion with Seymour, where life,
warmth, and love flourish in a bright, open, green landscape, vies
with the stark reality of her cold, dark, lifeless cell. She is "an insect
to be crushed"; earth is pitiless. But so is God, who remains as
silent as Seymour. Just as the Father in heaven, to whom Stuart
prays, fails to answer, so the husband on earth, to whom she writes,
does not reply. In the final lines of the poem, her notions of Seymour
and of God blur. The prayer Stuart begins to God transforms into a
farewell letter to Seymour and finally concludes as a benediction.
God, Seymour, and the King are similarly unyielding to her desire;
that is to say, the patriarchy is coldly unmovable. Still, the psycho-
logical depth of Hemans's depiction allows Arabella Stuart to emerge
as more than tradition's object of pathos or the stereotypical aban-

doned woman with a broken heart; her faith, fidelity, and suffering ennoble her, while her articulate protest implicitly impugns those responsible for her condition.

The tension Hemans sees between the ennobling power of love and the almost unbearable pain of its loss finds a voice in the dual epigraphs to *Records of Woman*: the first, by William Wordsworth, speaks to the force of woman's love; the second recounts the pain of Schiller's character Thekla on learning of the death of her lover.

Also central to *Records of Woman* are the complicated and sometimes contradictory attitudes about the woman poet and fame. "Properzia Rossi," like "Arabella Stuart," features a heroine whose frustrated need is to be heard, seen, and recognized by an unresponsive patriarchal authority. Rossi yearns to escape from artistic obscurity as much as Stuart desires freedom from physical bonds, although both poems are an exploration of woman's psyche under extreme stress. Their heroines struggle against an indifference that would reduce to a cipher all they are and can offer. In "Properzia Rossi," Hemans probes the internal reality of the female artist and points to the limits of art in her life. The artist's talent has not won her love, which she most ardently desires, but life without love is the material that she transforms into beauty. Her great disappointment is that art cannot fully embody her vision. Even so, the poem's conclusion highlights the power and the promise of art.

In the depths of her despair, Rossi describes fame as "worthless," a statement some see as evidence that Hemans believed women should not pursue fame. Nothing could be more untrue. Hemans was a highly ambitious artist who worked tirelessly to build her reputation. Read carefully, "Properzia Rossi" reflects and justifies this yearning after fame. In her last letter to a good friend, Rose Lawrence, penned at the end of her life, Hemans confessed, "My wish ever was to concentrate all my mental [energy] in the production of some more noble and [complete work:] something of pure and holy excellence, [(if there be] not too much presumption in the thought,) [which might] *permanently* take its place as the work of an English poetess.—I have always, hitherto, written as if in the breathing times of Autumn storms and billows.—perhaps it may not even yet be too late to accomplish what I wish."[25] In increasingly conservative Victorian culture, she well knew that this wish was unacceptable—something a woman must mask. One review, in fact, blasted Henry F. Chorley for making public in his biography, *Memorials of Mrs. Hemans* (1836), letters by Hemans that clearly show her desire for fame. It charges,

> Through the whole correspondence, and its accompanying commentaries there is exhibited by her a craving vanity, a restless and feverish anxiety for display, a desire to be always *en representation*, and all this under the studious affectation of very much disliking the eminence, on which she would remind her correspondents that she stands. . . . we find her constantly walking over to [Chorley's] house, with some adulatory letter in her pocket, or some story of the way in which her reputation has discovered her retreat, in order that she may explain to its members how disagreeable a thing is fame.[26]

Were Hemans's protestations against fame disingenuous? For Properzia Rossi, fame is no substitute for love, but fame is her one, last, ardent hope. The epigraph, penned by Hemans, prefigures the sentiments and shape of the poem. It opens with Rossi pleading, "Tell me no more, no more / Of my soul's lofty gifts! Are they not vain / To quench its haunting thirst for happiness?" It concludes, however, with the same concept that will close the poem "Yet it may be that death / Shall give my name a power to win such tears / As would have made life precious." As if in a hall of mirrors, Hemans paints Rossi painting the figure of Ariadne, about whom she declares "thou shalt wear / My form, my lineaments." Rossi is cheered with the thought that "I shall not perish all!"—that her creation, even after she is gone, will be capable of speaking to her beloved "of all my love and grief!" One day he will look at her work and be proud to acknowledge "'*Twas hers who lov'd me well!*"

"Joan of Arc," a companion poem, treats the tension between love and renown from a different angle. Unlike Properzia Rossi, Joan of Arc rides the crest of fame. She is a victorious woman mantled with power and authority. Yet triumph and glory have come at a steep price—the domestic circle whose loss she mourns. Like the Switzer's wife, Joan of Arc has given up an idyllic home, a choice she makes willingly but not without deep regret. In "The Grave of a Poetess," the most transparently self-referential poem in the sequence, Hemans contemplates her own grave and the promise of her own immortality as she ostensibly pays tribute to the Irish poet Mary Tighe. But it is in "The Effigies," a poem included in the "Miscellaneous Pieces" at the end of the volume, that Hemans provides both a commentary on and implicit celebration of her own "Records of Woman" series. This poem protests the obscurity of woman's historical record—the difficulty of discovering and reconstructing woman's traditional realm, the domestic. It asks of woman, "What bard hath sung of *thee*?" The answer, of course, is obvious—Hemans herself.

While the second part of the volume, "Miscellaneous Pieces," lacks the coherence of the "Records of Woman" series and is more uneven in its poetic achievement, it nevertheless contains some significant work. The tone shifts radically and rather unnervingly from the elegiac "Records of Woman" series to the celebratory "The Homes of England," which opens the "Miscellaneous Pieces" section. In the idealized world of this poem, there is no parting, sadness, or war. Homes are "stately," "merry," "blessed," "free," "fair," and "smiling." This is a harmonious, affluent world, free of rotting wood, privation, disease, and class conflict. Read within the context of a volume which, to this point, has featured intense human suffering, this poem seems a fairy tale—sanitized, chauvinistic and ironic. Still, removed from its ironizing context, "The Homes of England" became one of Hemans's most widely reprinted lyrics, as did "The Landing of the Pilgrim Fathers," which became a staple with her overseas audience. This poem celebrates the idealism of the American experiment and the religious freedom it made possible.

Other pieces in this section, however, echo the elegiac tone of "Records of Woman." In "The Lady of the Castle," a young woman's life is blighted by her mother's absence. Both the "Spanish Chapel" and "The Child's Last Sleep" deal with the pathos of infant death. The former offers a Christian consolation, while the latter explores more fully a loss that seems to defy understanding. Hemans achieves a startling effect by counterpoising the image of a peacefully sleeping child against that of an infant corpse, at one point disturbingly blurring the distinction. In "Roman Girl's Song," grief and nostalgia are monumental, for the singer mourns the loss not of an individual but of an entire civilization.

Hemans revisits and amplifies in this second section of the book the issue she raised in "Properzia Rossi" and "The Grave of a Poetess" concerning the character and role of the poet. "To Wordsworth" and "A Voyager's Dream of Land" are reverent imitations of a poet who is, for Hemans, the "True bard, and holy!" "The Sicilian Captive" tells of a woman whose song celebrates the lost land of her youth. Her poetic performance is liberating, restorative. Though she dies singing, she wins freedom from physical imprisonment both through song and death. Similarly, "The Mourner for the Barmecides" is a testament to the power of poetry. The protagonist literally sings for his life; he frees himself from a death sentence by moving his captors through song. "Tasso and his Sister" highlights the powerful bond between two siblings as well as the ill treatment the "bard of gifts divine" suffers at the hands of an unappreciative and insensitive public.

"The Palm-Tree," however, is crucial to the current critical debate about Hemans and aesthetic values. The poem is a defense of the "feminine" poetic sensibility. Here Hemans argues that strong devotion—the sentiment of daily life that is generally associated with women—should not be scorned, for it is the very source of such "masculine" attributes as courage and patriotism.

NOTES

1. In America "The Landing of the Pilgrim Fathers in New England" quickly became a classic.

2. Journals included the *Quarterly Review*, the *Gentleman's Magazine*, the *New Monthly Magazine*, *Blackwood's Edinburgh Magazine*, the *Eclectic Review*, the *Antijacobin Review*, the *Critical Review*, and the *European Magazine*. Critics such as Andrews Norton, David M. Moir, and William Gifford praised her highly.

3. For an inventory of lifetime sales by significant Romantic-era writers, see Paula R. Feldman, "Endurance and Forgetting: What the Evidence Suggests" in *Romanticism and Women Poets: Opening the Doors of Reception*, ed. Stephen C. Behrendt and Harriet Kramer Linkin (Lexington: University Press of Kentucky, 1999), 15-24.

4. (Oxford: Clarendon Press, 1996), 1, 4–6. McGann devotes a full chapter in his book to a consideration of Hemans.

5. "Reading Hemans, Aesthetics, and the Canon: An Online Discussion." Extracted, and slightly edited for the Web, from postings to the NASSR-L discussion list, 16–29 July 1997. Part 1: <http://orion.it.luc.edu/~sjones1/hemans2.htm>. The discussion was of such interest that on 21

July 1997, Steven E. Jones, editor of *Romantic Circles*, noted on the list, "NASSR-L members enjoyed a remarkable discussion . . . on Felicia Hemans, taste, aesthetics, the canon, and anthologies. With the permission of participants, the main thread on Hemans—a kind of slice of list-history—is now available on the Web (with added hyperlinks) at Romantic Circles . . . . The thread is also linked to a new user forum so that the discussion can continue on the Web."

6. Henry Fothergill Chorley, *Memorials of Mrs. Hemans, with Illustrations of her Literary Character from her Private Correspondence* (London, 1836), 1:20.

7. See Byron to John Murray, 30 September 1816 and 4 September 1817, in *"So late into the night,"* vol. 5 of *Byron's Letters and Journals*, ed. Leslie A. Marchand (London, 1976), 108, 262.

8. No. 172 (12 Feb. 1831): 104–5.

9. Quoted in Peter W. Trinder, *Mrs. Hemans* (Cardiff, 1984), 19.

10. Hemans to William Gifford, 17 Nov. 1819, quoted in Paula R. Feldman, "The Poet and the Profits: Felicia Hemans and the Literary Marketplace," *Keats-Shelley Journal* 46 (1997): 156.

11. Marian Evans, *The George Eliot Letters*, ed. Gordon S. Haight, 6 vols. (New Haven, 1954), 1:72.

12. Not only were the two poets close friends but Hemans was also a great admirer of Baillie's plays. She particularly liked Baillie's heroines, about whom she said, "Nothing in all her writings delights me so much as her general idea of what is beautiful in the female character. There is so much gentle fortitude, and deep self-devoting affection in the women whom she portrays, and they are so perfectly different from the pretty 'un-idea'd girls,' who seem to form the *beau ideal* of our whole sex in the works of some modern poets" (Hughes, "Memoir," 69).

13. Letter of 23 March 1828 to Mary Russell Mitford, quoted in Chorley, *Memorials of Mrs. Hemans*, 1: 160–61.

14. At least forty-four of the fifty-seven poems (or 77 percent) had been recently published separately in magazines, American books, or literary annuals, so journal editors contended that the volume did not contain enough new material to review.

15. One portrait, judged by her family to be the best likeness, inspired Hemans's poem "To my own portrait" and was given to her sister, Harriet Hughes, who used it for the frontispiece to the 1839 seven-volume edition of Hemans's *Works*; the other portrait went to Professor Andrews Norton in Boston. The portrait for Watts was later acquired by Fisher, proprietor of *The Drawing Room Scrapbook*; engravings from it appeared in that annual as well as in *The Christian Keepsake*. Hughes considered it an unsatisfactory likeness of her sister.

16. Letter of 11 July 1823, quoted in John Gibson Lockhart, *Memoirs of the Life of Sir Walter Scott*, 5 vols. (Boston, 1901), 4:126.

17. Hemans, journal entry, July 1829, quoted in Harriet Hughes, "Memoir of the Life and Writings of Mrs Hemans," in *The Works of Mrs Hemans; with a Memoir of Her Life, by Her Sister* (Edinburgh: William Blackwood and Sons, 1839), 1:191.

18. By the summer of 1832, she had moved to 36 Stephen's Green in order to avoid the street noise of her former home and by the spring of 1833 had moved again to 20 Dawson Street.

19. Many poets wrote tributes to her during her lifetime, and many eulogized her upon her death, including Wordsworth in his "Epitaphs" (no. 12, stanza 10), Letitia Elizabeth Landon in "Stanzas on the Death of Mrs. Hemans," Maria Abdy in "Lines Written on the Death of Mrs. Hemans," and Lydia Sigourney in "Monody on Mrs. Hemans."

20. This poem is one of those cited by Anna Jameson when she observes that Hemans's poems "could not have been written by a man. [Her protagonists'] love is without selfishness—their passion pure from sensual coarseness—their high heroism . . . unsullied by any base alloy of ambition." (Quoted in Chorley, *Memorials of Mrs. Hemans*, 1:138.)

21. Letter dated 8 April 1828, quoted in Chorley, *Memorials of Mrs. Hemans*, 1:142.

22. See, for example, "Costanza," "Madeline," and "Gertrude, or Fidelity till Death."

23. Quoted in Chorley, *Memorials of Mrs. Hemans*, 1:151. See also Hemans's unpublished letter to Dr. Samuel Butler, dated 19 February 1828, in which she observes, "I am about to lose . . . my only sister, and I may almost say, my only *companion*; since we have for years been linked together in a community of thought and pursuit, which I must never hope to have renewed. Unfortunately for me, interchange of thought is an habitual *want* of my mind, and I pine without it . . . so that I look with a feeling almost of alarm, to the loneliness (not literal, but *mental* loneliness) which seems awaiting me" (British Library, Add. MS 34587, f. 8).

24. Letter of 10 November 1828 to Mary Russell Mitford, quoted in Harriet Hughes, "Memoir of the Life and Writings of Mrs Hemans," in *The Works of Mrs Hemans; with a Memoir of Her Life, by Her Sister* (Edinburgh: William Blackwood and Sons, 1839), 1:156.

25. Dated Dublin, February 13, n.y.; text from the manuscript letter, in private collection.

26. *Dublin Review* (December 1836): 272–73.

FURTHER READING

Blain, Virginia. "'Thou with Earth's Music Answerest to the Sky': Felicia Hemans, Mary Anne Browne, and the Myth of Poetic Sisterhood." In *Women's Writing: the Elizabethan to Victorian Period* 2 (1995): 251–70.

Chorley, Henry Fothergill. *Memorials of Mrs. Hemans, with Illustrations of her Literary Character from her Private Correspondence*, 2 vols. London: Saunders and Otley, 1836.

Clarke, Norma. *Ambitious Heights: Writing, Friendship, Love: the Jewsbury Sisters, Felicia Hemans, and Jane Welsh Carlyle*. London: Routledge, 1990.

Eubanks, Kevin. "Minerva's Veil: Hemans, Critics, and the Construction of Gender." *European Romantic Review* 8, no. 4 (Fall 1997): 341–59.

Feldman, Paula R. "The Poet and the Profits: Felicia Hemans and the Literary Marketplace." *Keats-Shelley Journal* 46 (1997): 148–76.

Goslee, Nancy Moore. "Hemans's 'Red Indians': Reading Stereotypes." In *Romanticism, Race, and Imperial Culture*, edited by Alan Richardson and Sonia Hofkosh, 237–61. Bloomington, Indiana: Indiana University Press, 1996.

Harding, Anthony John. "Felicia Hemans and the Effacement of Woman." In *Romantic Women Writers: Voices and Countervoices*, edited by Paula R. Feldman and Theresa M. Kelley, 138–49. Hanover, N. H.: University Press of New England, 1995.

Hughes, H.[arriet] M.[ary] B.[rowne]. "Memoir of the Life and Writings of Mrs Hemans." In the *Works of Mrs Hemans; with a Memoir of her Life, by her Sister*, 7 vols. (Edinburgh: William Blackwood and Sons, 1839) 1: 1–315.

Lawrence, Mrs. [Rose D'Aguilar]. *The Last Autumn at a Favorite Residence, with Other Poems; and Recollections of Mrs. Hemans*. Liverpool: G. & J. Robinson, 1836.

Lootens, Tricia. "Hemans and her American Heirs: Nineteenth-Century Women's Poetry and National Identity." In *Women's Poetry, Late Romantic to Late Victorian: Gender and Genre, 1830–1900*, edited by Isobel Armstrong and Virginia Blain, 243–262. London: Macmillan, 1999.

———. "Hemans and Home: Victorianism, Feminine 'Internal Enemies,' and the Domestication of National Identity." *PMLA* 109 (1994): 238–53.

McGann, Jerome J. [as Anne Mack, J. J. Rome, and Georg Mannejc]. "Literary History, Romanticism, and Felicia Hemans." *Modern Language Quarterly* 54 (June 1993): 215–35.

Further Reading

————. *The Poetics of Sensibility: A Revolution in Literary Style*, 174–94. Oxford: Clarendon Press, 1996.

Mellor, Anne K. *Romanticism and Gender*. New York: Routledge, 1993.

Sweet, Nanora. "History, Imperialism, and the Aesthetics of the Beautiful: Hemans and the Post-Napoleonic Moment." In *At the Limits of Romanticism,* edited by M. A. Favret and N. J. Watson, 170–84. Bloomington: University of Indiana Press, 1994.

Trinder, Peter W. *Mrs Hemans*. Cardiff: University of Wales Press, 1984.

Wolfson, Susan. "'Domestic Affections' and 'the Spear of Minerva:' Felicia Hemans and the Dilemma of Gender." *Re-Visioning Romanticism: British Women Writers, 1776–1837,* edited by Carol Shiner Wilson and Joel Haefner, 128–66. Philadelphia: University of Pennsylvania Press, 1994.

————. "Gendering the Soul." In *Romantic Women Writers: Voices and Countervoices,* edited by Paula R. Feldman and Theresa M. Kelley, 33–68. Hanover, N. H.: University Press of New England, 1995.

————. "Men, Women, and 'Fame': Teaching Felicia Hemans." In *Approaches to Teaching British Women Poets of the Romantic Period,* edited by Stephen C. Behrendt and Harriet Kramer Linkin, 110 20. New York: Modern Language Association of America, 1997.

NOTE ON THE TEXT

The copy text is the 1828 first edition of *Records of Woman: With Other Poems* published in Edinburgh by William Blackwood and in London by Thomas Cadell. Contents of the first through the fifth editions (1828–37) are nearly identical, except for Hemans's addition in the second edition (1828) of "The Death Day of Körner," preserved in Blackwood's later reprintings. "The Captive Knight," which had appeared in all previous editions, was omitted from the "Records of Woman" section of *The Works of Mrs Hemans; with a Memoir of Her Life, by Her Sister,* published posthumously by Blackwood in 1839. That edition included among the "Miscellaneous Poems" of *Records of Woman* "Christmas Carol," "A Father Reading the Bible," and "The Meeting of the Brothers," none of which had appeared in previous editions. It was edited by members of Hemans's family and was the first collected edition brought out by Blackwood.

At least forty-four of the fifty-seven poems were published by Hemans previous to their inclusion in *Records of Woman: With Other Poems.* Often, although not always, Hemans made substantive changes to these texts before including them in her book. These substantive variants are noted, with their sources identified within square brackets using the following abbreviations:

Friendship's Offering [FO]
League of the Alps, Boston, 1826 [LA]
Literary Magnet [LM]
Literary Souvenir [LS]
Monthly Magazine [MM]
New Monthly Magazine [NMM]

Accidental variants, including spelling, punctuation, capitalization, italicization, and so forth, are not noted. After the first edition,

Hemans appears to have made no substantive emendations to the texts of individual poems.

To preserve the historical specificity of the copy text, the original spelling, capitalization, and punctuation have been retained in this edition. Some accidentals, however, such as line bars; font size; running heads; periods following titles, authors' names, and roman numerals; capitalization of authors' names or the first word of poems; or other design features, have not been retained. Printer's errors have been silently corrected, as have errors in the spelling of foreign language words. Titles of books have been uniformly set in italics. Corrections made in editions following 1828 (up to and including the 1839 *Works of Mrs Hemans; with a Memoir of her Life, by her Sister*) have been silently adopted for this text.

Hemans's own notes to the texts have been preserved and are marked (*Hemans's note.*) at the end to differentiate them from editorial notes, which are not signed. Editorial and authorial notes to poems appear at the end of the book and are, where possible, keyed to line numbers. Notes to titles, epigraphs, headnotes, and the like are keyed to significant words or phrases. Glosses are provided for unfamiliar words but are generally not repeated if used in more than one poem.

Hemans seems to have authored all unattributed epigraphs to the poems. In the 1839 *Works of Mrs Hemans*, epigraphs Hemans authored are the ones *not* enclosed in quotation marks.

RECORDS OF WOMAN

————Mightier far
Than strength of nerve or sinew, or the sway
Of magic potent over sun and star,
Is love, though oft to agony distrest,
And though his favourite seat be feeble woman's breast.
Wordsworth

Das ist das Los des Schönen auf der Erde!
Schiller

To
Mrs. Joanna Baillie,
this Volume,
as a Slight Token of
Grateful Respect and Admiration,
is Affectionately Inscribed,
by
the Author.

Arabella Stuart

"The Lady Arabella," as she has been frequently entitled, was descended from Margaret, eldest daughter of Henry VII, and consequently allied by birth to Elizabeth, as well as James I. This affinity to the throne proved the misfortune of her life, as the jealousies which it constantly excited in her royal relatives, who were anxious to prevent her marrying, shut her out from the enjoyment of that domestic happiness which her heart appears to have so fervently desired. By a secret, but early discovered union with William Seymour, son of Lord Beauchamp, she alarmed the cabinet of James, and the wedded lovers were immediately placed in separate confinement. From this they found means to concert a romantic plan of escape; and having won over a female attendant, by whose assistance she was disguised in male attire, Arabella, though faint from recent sickness and suffering, stole out in the night, and at last reached an appointed spot, where a boat and servants were in waiting. She embarked; and, at break of day, a French vessel, engaged to receive her, was discovered and gained. As Seymour, however, had not yet arrived, she was desirous that the vessel should lie at anchor for him; but this wish was overruled by her companions, who, contrary to her entreaties, hoisted sail, "which," says D'Israeli, "occasioned so fatal a termination to this romantic adventure. Seymour, indeed, had escaped from the Tower;—he reached the wharf, and found his confidential man waiting with a boat, and arrived at Lee. The time passed; the waves were rising; Arabella was not there; but in the distance he descried a vessel. Hiring a fisherman to take him on board, he discovered, to his grief, on hailing it, that it was not the French ship charged with his Arabella; in despair and confusion he found another ship from Newcastle, which for a large sum altered its course, and landed him in Flanders."—Arabella, meantime, whilst imploring her attendants to linger, and earnestly looking out for the expected boat of her husband, was overtaken in Calais Roads by a vessel in the King's service, and brought back to a captivity, under the suffering of which her mind and constitution gradually sank.— "What passed in that dreadful imprisonment, cannot perhaps be recovered for authentic history,—but enough is known;

that her mind grew impaired, that she finally lost her reason, and, if the duration of her imprisonment was short, that it was only terminated by her death. Some effusions, often begun and never ended, written and erased, incoherent and rational, yet remain among her papers."—D'Israeli's *Curiosities of Literature*————The following poem, meant as some record of her fate, and the imagined fluctuations of her thoughts and feelings, is supposed to commence during the time of her first imprisonment, whilst her mind was yet buoyed up by the consciousness of Seymour's affection, and the cherished hope of eventual deliverance.

> *And is not love in vain,*
> *Torture enough without a living tomb?*
>
> Byron

Fermossi al fin il cor che balzò tanto.

Pindemonte

I

'Twas but a dream!—I saw the stag leap free,
    Under the boughs where early birds were singing,
I stood, o'ershadow'd by the greenwood tree,
    And heard, it seemed, a sudden bugle ringing
Far thro' a royal forest: then the fawn
Shot, like a gleam of light, from grassy lawn
To secret covert; and the smooth turf shook,
And lilies quiver'd by the glade's lone brook,
And young leaves trembled, as, in fleet career,
A princely band, with horn, and hound, and spear,   10
Like a rich masque swept forth. I saw the dance
Of their white plumes, that bore a silvery glance
Into the deep wood's heart; and all pass'd by,
Save one—I met the smile of *one* clear eye,
Flashing out joy to mine.—Yes, *thou* wert there,
Seymour! a soft wind blew the clustering hair
Back from thy gallant brow, as thou didst rein
Thy courser, turning from that gorgeous train,
And fling, methought, thy hunting-spear away,
And, lightly graceful in thy green array,   20
Bound to my side; and we, that met and parted,
    Ever in dread of some dark watchful power,

Won back to childhood's trust, and, fearless-hearted,
  Blent the glad fulness of our thoughts that hour,
Ev'n like the mingling of sweet streams, beneath
Dim woven leaves, and midst the floating breath
Of hidden forest flowers.

II

'Tis past!—I wake,
  A captive, and alone, and far from thee,
My love and friend! Yet fostering, for thy sake,   30
  A quenchless hope of happiness to be;
And feeling still my woman's spirit strong,
In the deep faith which lifts from earthly wrong,
A heavenward glance. I know, I know our love
Shall yet call gentle angels from above,
By its undying fervour; and prevail,
Sending a breath, as of the spring's first gale,
Thro' hearts now cold; and, raising its bright face,
With a free gush of sunny tears erase
The characters of anguish; in this trust,   40
I bear, I strive, I bow not to the dust,
That I may bring thee back no faded form,
No bosom chill'd and blighted by the storm,
But all my youth's first treasures, when we meet,
Making past sorrow, by communion, sweet.

III

And thou too art in bonds!—yet droop thou not,
Oh, my belov'd!—there is *one* hopeless lot,
But one, and that not ours. Beside the dead
There sits the grief that mantles up its head,
Loathing the laughter and proud pomp of light,   50
When darkness, from the vainly-doting sight,
Covers its beautiful! If thou wert gone
  To the grave's bosom, with thy radiant brow,—
If thy deep-thrilling voice, with that low tone
  Of earnest tenderness, which now, ev'n now,
Seems floating thro' my soul, were music taken
For ever from this world,—oh! thus forsaken,

Could I bear on?—thou liv'st, thou liv'st, thou'rt mine!
With this glad thought I make my heart a shrine,
And by the lamp which quenchless there shall burn,   60
Sit, a lone watcher for the day's return.

IV

And lo! the joy that cometh with the morning,
    Brightly victorious o'er the hours of care!
I have not watch'd in vain, serenely scorning
    The wild and busy whispers of despair!
Thou hast sent tidings, as of heaven.—I wait
    The hour, the sign, for blessed flight to thee.
Oh! for the skylark's wing that seeks its mate
    As a star shoots!—but on the breezy sea
We shall meet soon.—To think of such an hour!   70
    Will not my heart, o'erburden'd by its bliss,
Faint and give way within me, as a flower
    Borne down and perishing by noontide's kiss?
Yet shall I *fear* that lot?—the perfect rest,
The full deep joy of dying on thy breast,
After long-suffering won? So rich a close
Too seldom crowns with peace affection's woes.

V

Sunset!—I tell each moment—from the skies
    The last red splendour floats along my wall,
Like a king's banner!—Now it melts, it dies!   80
    I see one star—I hear—'twas not the call,
Th' expected voice; my quick heart throbb'd too soon.
I must keep vigil till yon rising moon
Shower down less golden light. Beneath her beam
Thro' my lone lattice pour'd, I sit and dream
Of summer-lands afar, where holy love,
Under the vine, or in the citron-grove,
May breathe from terror.
                    Now the night grows deep,
And silent as its clouds, and full of sleep.   90
I hear my veins beat.—Hark! a bell's slow chime.
My heart strikes with it.—Yet again—'tis time!

‹ 10 ›

A step!—a voice!—or but a rising breeze?
Hark!—haste!—I come, to meet thee on the seas.

*   *   *   *   *   *   *   *   *

VI

Now never more, oh! never, in the worth
Of its pure cause, let sorrowing love on earth
Trust fondly—never more!—the hope is crush'd
That lit my life, the voice within me hush'd
That spoke sweet oracles; and I return
To lay my youth, as in a burial-urn,   100
Where sunshine may not find it.—All is lost!
No tempest met our barks—no billow toss'd;
Yet were they sever'd, ev'n as we must be,
That so have lov'd, so striven our hearts to free
From their close-coiling fate! In vain—in vain!
The dark links meet, and clasp themselves again,
And press out life.—Upon the deck I stood,
And a white sail came gliding o'er the flood,
Like some proud bird of ocean; then mine eye
Strained out, one moment earlier to descry   110
The form it ached for, and the bark's career
Seem'd slow to that fond yearning: It drew near,
Fraught with our foes!—What boots it to recall
The strife, the tears? Once more a prison-wall
Shuts the green hills and woodlands from my sight,
And joyous glance of waters to the light,
And thee, my Seymour, thee!

                    I will not sink!
   Thou, *thou* hast rent the heavy chain that bound thee;
And this shall be my strength—the joy to think   120
   That thou mayst wander with heaven's breath around thee,
And all the laughing sky! This thought shall yet
Shine o'er my heart, a radiant amulet,
Guarding it from despair. Thy bonds are broken,
And unto me, I know, thy true love's token
Shall one day be deliverance, tho' the years
Lie dim between, o'erhung with mists of tears.

VII

My friend, my friend! where art thou? Day by day,
Gliding, like some dark mournful stream, away,
My silent youth flows from me. Spring, the while,   130
   Comes and rains beauty on the kindling boughs
Round hall and hamlet; Summer, with her smile,
   Fills the green forest;—young hearts breathe their vows;
Brothers long parted meet; fair children rise
Round the glad board; Hope laughs from loving eyes:
All this is in the world!—These joys lie sown,
The dew of every path—On *one* alone
Their freshness may not fall—the stricken deer,
Dying of thirst with all the waters near.

VIII

Ye are from dingle and fresh glade, ye flowers!   140
   By some kind hand to cheer my dungeon sent;
O'er you the oak shed down the summer showers,
   And the lark's nest was where your bright cups bent,
Quivering to breeze and rain-drop, like the sheen
Of twilight stars. On you Heaven's eye hath been,
Thro' the leaves, pouring its dark sultry blue
Into your glowing hearts; the bee to you
Hath murmur'd, and the rill.—My soul grows faint
With passionate yearning, as its quick dreams paint
Your haunts by dell and stream,—the green, the free,   150
The full of all sweet sound,—the shut from me!

IX

There went a swift bird singing past my cell—
   O Love and Freedom! ye are lovely things!
With you the peasant on the hills may dwell,
   And by the streams; but I—the blood of kings,
A proud, unmingling river, thro' my veins
Flows in lone brightness,—and its gifts are chains!
Kings!—I had silent visions of deep bliss,
Leaving their thrones far distant, and for this
I am cast under their triumphal car,   160

An insect to be crush'd.—Oh! Heaven is far,—
Earth pitiless!

Dost thou forget me, Seymour? I am prov'd
So long, so sternly! Seymour, my belov'd!
There are such tales of holy marvels done
By strong affection, of deliverance won
Thro' its prevailing power! Are these things told
Till the young weep with rapture, and the old
Wonder, yet dare not doubt,—and thou, oh! thou,
   Dost thou forget me in my hope's decay?—   170
Thou canst not!—thro' the silent night, ev'n now,
   I, that need prayer so much, awake and pray
Still first for thee.—Oh! gentle, gentle friend!
How shall I bear this anguish to the end?

Aid!—comes there yet no aid?—the voice of blood
Passes Heaven's gate, ev'n ere the crimson flood
Sinks thro' the greensward!—is there not a cry
From the wrung heart, of power, thro' agony,
To pierce the clouds? Hear, Mercy! hear me! None
That bleed and weep beneath the smiling sun,   180
Have heavier cause!—yet hear!—my soul grows dark—
Who hears the last shriek from the sinking bark,
On the mid seas, and with the storm alone,
And bearing to th' abyss, unseen, unknown,
Its freight of human hearts?—th' o'ermastering wave!
Who shall tell how it rush'd—and none to save?

Thou hast forsaken me! I feel, I know,
There would be rescue if this were not so.
Thou'rt at the chase, thou'rt at the festive board,
Thou'rt where the red wine free and high is pour'd,   190
Thou'rt where the dancers meet!—a magic glass
Is set within my soul, and proud shapes pass,
Flushing it o'er with pomp from bower and hall;—
I see one shadow, stateliest there of all,—
Thine!—What dost *thou* amidst the bright and fair,

Whispering light words, and mocking my despair?
It is not well of thee!—my love was more
Than fiery song may breathe, deep thought explore,
And there thou smilest, while my heart is dying,
With all its blighted hopes around it lying;   200
Ev'n thou, on whom they hung their last green leaf—
Yet smile, smile on! too bright art thou for grief!

Death!—what, is death a lock'd and treasur'd thing,
Guarded by swords of fire? a hidden spring,
A fabled fruit, that I should thus endure,
As if the world within me held no cure?
Wherefore not spread free wings—Heaven, Heaven! controul
These thoughts—they rush—I look into my soul
As down a gulph, and tremble at th' array
Of fierce forms crowding it! Give strength to pray,   210
So shall their dark host pass.

                The storm is still'd.
  Father in Heaven! Thou, only thou, canst sound
The heart's great deep, with floods of anguish fill'd,
  For human line too fearfully profound.
Therefore, forgive, my Father! if Thy child,
Rock'd on its heaving darkness, hath grown wild,
And sinn'd in her despair! It well may be,
That Thou wouldst lead my spirit back to Thee,
By the crush'd hope too long on this world pour'd,   220
The stricken love which hath perchance ador'd
A mortal in Thy place! Now let me strive
With Thy strong arm no more! Forgive, forgive!
Take me to peace!

            And peace at last is nigh.
  A sign is on my brow, a token sent
Th' o'erwearied dust, from home: no breeze flits by,
  But calls me with a strange sweet whisper, blent
Of many mysteries.

Hark! the warning tone   230
Deepens—its word is *Death*. Alone, alone,
And sad in youth, but chasten'd, I depart,
Bowing to heaven. Yet, yet my woman's heart
Shall wake a spirit and a power to bless,
Ev'n in this hour's o'ershadowing fearfulness,
Thee, its first love!—oh! tender still, and true!
Be it forgotten if mine anguish threw
Drops from its bitter fountain on thy name,
Tho' but a moment.

      Now, with fainting frame,   240
With soul just lingering on the flight begun,
To bind for thee its last dim thoughts in one,
I bless thee! Peace be on thy noble head,
Years of bright fame, when I am with the dead!
I bid this prayer survive me, and retain
Its might, again to bless thee, and again!
Thou hast been gather'd into my dark fate
Too much; too long, for my sake, desolate
Hath been thine exiled youth; but now take back,
From dying hands, thy freedom, and re-track   250
(After a few kind tears for her whose days
Went out in dreams of thee) the sunny ways
Of hope, and find thou happiness! Yet send,
Ev'n then, in silent hours a thought, dear friend!
Down to my voiceless chamber; for thy love
Hath been to me all gifts of earth above,
Tho' bought with burning tears! It is the sting
Of death to leave that vainly-precious thing
In this cold world! What were it then, if thou,
With thy fond eyes, wert gazing on me now?   260
Too keen a pang!—Farewell! and yet once more,
Farewell!—the passion of long years I pour
Into that word: thou hear'st not,—but the woe
And fervour of its tones may one day flow
To thy heart's holy place; there let them dwell—
We shall o'ersweep the grave to meet—Farewell!

‹ 15 ›

"The breaking waves dashed high / On a stern and rock-bound coast."
Illustration by L.B. Humphrey to Hemans's "The Pilgrim Fathers in New
England" in *The Breaking Waves Dashed High* (Boston: Lee and Shepard;
New York: Charles T. Dillingham, 1879).

THE BRIDE OF THE GREEK ISLE

Fear!—I'm a Greek, and how should I fear death?
A slave, and wherefore should I dread my freedom?

*   *   *   *   *   *

I will not live degraded.

Sardanapalus

Come from the woods with the citron-flowers,
Come with your lyres for the festal hours,
Maids of bright Scio! They came, and the breeze
Bore their sweet songs o'er the Grecian seas;—
They came, and Eudora stood rob'd and crown'd,
The bride of the morn, with her train around.
Jewels flash'd out from her braided hair,
Like starry dews midst the roses there;
Pearls on her bosom quivering shone,
Heav'd by her heart thro' its golden zone;   10
But a brow, as those gems of the ocean pale,
Gleam'd from beneath her transparent veil;
Changeful and faint was her fair cheek's hue,
Tho' clear as a flower which the light looks through;
And the glance of her dark resplendent eye,
For the aspect of woman at times too high,
Lay floating in mists, which the troubled stream
Of the soul sent up o'er its fervid beam.

She look'd on the vine at her father's door,
Like one that is leaving his native shore;   20
She hung o'er the myrtle once call'd her own,
As it greenly wav'd by the threshold stone;

‹ 17 ›

She turn'd—and her mother's gaze brought back
Each hue of her childhood's faded track.
Oh! hush the song, and let her tears
Flow to the dream of her early years!
Holy and pure are the drops that fall
When the young bride goes from her father's hall;
She goes unto love yet untried and new,
She parts from love which hath still been true;   30
Mute be the song and the choral strain,
Till her heart's deep well-spring is clear again!
She wept on her mother's faithful breast,
Like a babe that sobs itself to rest;
She wept—yet laid her hand awhile
In *his* that waited her dawning smile,
Her soul's affianced, nor cherish'd less
For the gush of nature's tenderness!
She lifted her graceful head at last—
The choking swell of her heart was past;   40
And her lovely thoughts from their cells found way
In the sudden flow of a plaintive lay.

The Bride's Farewell

Why do I weep?—to leave the vine
   Whose clusters o'er me bend,—
The myrtle—yet, oh! call it mine!—
   The flowers I lov'd to tend.
A thousand thoughts of all things dear,
   Like shadows o'er me sweep,
I leave my sunny childhood here,   50
   Oh, therefore let me weep!

I leave thee, sister! we have play'd
   Thro' many a joyous hour,
Where the silvery green of the olive shade
   Hung dim o'er fount and bower.
Yes, thou and I, by stream, by shore,
   In song, in prayer, in sleep,

Have been as we may be no more—
    Kind sister, let me weep!

I leave thee, father! Eve's bright moon   60
    Must now light other feet,
With the gather'd grapes, and the lyre in tune,
    Thy homeward step to greet.
Thou in whose voice, to bless thy child,
    Lay tones of love so deep,
Whose eye o'er all my youth hath smiled—
    I leave thee! let me weep!

Mother! I leave thee! on thy breast,
    Pouring out joy and woe,
I have found that holy place of rest   70
    Still changeless,   yet I go!
Lips, that have lull'd me with your strain,
    Eyes, that have watch'd my sleep!
Will earth give love like *yours* again?
    Sweet mother! let me weep!

And like a slight young tree, that throws
The weight of rain from its drooping boughs,
Once more she wept. But a changeful thing
Is the human heart, as a mountain spring,
That works its way, thro' the torrent's foam,   80
To the bright pool near it, the lily's home!
It is well!—the cloud, on her soul that lay,
Hath melted in glittering drops away.
Wake again, mingle, sweet flute and lyre!
She turns to her lover, she leaves her sire.
Mother! on earth it must still be so,
Thou rearest the lovely to see them go!

They are moving onward, the bridal throng,
Ye may track their way by the swells of song;
Ye may catch thro' the foliage their white robes' gleam,   90
Like a swan midst the reeds of a shadowy stream.

Their arms bear up garlands, their gliding tread
Is over the deep-vein'd violet's bed;
They have light leaves around them, blue skies above,
An arch for the triumph of youth and love!

II

Still and sweet was the home that stood
In the flowering depths of a Grecian wood,
With the soft green light o'er its low roof spread,
As if from the glow of an emerald shed,
Pouring thro' lime-leaves that mingled on high,   100
Asleep in the silence of noon's clear sky.
Citrons amidst their dark foliage glow'd,
Making a gleam round the lone abode;
Laurels o'erhung it, whose faintest shiver
Scatter'd out rays like a glancing river;
Stars of the jasmine its pillars crown'd,
Vine-stalks its lattice and walls had bound,
And brightly before it a fountain's play
Flung showers thro' a thicket of glossy bay,
To a cypress which rose in that flashing rain,   110
Like one tall shaft of some fallen fane.

And thither Ianthis had brought his bride,
And the guests were met by that fountain-side;
They lifted the veil from Eudora's face,
It smiled out softly in pensive grace,
With lips of love, and a brow serene,
Meet for the soul of the deep wood-scene.—
Bring wine, bring odours!—the board is spread—
Bring roses! a chaplet for every head!
The wine-cups foam'd, and the rose was shower'd   120
On the young and fair from the world embower'd,
The sun look'd not on them in that sweet shade,
The winds amid scented boughs were laid;
But there came by fits, thro' some wavy tree,
A sound and a gleam of the moaning sea.

Hush! be still!—was that no more
Than the murmur from the shore?
Silence!—did thick rain-drops beat
On the grass like trampling feet?—
Fling down the goblet, and draw the sword!   130
The groves are filled with a pirate-horde!
Thro' the dim olives their sabres shine;—
Now must the red blood stream for wine!

The youths from the banquet to battle sprang,
The woods with the shriek of the maidens rang;
Under the golden-fruited boughs
There were flashing poniards, and darkening brows,
Footsteps, o'er garland and lyre that fled;
And the dying soon on a greensward bed.

Eudora, Eudora! *thou* dost not fly!—   140
She saw but Ianthis before her lie,
With the blood from his breast in a gushing flow,
Like a child's large tears in its hour of woe,
And a gathering film in his lifted eye,
That sought his young bride out mournfully.—
She knelt down beside him, her arms she wound,
Like tendrils, his drooping neck around,
As if the passion of that fond grasp
Might chain in life with its ivy-clasp.

But they tore her thence in her wild despair,   150
The sea's fierce rovers—they left him there;
They left to the fountain a dark-red vein,
And on the wet violets a pile of slain,
And a hush of fear thro' the summer-grove,—
So clos'd the triumph of youth and love!

III
Gloomy lay the shore that night,
When the moon, with sleeping light,
Bath'd each purple Sciote hill,—

Gloomy lay the shore, and still.
O'er the wave no gay guitar   160
Sent its floating music far;
No glad sound of dancing feet
Woke, the starry hours to greet.
But a voice of mortal woe,
In its changes wild or low,
Thro' the midnight's blue repose,
From the sea-beat rocks arose,
As Eudora's mother stood
Gazing o'er th' Aegean flood,
With a fix'd and straining eye—   170
Oh! was the spoilers' vessel nigh?
Yes! there, becalm'd in silent sleep,
Dark and alone on a breathless deep,
On a sea of molten silver dark,
Brooding it frown'd that evil bark!
There its broad pennon a shadow cast,
Moveless and black from the tall still mast,
And the heavy sound of its flapping sail,
Idly and vainly wooed the gale.
Hush'd was all else—had ocean's breast   180
Rock'd e'en Eudora that hour to rest?

To rest?—the waves tremble!—what piercing cry
Bursts from the heart of the ship on high?
What light through the heavens, in a sudden spire,
Shoots from the deck up? Fire! 'tis fire!
There are wild forms hurrying to and fro,
Seen darkly clear on that lurid glow;
There are shout, and signal-gun, and call,
And the dashing of water,—but fruitless all!
Man may not fetter, nor ocean tame   190
The might and wrath of the rushing flame!
It hath twined the mast like a glittering snake,
That coils up a tree from a dusky brake;
It hath touch'd the sails, and their canvass rolls
Away from its breath into shrivell'd scrolls;

It hath taken the flag's high place in air,
And redden'd the stars with its wavy glare,
And sent out bright arrows, and soar'd in glee,
To a burning mount midst the moonlight sea.
The swimmers are plunging from stern and prow—   200
Eudora, Eudora! where, where art thou?
The slave and his master alike are gone.—
Mother! who stands on the deck alone?
The child of thy bosom!—and lo! a brand
Blazing up high in her lifted hand!
And her veil flung back, and her free dark hair
Sway'd by the flames as they rock and flare,
And her fragile form to its loftiest height
Dilated, as if by the spirit's might,
And her eye with an eagle-gladness fraught,—   210
Oh! could this work be of woman wrought?
Yes! 'twas her deed!—by that haughty smile
It was hers!—She hath kindled her funeral pile!
Never might shame on that bright head be,
Her blood was the Greek's, and hath made her free.

Proudly she stands, like an Indian bride
On the pyre with the holy dead beside;
But a shriek from her mother hath caught her ear,
As the flames to her marriage-robe draw near,
And starting, she spreads her pale arms in vain   220
To the form they must never infold again.

One moment more, and her hands are clasp'd,
Fallen is the torch they had wildly grasp'd,
Her sinking knee unto Heaven is bow'd,
And her last look rais'd thro' the smoke's dim shroud,
And her lips as in prayer for her pardon move—
Now the night gathers o'er youth and love!

"The Switzer's Wife." Illustration by the Society of Decorative Art; published in *The Poetical Works of Mrs Felicia Hemans*, ed. William Michael Rossetti (London: Ward, Lock, and Co., [ca. 1882]).

THE SWITZER'S WIFE

Werner Stauffacher, one of the three confederates of the field of Grutli, had been alarmed by the envy with which the Austrian Bailiff, Landenberg, had noticed the appearance of wealth and comfort which distinguished his dwelling. It was not, however, until roused by the entreaties of his wife, a woman who seems to have been of an heroic spirit, that he was induced to deliberate with his friends upon the measures by which Switzerland was finally delivered.

> Nor look nor tone revealeth aught
> Save woman's quietness of thought;
> And yet around her is a light
> Of inward majesty and might.
>
> M. J. J.

> Wer solch ein Herz an seinen Busen drückt,
> Der kann für Herd und Hof mit Freuden fechten.
>
> Wilhelm Tell

It was the time when children bound to meet
   Their father's homeward step from field or hill,
And when the herd's returning bells are sweet
   In the Swiss valleys, and the lakes grow still,
And the last note of that wild horn swells by,
Which haunts the exile's heart with melody.

And lovely smil'd full many an Alpine home,
   Touch'd with the crimson of the dying hour,
Which lit its low roof by the torrent's foam,
   And pierced its lattice thro' the vine-hung bower;   10
But one, the loveliest o'er the land that rose,
Then first look'd mournful in its green repose.

For Werner sat beneath the linden-tree,
   That sent its lulling whispers through his door,
Ev'n as man sits whose heart alone would be

With some deep care, and thus can find no more
Th' accustom'd joy in all which evening brings,
Gathering a household with her quiet wings.

His wife stood hush'd before him,—sad, yet mild
    In her beseeching mien;—he mark'd it not.   20
The silvery laughter of his bright-hair'd child
    Rang from the greensward round the shelter'd spot,
But seem'd unheard; until at last the boy
Rais'd from his heap'd up flowers a glance of joy,

And met his father's face: but then a change
    Pass'd swiftly o'er the brow of infant glee,
And a quick sense of something dimly strange
    Brought him from play to stand beside the knee
So often climb'd, and lift his loving eyes
That shone through clouds of sorrowful surprise.   30

Then the proud bosom of the strong man shook;
    But tenderly his babe's fair mother laid
Her hand on his, and with a pleading look,
    Thro' tears half quivering, o'er him bent, and said,
"What grief, dear friend, hath made thy heart its prey,
That thou shouldst turn thee from our love away?

"It is too sad to see thee thus, my friend!
    Mark'st thou the wonder on thy boy's fair brow,
Missing the smile from thine? Oh! cheer thee! bend
    To his soft arms, unseal thy thoughts e'en now!   40
Thou dost not kindly to withhold the share
Of tried affection in thy secret care."

He looked up into that sweet earnest face,
    But sternly, mournfully: not yet the band
Was loosen'd from his soul; its inmost place
    Not yet unveil'd by love's o'ermastering hand.
"Speak low!" he cried, and pointed where on high
The white Alps glitter'd thro' the solemn sky:

"We must speak low amidst our ancient hills
    And their free torrents; for the days are come   50
When tyranny lies couch'd by forest-rills,
    And meets the shepherd in his mountain-home.
Go, pour the wine of our own grapes in fear,
Keep silence by the hearth! its foes are near.

"The envy of th' oppressor's eye hath been
    Upon my heritage. I sit to-night
Under my household tree, if not serene,
    Yet with the faces best-belov'd in sight:
To-morrow eve may find me chain'd, and thee—
How can I bear the boy's young smiles to see?"   60

The bright blood left that youthful mother's cheek;
    Back on the linden-stem she lean'd her form,
And her lip trembled, as it strove to speak,
    Like a frail harp-string, shaken by the storm.
'Twas but a moment, and the faintness pass'd,
And the free Alpine spirit woke at last.

And she, that ever thro' her home had mov'd
    With the meek thoughtfulness and quiet smile
Of woman, calmly loving and belov'd,
    And timid in her happiness the while,   70
Stood brightly forth, and stedfastly, that hour,
Her clear glance kindling into sudden power.

Ay, pale she stood, but with an eye of light,
    And took her fair child to her holy breast,
And lifted her soft voice, that gather'd might
    As it found language:—"Are we thus oppress'd?
Then must we rise upon our mountain-sod,
And man must arm, and woman call on God!

"I know what thou wouldst do,—and be it done!
    Thy soul is darken'd with its fears for me.   80
Trust me to Heaven, my husband!—this, thy son,

The babe whom I have born thee, must be free!
And the sweet memory of our pleasant hearth
May well give strength—if aught be strong on earth.

"Thou hast been brooding o'er the silent dread
    Of my desponding tears; now lift once more,
My hunter of the hills! thy stately head,
    And let thine eagle glance my joy restore!
I can bear all, but seeing *thee* subdued,—
Take to thee back thine own undaunted mood.   90

"Go forth beside the waters, and along
    The chamois-paths, and thro' the forests go;
And tell, in burning words, thy tale of wrong
    To the brave hearts that midst the hamlets glow.
God shall be with thee, my belov'd!—Away!
Bless but thy child, and leave me,—I can pray!"

He sprang up like a warrior-youth awaking
    To clarion-sounds upon the ringing air;
He caught her to his breast, while proud tears breaking
    From his dark eyes, fell o'er her braided hair,—   100
And "Worthy art thou," was his joyous cry,
"That man for thee should gird himself to die.

"My bride, my wife, the mother of my child!
    Now shall thy name be armour to my heart;
And this our land, by chains no more defiled,
    Be taught of thee to choose the better part!
I go—thy spirit on my words shall dwell,
Thy gentle voice shall stir the Alps—Farewell!"

And thus they parted, by the quiet lake,
    In the clear starlight: he, the strength to rouse   110
Of the free hills; she, thoughtful for his sake,
    To rock her child beneath the whispering boughs
Singing its blue, half-curtain'd eyes to sleep,
With a low hymn, amidst the stillness deep.

PROPERZIA ROSSI

Properzia Rossi, a celebrated female sculptor of Bologna, possessed also of talents for poetry and music, died in consequence of an unrequited attachment.—A painting by Ducis, represents her showing her last work, a basso-relievo of Ariadne, to a Roman Knight, the object of her affection, who regards it with indifference.

——Tell me no more, no more
Of my soul's lofty gifts! Are they not vain
To quench its haunting thirst for happiness?
Have I not lov'd, and striven, and fail'd to bind
One true heart unto me, whereon my own
Might find a resting-place, a home for all
Its burden of affections? I depart,
Unknown, tho' Fame goes with me; I must leave
The earth unknown. Yet it may be that death
Shall give my name a power to win such tears
As would have made life precious.

I

One dream of passion and of beauty more!
And in its bright fulfilment let me pour
My soul away! Let earth retain a trace
Of that which lit my being, tho' its race
Might have been loftier far.—Yet one more dream!
From my deep spirit one victorious gleam
Ere I depart! For thee alone, for thee!
May this last work, this farewell triumph be,
Thou, lov'd so vainly! I would leave enshrined
Something immortal of my heart and mind,   10
That yet may speak to thee when I am gone,
Shaking thine inmost bosom with a tone
Of lost affection;—something that may prove
What she hath been, whose melancholy love
On thee was lavish'd; silent pang and tear,
And fervent song, that gush'd when none were near,

And dream by night, and weary thought by day,
Stealing the brightness from her life away,—
While thou——Awake! not yet within me die,
Under the burden and the agony   20
Of this vain tenderness,—my spirit, wake!
Ev'n for thy sorrowful affection's sake,
Live! in thy work breathe out!—that he may yet,
Feeling sad mastery there, perchance regret
Thine unrequited gift.

II
It comes,—the power
Within me born, flows back; my fruitless dower
That could not win me love. Yet once again
I greet it proudly, with its rushing train
Of glorious images:—they throng—they press—   30
A sudden joy lights up my loneliness,—
I shall not perish all!
The bright work grows
Beneath my hand, unfolding, as a rose,
Leaf after leaf, to beauty; line by line,
I fix my thought, heart, soul, to burn, to shine,
Thro' the pale marble's veins. It grows—and now
I give my own life's history to thy brow,
Forsaken Ariadne! thou shalt wear
My form, my lineaments; but oh! more fair,   40
Touch'd into lovelier being by the glow
Which in me dwells, as by the summer-light
All things are glorified. From thee my woe
Shall yet look beautiful to meet his sight,
When I am pass'd away. Thou art the mould
Wherein I pour the fervent thoughts, th' untold,
The self-consuming! Speak to him of me,
Thou, the deserted by the lonely sea,
With the soft sadness of thine earnest eye,
Speak to him, lorn one! deeply, mournfully,   50
Of all my love and grief! Oh! could I throw
Into thy frame a voice, a sweet, and low,

And thrilling voice of song! when he came nigh,
To send the passion of its melody
Thro' his pierc'd bosom—on its tones to bear
My life's deep feeling, as the southern air
Wafts the faint myrtle's breath,—to rise, to swell,
To sink away in accents of farewell,
Winning but one, *one* gush of tears, whose flow
Surely my parted spirit yet might know,   60
If love be strong as death!

III
Now fair thou art,
Thou form, whose life is of my burning heart!
Yet all the vision that within me wrought,
    I cannot make thee! Oh! I might have given
Birth to creations of far nobler thought,
    I might have kindled, with the fire of heaven,
Things not of such as die! But I have been
Too much alone; a heart whereon to lean,
With all these deep affections, that o'erflow   70
My aching soul, and find no shore below;
An eye to be my star, a voice to bring
Hope o'er my path, like sounds that breathe of spring,
These are denied me—dreamt of still in vain,—
Therefore my brief aspirings from the chain,
Are ever but as some wild fitful song,
Rising triumphantly, to die ere long
In dirge-like echoes.

IV
Yet the world will see
Little of this, my parting work, in thee,   80
    Thou shalt have fame! Oh, mockery! give the reed
From storms a shelter,—give the drooping vine
Something round which its tendrils may entwine,—
    Give the parch'd flower a rain-drop, and the meed
Of love's kind words to woman! Worthless fame!
That in *his* bosom wins not for my name

Th' abiding-place it ask'd! Yet how my heart,
In its own fairy world of song and art,
Once beat for praise!—Are those high longings o'er?
That which I have been can I be no more?—   90
Never, oh! never more; tho' still thy sky
Be blue as then, my glorious Italy!
And tho' the music, whose rich breathings fill
Thine air with soul, be wandering past me still,
And tho' the mantle of thy sunlight streams,
Unchang'd on forms, instinct with poet-dreams;
Never, oh! never more! Where'er I move,
The shadow of this broken-hearted love
Is on me and around! Too well *they* know,
    Whose life is all within, too soon and well,   100
When there the blight hath settled;—but I go
    Under the silent wings of peace to dwell;
From the slow wasting, from the lonely pain,
The inward burning of those words—*"in vain,"*
    Sear'd on the heart—I go. 'Twill soon be past.
Sunshine, and song, and bright Italian heaven,
    And thou, oh! thou, on whom my spirit cast
Unvalued wealth,—who know'st not what was given
In that devotedness,—the sad, and deep,
And unrepaid—farewell! If I could weep   110
Once, only once, belov'd one! on thy breast,
Pouring my heart forth ere I sink to rest!
But that were happiness, and unto me
Earth's gift is *fame*. Yet I was form'd to be
So richly blest! With thee to watch the sky,
Speaking not, feeling but that thou wert nigh;
With thee to listen, while the tones of song
Swept ev'n as part of our sweet air along,
To listen silently;—with thee to gaze
On forms, the deified of olden days,   120
This had been joy enough;—and hour by hour,
From its glad well-springs drinking life and power,
How had my spirit soar'd, and made its fame
    A glory for thy brow!—Dreams, dreams!—the fire

Burns faint within me. Yet I leave my name—
    As a deep thrill may linger on the lyre
When its full chords are hush'd—awhile to live,
And one day haply in thy heart revive
Sad thoughts of me:—I leave it, with a sound,
A spell o'er memory, mournfully profound,   130
I leave it, on my country's air to dwell,—
Say proudly yet—"'Twas hers who lov'd me well!"

GERTRUDE,
OR FIDELITY TILL DEATH

The Baron Von Der Wart, accused, though it is believed unjustly, as an accomplice in the assassination of the Emperor Albert, was bound alive on the wheel, and attended by his wife Gertrude, throughout his last agonizing hours, with the most heroic devotedness. Her own sufferings, with those of her unfortunate husband, are most affectingly described in a letter which she afterwards addressed to a female friend, and which was published some years ago, at Haarlem, in a book entitled *Gertrude Von Der Wart, or Fidelity unto Death*.

    Dark lowers our fate,
And terrible the storm that gathers o'er us;
But nothing, till that latest agony
Which severs thee from nature, shall unloose
This fix'd and sacred hold. In thy dark prison-house,
In the terrific face of armed law,
Yea, on the scaffold, if it needs must be,
I never will forsake thee.
                        Joanna Baillie

Her hands were clasp'd, her dark eyes rais'd,
    The breeze threw back her hair;
Up to the fearful wheel she gaz'd—
    All that she lov'd was there.

The night was round her clear and cold,
    The holy heaven above,
Its pale stars watching to behold
    The might of earthly love.

"And bid me not depart," she cried,
    "My Rudolph, say not so!   10
This is no time to quit thy side,
    Peace, peace! I cannot go.
Hath the world aught for *me* to fear,
    When death is on thy brow?
The world! what means it?—*mine* is *here*—
    I will not leave thee now.

"I have been with thee in thine hour
    Of glory and of bliss;
Doubt not its memory's living power
    To strengthen me thro' *this!*   20
And thou, mine honour'd love and true,
    Bear on, bear nobly on!
We have the blessed heaven in view,
    Whose rest shall soon be won."

And were not these high words to flow
    From woman's breaking heart?
Thro' all that night of bitterest woe
    She bore her lofty part;
But oh! with such a glazing eye,
    With such a curdling cheek—   30
Love, love! of mortal agony,
    Thou, only *thou* shouldst speak!

The wind rose high,—but with it rose
    Her voice, that he might hear:
Perchance that dark hour brought repose
    To happy bosoms near;
While she sat striving with despair
    Beside his tortured form,

And pouring her deep soul in prayer
    Forth on the rushing storm.   40

She wiped the death-damps from his brow,
    With her pale hands and soft,
Whose touch upon the lute-chords low,
    Had still'd his heart so oft.
She spread her mantle o'er his breast,
    She bath'd his lips with dew,
And on his cheek such kisses press'd
    As hope and joy ne'er knew.

Oh! lovely are ye, Love and Faith,
    Enduring to the last!   50
She had her meed—one smile in death—
    And his worn spirit pass'd.
While ev'n as o'er a martyr's grave
    She knelt on that sad spot,
And, weeping, bless'd the God who gave
    Strength to forsake it not!

IMELDA

—*Sometimes*
The young forgot the lessons they had learnt,
And lov'd when they should hate,—like thee, Imelda!
Italy, a Poem

Passa la bella Donna, e par che dorma.
Tasso

We have the myrtle's breath around us here,
    Amidst the fallen pillars;—this hath been
Some Naiad's fane of old. How brightly clear,
    Flinging a vein of silver o'er the scene,

Up thro' the shadowy grass, the fountain wells,
　　And music with it, gushing from beneath
The ivied altar!—that sweet murmur tells
　　The rich wild flowers no tale of woe or death;
Yet once the wave was darken'd, and a stain
Lay deep, and heavy drops—but not of rain—　　　　10
On the dim violets by its marble bed,
And the pale shining water-lily's head.

Sad is that legend's truth.—A fair girl met
　　One whom she lov'd, by this lone temple's spring,
Just as the sun behind the pine-grove set,
　　And eve's low voice in whispers woke, to bring
All wanderers home. They stood, that gentle pair,
　　With the blue heaven of Italy above,
And citron-odours dying on the air,
　　And light leaves trembling round, and early love　　20
Deep in each breast.—What reck'd *their* souls of strife
Between their fathers? Unto them young life
Spread out the treasures of its vernal years;
And if they wept, they wept far other tears
Than the cold world wrings forth. They stood, that hour,
Speaking of hope, while tree, and fount, and flower,
And star, just gleaming thro' the cypress boughs,
Seem'd holy things, as records of their vows.

But change came o'er the scene. A hurrying tread
　　Broke on the whispery shades. Imelda knew　　　　30
The footstep of her brother's wrath, and fled
　　Up where the cedars make yon avenue
Dim with green twilight: pausing there, she caught—
Was it the clash of swords?—a swift dark thought
　　Struck down her lip's rich crimson as it pass'd,
And from her eye the sunny sparkle took
One moment with its fearfulness, and shook
　　Her slight frame fiercely, as a stormy blast
Might rock the rose. Once more, and yet once more,
She still'd her heart to listen,—all was o'er;　　　　40

Sweet summer winds alone were heard to sigh,
Bearing the nightingale's deep spirit by.

That night Imelda's voice was in the song,
Lovely it floated thro' the festive throng,
Peopling her father's halls. That fatal night
Her eye look'd starry in its dazzling light,
And her cheek glow'd with beauty's flushing dyes,
Like a rich cloud of eve in southern skies,
A burning, ruby cloud. There were, whose gaze
Follow'd her form beneath the clear lamp's blaze,   50
And marvell'd at its radiance. But a few
Beheld the brightness of that feverish hue,
With something of dim fear; and in that glance
    Found strange and sudden tokens of unrest,
Startling to meet amidst the mazy dance,
    Where thought, if present, an unbidden guest,
Comes not unmask'd. Howe'er this were, the time
Sped as it speeds with joy, and grief, and crime
Alike: and when the banquet's hall was left
Unto its garlands of their bloom bereft,   60
When trembling stars look'd silvery in their wane,
And heavy flowers yet slumber'd, once again
There stole a footstep, fleet, and light, and lone,
Thro' the dim cedar shade; the step of one
That started at a leaf, of one that fled,
Of one that panted with some secret dread:—
What did Imelda there? She sought the scene
Where love so late with youth and hope had been;
Bodings were on her soul—a shuddering thrill
Ran thro' each vein, when first the Naiad's rill   70
Met her with melody—sweet sounds and low;
We hear them yet, they live along its flow—
Her voice is music lost! The fountain-side
She gain'd—the wave flash'd forth—'twas darkly dyed
Ev'n as from warrior-hearts; and on its edge,
    Amidst the fern, and flowers, and moss-tufts deep,
There lay, as lull'd by stream and rustling sedge,

A youth, a graceful youth. "Oh! dost thou sleep?
"Azzo!" she cried, "my Azzo! is this rest?"
But then her low tones falter'd:—"On thy breast 80
Is the stain,—yes, 'tis blood!—and that cold cheek—
That moveless lip!—thou dost not slumber?—speak,
Speak, Azzo, my belov'd!—no sound—no breath—
What hath come thus between our spirits?—Death!
Death?—I but dream—I dream!"—and there she stood,
A faint, frail trembler, gazing first on blood,
With her fair arm around yon cypress thrown,
Her form sustain'd by that dark stem alone,
And fading fast, like spell-struck maid of old,
Into white waves dissolving, clear and cold; 90
When from the grass her dimm'd eye caught a gleam—
'Twas where a sword lay shiver'd by the stream,—
Her brother's sword!—she knew it; and she knew
'Twas with a venom'd point that weapon slew!
Woe for young love! But love is strong. There came
Strength upon woman's fragile heart and frame,
There came swift courage! On the dewy ground
She knelt, with all her dark hair floating round,
Like a long silken stole; she knelt, and press'd
Her lips of glowing life to Azzo's breast, 100
Drawing the poison forth. A strange, sad sight!
Pale death, and fearless love, and solemn night!—
So the moon saw them last.
                    The morn came singing
    Thro' the green forests of the Appenines,
With all her joyous birds their free flight winging,
    And steps and voices out amongst the vines.
What found that day-spring *here?* Two fair forms laid
Like sculptured sleepers; from the myrtle shade
Casting a gleam of beauty o'er the wave, 110
Still, mournful, sweet. Were such things for the grave?
Could it be so indeed? That radiant girl,
Deck'd as for bridal hours!—long braids of pearl
Amidst her shadowy locks were faintly shining,
    As tears might shine, with melancholy light;

And there was gold her slender waist entwining;
    And her pale graceful arms—how sadly bright!
And fiery gems upon her breast were lying,
And round her marble brow red roses dying.—
But she died first!—the violet's hue had spread   120
    O'er her sweet eyelids with repose oppress'd,
She had bow'd heavily her gentle head,
    And, on the youth's hush'd bosom, sunk to rest.
So slept they well!—the poison's work was done;
Love with true heart had striven—but Death had won.

EDITH, A TALE OF THE WOODS

Du Heilige! rufe dein Kind zurück!
Ich habe genossen das irdische Glück,
Ich habe gelebt und geliebet.
                       Wallenstein

The woods—oh! solemn are the boundless woods
    Of the great Western World, when day declines,
And louder sounds the roll of distant floods,
    More deep the rustling of the ancient pines;
When dimness gathers on the stilly air,
    And mystery seems o'er every leaf to brood,
Awful it is for human heart to bear
    The might and burden of the solitude!
Yet, in that hour, midst those green wastes, there sate
One young and fair; and oh! how desolate!   10
But undismay'd; while sank the crimson light,
And the high cedars darken'd with the night.
Alone she sate: tho' many lay around,
They, pale and silent on the bloody ground,
Were sever'd from her need and from her woe,
    Far as Death severs Life. O'er that wild spot

"Ay, call it holy ground, / The soil where first they trod—." Illustration by L.B. Humphrey to Hemans's "The Pilgrim Fathers in New England" in *The Breaking Waves Dashed High* (Boston: Lee and Shepard; New York: Charles T. Dillingham, 1879).

Combat had rag'd, and brought the valiant low,
    And left them, with the history of their lot,
Unto the forest oaks. A fearful scene
For her whose home of other days had been   20
Midst the fair halls of England! but the love
    Which fill'd her soul was strong to cast out fear,
And by its might upborne all else above,
    She shrank not—mark'd not that the dead were near.
Of him alone she thought, whose languid head
    Faintly upon her wedded bosom fell;
Memory of aught but him on earth was fled,
    While heavily she felt his life-blood well
Fast o'er her garments forth, and vainly bound
With her torn robe and hair the streaming wound,   30
Yet hoped, still hoped!—Oh! from such hope how long
    Affection woos the whispers that deceive,
Ev'n when the pressure of dismay grows strong,
    And we, that weep, watch, tremble, ne'er believe
The blow indeed can fall! So bow'd she there,
Over the dying, while unconscious prayer
Fill'd all her soul. Now pour'd the moonlight down,
Veining the pine-stems thro' the foliage brown,
And fire-flies, kindling up the leafy place,
Cast fitful radiance o'er the warrior's face,   40
Whereby she caught its changes: to her eye,
    The eye that faded look'd through gathering haze,
Whence love, o'ermastering mortal agony,
    Lifted a long deep melancholy gaze,
When voice was not: that fond sad meaning pass'd—
She knew the fulness of her woe at last!
One shriek the forests heard,—and mute she lay,
And cold; yet clasping still the precious clay
To her scarce-heaving breast. O Love and Death!
Ye have sad meetings on this changeful earth,   50
Many and sad! but airs of heavenly breath
Shall melt the links which bind you, for your birth
Is far apart.

                    Now light, of richer hue
Than the moon sheds, came flushing mist and dew;
The pines grew red with morning; fresh winds play'd,
Bright-colour'd birds with splendour cross'd the shade,
Flitting on flower-like wings; glad murmurs broke
        From reed, and spray, and leaf, the living strings
Of earth's Æolian lyre, whose music woke   60
        Into young life and joy all happy things.
And she too woke from that long dreamless trance,
The widow'd Edith: fearfully her glance
Fell, as in doubt, on faces dark and strange,
And dusky forms. A sudden sense of change
Flash'd o'er her spirit, ev'n ere memory swept
The tide of anguish back with thoughts that slept;
Yet half instinctively she rose, and spread
Her arms, as 'twere for something lost or fled,
Then faintly sank again. The forest-bough,   70
With all its whispers, wav'd not o'er her now,—
Where was she? Midst the people of the wild,
        By the red hunter's fire: an aged chief,
Whose home look'd sad—for therein play'd no child—
        Had borne her, in the stillness of her grief,
To that lone cabin of the woods; and there,
Won by a form so desolately fair,
Or touch'd with thoughts from some past sorrow sprung,
O'er her low couch an Indian matron hung,
While in grave silence, yet with earnest eye,   80
The ancient warrior of the waste stood by,
Bending in watchfulness his proud grey head,
        And leaning on his bow.

                    And life return'd,
Life, but with all its memories of the dead,
        To Edith's heart; and well the sufferer learn'd
Her task of meek endurance, well she wore
The chasten'd grief that humbly can adore,
Midst blinding tears. But unto that old pair,
Ev'n as a breath of spring's awakening air,   90

Her presence was; or as a sweet wild tune
Bringing back tender thoughts, which all too soon
Depart with childhood. Sadly they had seen
 A daughter to the land of spirits go,
And ever from that time her fading mien,
 And voice, like winds of summer, soft and low,
Had haunted their dim years; but Edith's face
Now look'd in holy sweetness from her place,
And they again seem'd parents. Oh! the joy,   100
The rich, deep blessedness—tho' earth's alloy,
Fear, that still bodes, be there—of pouring forth
The heart's whole power of love, its wealth and worth
Of strong affection, in one healthful flow,
On something all its own!—that kindly glow,
Which to shut inward is consuming pain,
Gives the glad soul its flowering time again,
When, like the sunshine, freed.—And gentle cares
Th' adopted Edith meekly gave for theirs
Who lov'd her thus:—her spirit dwelt, the while,
With the departed, and her patient smile   110
Spoke of farewells to earth;—yet still she pray'd,
Ev'n o'er her soldier's lowly grave, for aid
One purpose to fulfil, to leave one trace
Brightly recording that her dwelling-place
Had been among the wilds; for well she knew
The secret whisper of her bosom true,
Which warn'd her hence.
     And now, by many a word
Link'd unto moments when the heart was stirr'd,
By the sweet mournfulness of many a hymn,   120
Sung when the woods at eve grew hush'd and dim,
By the persuasion of her fervent eye,
All eloquent with child-like piety,
By the still beauty of her life, she strove
To win for heaven, and heaven-born truth, the love
Pour'd out on her so freely.—Nor in vain
Was that soft-breathing influence to enchain
The soul in gentle bonds: by slow degrees

Light follow'd on, as when a summer breeze
Parts the deep masses of the forest shade   130
And lets the sunbeam through:—her voice was made
Ev'n such a breeze; and she, a lowly guide,
By faith and sorrow rais'd and purified,
So to the Cross her Indian fosterers led,
Until their prayers were one. When morning spread
O'er the blue lake, and when the sunset's glow
Touch'd into golden bronze the cypress-bough,
And when the quiet of the Sabbath time
Sank on her heart, tho' no melodious chime
Waken'd the wilderness, their prayers were one.   140
—Now might she pass in hope, her work was done.
And she *was* passing from the woods away;
The broken flower of England might not stay
Amidst those alien shades; her eye was bright
Ev'n yet with something of a starry light,
But her form wasted, and her fair young cheek
Wore oft and patiently a fatal streak,
A rose whose root was death. The parting sigh
Of autumn thro' the forests had gone by,
And the rich maple o'er her wanderings lone   150
Its crimson leaves in many a shower had strown,
Flushing the air; and winter's blast had been
Amidst the pines; and now a softer green
Fring'd their dark boughs; for spring again had come,
The sunny spring! but Edith to her home
Was journeying fast. Alas! we think it sad
To part with life, when all the earth looks glad
In her young lovely things, when voices break
Into sweet sounds, and leaves and blossoms wake:
Is it not brighter then, in that far clime   160
Where graves are not, nor blights of changeful time,
If *here* such glory dwell with passing blooms,
Such golden sunshine rest around the tombs?
So thought the dying one. 'Twas early day,
And sounds and odours with the breezes' play,
Whispering of spring-time, thro' the cabin-door,

Unto her couch life's farewell sweetness bore;
Then with a look where all her hope awoke,
"My father!"—to the grey-hair'd chief she spoke—
"Know'st thou that I depart?"—"I know, I know,"   170
He answer'd mournfully, "that thou must go
To thy belov'd, my daughter!"—"Sorrow not
        For me, kind mother!" with meek smiles once more
She murmur'd in low tones; "one happy lot
        Awaits us, friends! upon the better shore;
For we have pray'd together in one trust,
And lifted our frail spirits from the dust,
To God, who gave them. Lay me by mine own,
Under the cedar-shade: where he is gone
Thither I go. There will my sisters be,   180
And the dead parents, lisping at whose knee
My childhood's prayer was learn'd,—the Saviour's prayer
Which now *ye* know,—and I shall meet you there,
Father, and gentle mother!—ye have bound
The bruised reed, and mercy shall be found
By Mercy's children."—From the matron's eye
Dropp'd tears, her sole and passionate reply;
But Edith felt them not; for now a sleep,
Solemnly beautiful, a stillness deep,
Fell on her settled face. Then, sad and slow,   190
And mantling up his stately head in woe,
"Thou'rt passing hence," he sang, that warrior old,
In sounds like those by plaintive waters roll'd.

        "Thou'rt passing from the lake's green side,
            And the hunter's hearth away;
        For the time of flowers, for the summer's pride,
            Daughter! thou canst not stay.

        Thou'rt journeying to thy spirit's home,
            Where the skies are ever clear;
        The corn-month's golden hours will come,   200
            But they shall not find thee here.

And we shall miss thy voice, my bird!
  Under our whispering pine;
Music shall midst the leaves be heard,
  But not a song like thine.

A breeze that roves o'er stream and hill,
  Telling of winter gone,
Hath such sweet falls—yet caught we still
  A farewell in its tone.

But thou, my bright one! thou shalt be   210
  Where farewell sounds are o'er;
Thou, in the eyes thou lov'st, shalt see
  No fear of parting more.

The mossy grave thy tears have wet,
  And the wind's wild moanings by,
Thou with thy kindred shalt forget,
  Midst flowers—not such as die.

The shadow from thy brow shall melt,
  The sorrow from thy strain,
But where thine earthly smile hath dwelt,   220
  Our hearts shall thirst in vain.

Dim will our cabin be, and lone,
  When thou, its light, art fled;
Yet hath thy step the pathway shown
  Unto the happy dead.

And we will follow thee, our guide!
  And join that shining band;
Thou'rt passing from the lake's green side—
  Go to the better land!"

The song had ceas'd—the listeners caught no breath,   230
That lovely sleep had melted into death.

THE INDIAN CITY

What deep wounds ever clos'd without a scar?
The heart's bleed longest, and but heal to wear
That which disfigures it.

Childe Harold

I

Royal in splendour went down the day
On the plain where an Indian city lay,
With its crown of domes o'er the forest high,
Red as if fused in the burning sky,
And its deep groves pierced by the rays which made
A bright stream's way thro' each long arcade,
Till the pillar'd vaults of the Banian stood,
Like torch-lit aisles midst the solemn wood,
And the plantain glitter'd with leaves of gold,
As a tree midst the genii-gardens old,   10
And the cypress lifted a blazing spire,
And the stems of the cocoas were shafts of fire.
Many a white pagoda's gleam
Slept lovely round upon lake and stream,
Broken alone by the lotus-flowers,
As they caught the glow of the sun's last hours,
Like rosy wine in their cups, and shed
Its glory forth on their crystal bed.
Many a graceful Hindoo maid,
With the water-vase from the palmy shade,   20
Came gliding light as the desert's roe,
Down marble steps to the tanks below;
And a cool sweet plashing was ever heard,
As the molten glass of the wave was stirr'd;
And a murmur, thrilling the scented air,
Told where the Bramin bow'd in prayer.

There wandered a noble Moslem boy
Thro' the scene of beauty in breathless joy;

He gazed where the stately city rose
Like a pageant of clouds in its red repose;   30
He turn'd where birds thro' the gorgeous gloom
Of the woods went glancing on starry plume;
He track'd the brink of the shining lake,
By the tall canes feathered in tuft and brake,
Till the path he chose, in its mazes wound
To the very heart of the holy ground.

And there lay the water, as if enshrin'd
In a rocky urn from the sun and wind,
Bearing the hues of the grove on high,
Far down thro' its dark still purity.   40
The flood beyond, to the fiery west
Spread out like a metal-mirror's breast,
But that lone bay, in its dimness deep,
Seem'd made for the swimmer's joyous leap,
For the stag athirst from the noontide chase,
For all free things of the wild-wood's race.

Like a falcon's glance on the wide blue sky,
Was the kindling flash of the boy's glad eye,
Like a sea-bird's flight to the foaming wave,
From the shadowy bank was the bound he gave;   50
Dashing the spray-drops, cold and white,
O'er the glossy leaves in his young delight,
And bowing his locks to the waters clear—
Alas! he dreamt not that fate was near.

His mother look'd from her tent the while,
O'er heaven and earth with a quiet smile:
She, on her way unto Mecca's fane,
Had stay'd the march of her pilgrim-train,
Calmly to linger a few brief hours,
In the Bramin city's glorious bowers;   60
For the pomp of the forest, the wave's bright fall,
The red gold of sunset—she lov'd them all.

II

The moon rose clear in the splendour given
To the deep-blue night of an Indian heaven;
The boy from the high-arch'd woods came back—
Oh! what had he met in his lonely track?
The serpent's glance, thro' the long reeds bright?
The arrowy spring of the tiger's might?
No!—yet as one by a conflict worn,
With his graceful hair all soil'd and torn,   70
And a gloom on the lids of his darken'd eye,
And a gash on his bosom—he came to die!
He look'd for the face to his young heart sweet,
And found it, and sank at his mother's feet.

"Speak to me!—whence doth the swift blood run?
What hath befall'n thee, my child, my son?"
The mist of death on his brow lay pale,
But his voice just linger'd to breathe the tale,
Murmuring faintly of wrongs and scorn,
And wounds from the children of Brahma born: 80
This was the doom for a Moslem found
With foot profane on their holy ground,
This was for sullying the pure waves free
Unto them alone—'twas their God's decree.

A change came o'er his wandering look—
The mother shriek'd not then, nor shook:
Breathless she knelt in her son's young blood,
Rending her mantle to staunch its flood;
But it rush'd like a river which none may stay,
Bearing a flower to the deep away.   90
That which our love to the earth would chain,
Fearfully striving with Heaven in vain,
That which fades from us, while yet we hold,
Clasp'd to our bosoms, its mortal mould,
Was fleeting before her, afar and fast;
One moment—the soul from the face had pass'd!

Are there no words for that common woe?
—Ask of the thousands, its depths that know!
The boy had breathed, in his dreaming rest,
Like a low-voiced dove, on her gentle breast;   100
He had stood, when she sorrow'd, beside her knee,
Painfully stilling his quick heart's glee;
He had kiss'd from her cheek the widow's tears,
With the loving lip of his infant years;
He had smil'd o'er her path like a bright spring-day—
Now in his blood on the earth he lay!
Murder'd!—Alas! and we love so well
In a world where anguish like this can dwell!

She bow'd down mutely o'er her dead—
They that stood round her watch'd in dread;   110
They watch'd—she knew not they were by—
Her soul sat veil'd in its agony.
On the silent lip she press'd no kiss,
Too stern was the grasp of her pangs for this;
She shed no tear as her face bent low,
O'er the shining hair of the lifeless brow;
She look'd but into the half-shut eye,
With a gaze that found there no reply,
And shrieking, mantled her head from sight,
And fell, struck down by her sorrow's might!   120

And what deep change, what work of power,
Was wrought on her secret soul that hour?
How rose the lonely one?—She rose
Like a prophetess from dark repose!
And proudly flung from her face the veil,
And shook the hair from her forehead pale,
And 'midst her wondering handmaids stood,
With the sudden glance of a dauntless mood.
Ay, lifting up to the midnight sky
A brow in its regal passion high,   130
With a close and rigid grasp she press'd
The blood-stain'd robe to her heaving breast,

And said—"Not yet—not yet I weep,
Not yet my spirit shall sink or sleep,
Not till yon city, in ruins rent,
Be piled for its victim's monument.
—Cover his dust! bear it on before!
It shall visit those temple-gates once more."

And away in the train of the dead she turn'd,
The strength of her step was the heart that burn'd;   140
And the Bramin groves in the starlight smil'd,
As the mother pass'd with her slaughter'd child.

III
Hark! a wild sound of the desert's horn
Thro' the woods round the Indian city borne,
A peal of the cymbal and tambour afar—
War! 'tis the gathering of Moslem war!
The Bramin look'd from the leaguer'd towers—
He saw the wild archer amidst his bowers;
And the lake that flash'd through the plantain shade,
As the light of the lances along it play'd;   150
And the canes that shook as if winds were high,
When the fiery steed of the waste swept by;
And the camp as it lay, like a billowy sea,
Wide round the sheltering Banian tree.

There stood one tent from the rest apart—
That was the place of a wounded heart.
—Oh! deep is a wounded heart, and strong
A voice that cries against mighty wrong;
And full of death, as a hot wind's blight,
Doth the ire of a crush'd affection light.   160

Maimuna from realm to realm had pass'd,
And her tale had rung like a trumpet's blast.
There had been words from her pale lips pour'd,
Each one a spell to unsheath the sword.
The Tartar had sprung from his steed to hear,

And the dark chief of Araby grasp'd his spear,
Till a chain of long lances begirt the wall,
And a vow was recorded that doom'd its fall.
Back with the dust of her son she came,
When her voice had kindled that lightning flame;   170
She came in the might of a queenly foe,
Banner, and javelin, and bended bow;
But a deeper power on her forehead sate—
There sought the warrior his star of fate;
Her eye's wild flash through the tented line
Was hail'd as a spirit and a sign,
And the faintest tone from her lip was caught,
As a Sybil's breath of prophetic thought.

Vain, bitter glory!—the gift of grief,
That lights up vengeance to find relief,   180
Transient and faithless!—it cannot fill
So the deep void of the heart, nor still
The yearning left by a broken tie,
That haunted fever of which we die!

Sickening she turn'd from her sad renown,
As a king in death might reject his crown;
Slowly the strength of the walls gave way—
She wither'd faster, from day to day.
All the proud sounds of that banner'd plain,
To stay the flight of her soul were vain;   190
Like an eagle caged, it had striven, and worn
The frail dust ne'er for such conflicts born,
Till the bars were rent, and the hour was come
For its fearful rushing thro' darkness home.

The bright sun set in his pomp and pride,
As on that eve when the fair boy died;
She gazed from her couch, and a softness fell
O'er her weary heart with the day's farewell;
She spoke, and her voice in its dying tone
Had an echo of feelings that long seem'd flown.   200

She murmur'd a low sweet cradle song,
Strange midst the din of a warrior throng,
A song of the time when her boy's young cheek
Had glow'd on her breast in its slumber meek;
But something which breathed from that mournful strain
Sent a fitful gust o'er her soul again,
And starting as if from a dream, she cried—
"Give him proud burial at my side!
There, by yon lake, where the palm boughs wave,
When the temples are fallen, make there our grave."   210

And the temples fell, tho' the spirit pass'd,
That stay'd not for victory's voice at last;
When the day was won for the martyr-dead,
For the broken heart, and the bright blood shed.

Thro' the gates of the vanquish'd the Tartar steed
Bore in the avenger with foaming speed;
Free swept the flame thro' the idol-fanes,
And the streams glow'd red, as from warrior-veins,
And the sword of the Moslem, let loose to slay,
Like the panther leapt on its flying prey,   220
Till a city of ruin begirt the shade,
Where the boy and his mother at rest were laid.

Palace and tower on that plain were left,
Like fallen trees by the lightning cleft;
The wild vine mantled the stately square,
The Rajah's throne was the serpent's lair,
And the jungle grass o'er the altar sprung—
This was the work of one deep heart wrung!

THE PEASANT GIRL
OF THE RHONE

—There is but one place in the world:
Thither where he lies buried!

*   *   *   *   *   *   *   *

There, there is all that still remains of him,
That single spot is the whole earth to me.

Coleridge's Wallenstein

Alas! our young affections run to waste,
Or water but the desert.

Childe Harold

There went a warrior's funeral thro' the night,
A waving of tall plumes, a ruddy light
Of torches, fitfully and wildly thrown
From the high woods, along the sweeping Rhone,
Far down the waters. Heavily and dead,
Under the moaning trees the horse-hoof's tread
In muffled sounds upon the greensward fell,
As chieftains pass'd; and solemnly the swell
Of the deep requiem, o'er the gleaming river
Borne with the gale, and with the leaves low shiver,   10
Floated and died. Proud mourners there, yet pale,
    Wore man's mute anguish sternly;—but of *one*
Oh! who shall speak? What words *his* brow unveil?
    A father following to the grave his son!
That is no grief to picture! Sad and slow,
    Thro' the wood-shadows moved the knightly train,
With youth's fair form upon the bier laid low,
    Fair even when found, amidst the bloody slain,
Stretch'd by its broken lance. They reached the lone
    Baronial chapel, where the forest gloom   20
Fell heaviest, for the massy boughs had grown
    Into thick archways, as to vault the tomb.

Stately they trod the hollow ringing aisle,
A strange deep echo shuddered thro' the pile,
Till crested heads at last, in silence bent
Round the De Couci's antique monument,
When dust to dust was given:—and Aymer slept
    Beneath the drooping banners of his line,
Whose broider'd folds the Syrian wind had swept
    Proudly and oft o'er fields of Palestine: 30
So the sad rite was clos'd.—The sculptor gave
Trophies, ere long, to deck that lordly grave,
And the pale image of a youth, arrayed
As warriors are for fight, but calmly laid
    In slumber on his shield.—Then all was done,
All still, around the dead.—His name was heard
Perchance when wine-cups flow'd, and hearts were stirr'd
    By some old song, or tale of battle won,
Told round the hearth: but in his father's breast
Manhood's high passions woke again, and press'd   40
On to their mark; and in his friend's clear eye
There dwelt no shadow of a dream gone by;
And with the brethren of his fields, the feast
Was gay as when the voice whose sounds had ceas'd
Mingled with theirs.—Ev'n thus life's rushing tide
Bears back affection from the grave's dark side:
Alas! to think of this!—the heart's void place
    Filled up so soon!—so like a summer-cloud,
All that we lov'd to pass and leave no trace!—
    He lay forgotten in his early shroud.   50
Forgotten?—not of all!—the sunny smile
Glancing in play o'er that proud lip erewhile,
And the dark locks whose breezy waving threw
A gladness round, whene'er their shade withdrew
From the bright brow; and all the sweetness lying
    Within that eagle-eye's jet radiance deep,
And all the music with that young voice dying,
    Whose joyous echoes made the quick heart leap
As at a hunter's bugle—these things lived
Still in one breast, whose silent love survived   60

The pomps of kindred sorrow.—Day by day,
On Aymer's tomb fresh flowers in garlands lay,
Thro' the dim fane soft summer-odours breathing,
And all the pale sepulchral trophies wreathing,
And with a flush of deeper brilliance glowing
In the rich light, like molten rubies flowing
Thro' storied windows down. The violet there
Might speak of love—a secret love and lowly,
And the rose image all things fleet and fair,
And the faint passion-flower, the sad and holy,   70
Tell of diviner hopes. But whose light hand,
As for an altar, wove the radiant band?
Whose gentle nurture brought, from hidden dells,
That gem-like wealth of blossoms and sweet bells,
To blush thro' every season?—Blight and chill
Might touch the changing woods, but duly still,
For years, those gorgeous coronals renewed,
    And brightly clasping marble spear and helm,
Even thro' mid-winter, filled the solitude
    With a strange smile, a glow of summer's realm.   80
Surely some fond and fervent heart was pouring
Its youth's vain worship on the dust, adoring
In lone devotedness!

                One spring-morn rose,
    And found, within that tomb's proud shadow laid—
Oh! not as midst the vineyards, to repose
    From the fierce noon—a dark-hair'd peasant maid:
Who could reveal her story?—That still face
    Had once been fair; for on the clear arch'd brow,
And the curv'd lip, there lingered yet such grace   90
    As sculpture gives its dreams; and long and low
The deep black lashes, o'er the half-shut eye—
For death was on its lids—fell mournfully.
But the cold cheek was sunk, the raven hair
Dimm'd, the slight form all wasted, as by care.
Whence came that early blight?—*Her* kindred's place
Was not amidst the high De Couci race;

Yet there her shrine had been!—She grasp'd a wreath—
The tomb's last garland!—This was love in death!

Indian Woman's Death Song

An Indian woman, driven to despair by her husband's desertion of
her for another wife, entered a canoe with her children, and rowed it
down the Mississippi towards a cataract. Her voice was heard from the
shore singing a mournful death-song, until overpowered by the sound of
the waters in which she perished. The tale is related in Long's *Expedition
to the Source of St Peter's River*.

> *Non, je ne puis vivre avec un coeur brisé. Il faut que je retrouve la joie,
> et que je m'unisse aux esprits libres de l'air.*
>
> Bride of Messina,
> Translated by Madame de Staël

> *Let not my child be a girl, for very sad is the life of a woman.*
>
> The Prairie

Down a broad river of the western wilds,
Piercing thick forest glooms, a light canoe
Swept with the current: fearful was the speed
Of the frail bark, as by a tempest's wing
Borne leaf-like on to where the mist of spray
Rose with the cataract's thunder.—Yet within,
Proudly, and dauntlessly, and all alone,
Save that a babe lay sleeping at her breast,
A woman stood: upon her Indian brow
Sat a strange gladness, and her dark hair wav'd   10
As if triumphantly. She press'd her child,
In its bright slumber, to her beating heart,
And lifted her sweet voice, that rose awhile
Above the sound of waters, high and clear,
Wafting a wild proud strain, her song of death.

Roll swiftly to the Spirit's land, thou mighty stream and free!
Father of ancient waters, roll! and bear our lives with thee!
The weary bird that storms have toss'd, would seek the sunshine's
    calm,
And the deer that hath the arrow's hurt, flies to the woods of
    balm.

Roll on!—my warrior's eye hath look'd upon another's face,   20
And mine hath faded from his soul, as fades a moonbeam's trace;
My shadow comes not o'er his path, my whisper to his dream,
He flings away the broken reed—roll swifter yet, thou stream!

The voice that spoke of other days is hush'd within *his* breast,
But *mine* its lonely music haunts, and will not let me rest;
It sings a low and mournful song of gladness that is gone,
I cannot live without that light—Father of waves! roll on!

Will he not miss the bounding step that met him from the chase?
The heart of love that made his home an ever sunny place?
The hand that spread the hunter's board, and deck'd his couch of
    yore?—   30
He will not!—roll, dark foaming stream, on to the better shore!

Some blessed fount amidst the woods of that bright land must
    flow,
Whose waters from my soul may lave the memory of this woe;
Some gentle wind must whisper there, whose breath may waft
    away
The burden of the heavy night, the sadness of the day.

And thou, my babe! tho' born, like me, for woman's weary lot,
Smile!—to that wasting of the heart, my own! I leave thee not;
Too bright a thing art *thou* to pine in aching love away,
Thy mother bears thee far, young Fawn! from sorrow and decay.

She bears thee to the glorious bowers where none are heard to
    weep,   40
And where th' unkind one hath no power again to trouble sleep;

And where the soul shall find its youth, as wakening from a
    dream,—
One moment, and that realm is ours—On, on, dark rolling stream!

Joan of Arc, in Rheims

Jeanne d'Arc avait eu la joie de voir à Chalons quelques amis de son
enfance. Une joie plus ineffable encore l'attendait à Rheims, au sein de
son triomphe: Jacques d'Arc, son père s'y trouva, aussitôt que des troupes
de Charles VII y furent entrées; et comme les deux frères de notre Héroïne
l'avaient accompagnée, elle se vit, pour un instant au milieu de sa famille,
dans les bras d'un père vertueux.

Vie de Jeanne d'Arc

Thou hast a charmed cup, O Fame!
   A draught that mantles high,
And seems to lift this earth-born frame
   Above mortality:
Away! to me—a woman—bring
Sweet waters from affection's spring.

That was a joyous day in Rheims of old,
When peal on peal of mighty music roll'd
Forth from her throng'd cathedral; while around,
A multitude, whose billows made no sound,
Chain'd to a hush of wonder, tho' elate
With victory, listen'd at their temple's gate.
And what was done within?—within, the light
   Thro' the rich gloom of pictured windows flowing,
Tinged with soft awfulness a stately sight,
   The chivalry of France, their proud heads bowing   10
In martial vassalage!—while midst that ring,
And shadow'd by ancestral tombs, a king
Receiv'd his birthright's crown. For this, the hymn
   Swell'd out like rushing waters, and the day
With the sweet censer's misty breath grew dim,
   As thro' long aisles it floated o'er th' array

Of arms and sweeping stoles. But who, alone
And unapproach'd, beside the altar-stone,
With the white banner, forth like sunshine streaming,
And the gold helm, thro' clouds of fragrance gleaming,   20
Silent and radiant stood?—the helm was rais'd,
And the fair face reveal'd, that upward gaz'd,
      Intensely worshipping:—a still, clear face,
Youthful, but brightly solemn!—Woman's cheek
And brow were there, in deep devotion meek,
      Yet glorified with inspiration's trace
On its pure paleness; while, enthron'd above,
The pictur'd virgin, with her smile of love,
Seem'd bending o'er her votaress.—That slight form!
Was that the leader thro' the battle storm?   30
Had the soft light in that adoring eye,
Guided the warrior where the swords flash'd high?
'Twas so, even so!—and thou, the shepherd's child,
Joanne, the lowly dreamer of the wild!
Never before, and never since that hour,
Hath woman, mantled with victorious power,
Stood forth as *thou* beside the shrine didst stand,
Holy amidst the knighthood of the land;
And beautiful with joy and with renown,
Lift thy white banner o'er the olden crown,   40
Ransom'd for France by thee!

                    The rites are done.
Now let the dome with trumpet-notes be shaken,
And bid the echoes of the tombs awaken,
      And come thou forth, that Heaven's rejoicing sun
May give thee welcome from thine own blue skies,
      Daughter of victory!—A triumphant strain,
A proud rich stream of warlike melodies,
      Gush'd thro' the portals of the antique fane,
And forth she came.—Then rose a nation's sound—   50
Oh! what a power to bid the quick heart bound,
The wind bears onward with the stormy cheer
Man gives to glory on her high career!

Is there indeed such power?—far deeper dwells
In one kind household voice, to reach the cells
Whence happiness flows forth!—The shouts that fill'd
The hollow heaven tempestuously, were still'd
One moment; and in that brief pause, the tone,
As of a breeze that o'er her home had blown,
Sank on the bright maid's heart.—"Joanne!"—Who spoke   60
    Like those whose childhood with *her* childhood grew
Under one roof?—"Joanne!"—*that* murmur broke
    With sounds of weeping forth!—She turn'd—She knew
Beside her, mark'd from all the thousands there,
In the calm beauty of his silver hair,
The stately shepherd; and the youth, whose joy
From his dark eye flash'd proudly; and the boy,
The youngest-born, that ever lov'd her best:
"Father! and ye, my brothers!"—On the breast
Of that grey sire she sank—and swiftly back,   70
Ev'n in an instant, to their native track
Her free thoughts flowed.—She saw the pomp no more—
The plumes, the banners:—to her cabin-door,
And to the Fairy's fountain in the glade,
Where her young sisters by her side had play'd,
And to her hamlet's chapel, where it rose
Hallowing the forest unto deep repose,
Her spirit turn'd.—The very wood-note, sung
    In early spring-time by the bird, which dwelt
Where o'er her father's roof the beech-leaves hung,   80
    Was in her heart; a music heard and felt,
Winning her back to nature.—She unbound
    The helm of many battles from her head,
And, with her bright locks bow'd to sweep the ground,
    Lifting her voice up, wept for joy, and said,—
"Bless me, my father, bless me! and with thee,
To the still cabin and the beechen-tree,
Let me return!"
                    Oh! never did thine eye
Thro' the green haunts of happy infancy   90
Wander again, Joanne!—too much of fame

Had shed its radiance on thy peasant-name;
And bought alone by gifts beyond all price,
The trusting heart's repose, the paradise
Of home with all its loves, doth fate allow
The crown of glory unto woman's brow.

Felicia Hemans from a portrait painted in the autumn of 1828 by William
E. West and later engraved by Edward Scriven for the frontispiece to vol-
ume one of *The Works of Mrs. Hemans; with a memoir of her life by her
sister* (Harriet Hughes), published in seven volumes in 1839 for Thomas
Cadell, London.

PAULINE

To die for what we love!—Oh! there is power
In the true heart, and pride, and joy, for *this;*
It is to *live* without the vanish'd light
That strength is needed.

    Così trapassa al trapassar d'un Giorno
    Della vita mortal il fiore e'l verde.
                         Tasso

Along the star-lit Seine went music swelling,
    Till the air thrill'd with its exulting mirth;
Proudly it floated, even as if no dwelling
    For cares or stricken hearts were found on earth;
And a glad sound the measure lightly beat,
A happy chime of many dancing feet.

For in a palace of the land that night,
    Lamps, and fresh roses, and green leaves were hung,
And from the painted walls a stream of light
    On flying forms beneath soft splendour flung: 10
But loveliest far amidst the revel's pride
Was one, the lady from the Danube-side.

Pauline, the meekly bright!—tho' now no more
    Her clear eye flash'd with youth's all tameless glee,
Yet something holier than its dayspring wore,
    There in soft rest lay beautiful to see;
A charm with graver, tenderer, sweetness fraught—
The blending of deep love and matron thought.

Thro' the gay throng she moved, serenely fair,
    And such calm joy as fills a moonlight sky,   20
Sate on her brow beneath its graceful hair,
    As her young daughter in the dance went by,

Felicity Dorothea Wagner Browne, mother of Felicia Hemans. Engraving, by Edward Scriven, published as the frontispiece to volume 2 of *The Works of Mrs Hemans; with a Memoir of her Life, by her Sister* (Edinburgh: William Blackwood, 1839).

With the fleet step of one that yet hath known
Smiles and kind voices in this world alone.

Lurk'd there no secret boding in her breast?
    Did no faint whisper warn of evil nigh?
Such oft awake when most the heart seems blest
    Midst the light laughter of festivity:
Whence come those tones!—Alas! enough we know,
To mingle fear with all triumphal show!   30

Who spoke of evil, when young feet were flying
    In fairy rings around the echoing hall?
Soft airs thro' braided locks in perfume sighing,
    Glad pulses beating unto music's call?
Silence!—the minstrels pause—and hark! a sound,
A strange quick rustling which their notes had drown'd!

And lo! a light upon the dancers breaking—
    Not such their clear and silvery lamps had shed!
From the gay dream of revelry awaking,
    One moment holds them still in breathless dread;   40
The wild fierce lustre grows—then bursts a cry—
Fire! thro' the hall and round it gathering—fly!

And forth they rush—as chased by sword and spear—
    To the green coverts of the garden-bowers;
A gorgeous masque of pageantry and fear,
    Startling the birds and trampling down the flowers:
While from the dome behind, red sparkles driven
Pierce the dark stillness of the midnight heaven.

And where is she, Pauline?—the hurrying throng
    Have swept her onward, as a stormy blast   50
Might sweep some faint o'erwearied bird along—
    Till now the threshold of that death is past,
And free she stands beneath the starry skies,
Calling her child—but no sweet voice replies.

"Bertha! where art thou?—Speak, oh! speak, my own!"
    Alas! unconscious of her pangs the while,
The gentle girl, in fear's cold grasp alone,
    Powerless hath sunk within the blazing pile;
A young bright form, deck'd gloriously for death,
With flowers all shrinking from the flame's fierce breath!   60

But oh! thy strength, deep love!—there is no power
    To stay the mother from that rolling grave,
Tho' fast on high the fiery volumes tower,
    And forth, like banners, from each lattice wave
Back, back she rushes thro' a host combined—
Mighty is anguish, with affection twined!

And what bold step may follow, midst the roar
    Of the red billows, o'er their prey that rise?
None!—Courage there stood still—and never more
    Did those fair forms emerge on human eyes!   70
Was one brief meeting theirs, one wild farewell?
And died they heart to heart?—Oh! who can tell?

Freshly and cloudlessly the morning broke
    On that sad palace, midst its pleasure-shades;
Its painted roofs had sunk—yet black with smoke
    And lonely stood its marble colonnades:
But yester-eve their shafts with wreaths were bound—
Now lay the scene one shrivell'd scroll around!

And bore the ruins no recording trace
    Of all that woman's heart had dared and done?   80
Yes! there were gems to mark its mortal place,
    That forth from dust and ashes dimly shone!
Those had the mother on her gentle breast,
Worn round her child's fair image, there at rest.

And they were all!—the tender and the true
    Left this alone her sacrifice to prove,
Hallowing the spot where mirth once lightly flew,
    To deep, lone, chasten'd thoughts of grief and love.

Oh! we have need of patient faith below,
To clear away the mysteries of such woe!   90

JUANA

Juana, mother of the Emperor Charles V, upon the death of her husband, Philip the Handsome of Austria, who had treated her with uniform neglect, had his body laid upon a bed of state in a magnificent dress, and being possessed with the idea that it would revive, watched it for a length of time incessantly, waiting for the moment of returning life.

It is but dust thou look'st upon. This love,
This wild and passionate idolatry,
What doth it in the shadow of the grave?
Gather it back within thy lonely heart,
So must it ever end: too much we give
Unto the things that perish.

The night-wind shook the tapestry round an ancient palace-room,
And torches, as it rose and fell, waved thro' the gorgeous gloom,
And o'er a shadowy regal couch threw fitful gleams and red,
Where a woman with long raven hair sat watching by the dead.

Pale shone the features of the dead, yet glorious still to see,
Like a hunter or a chief struck down while his heart and step
    were free;
No shroud he wore, no robe of death, but there majestic lay,
Proudly and sadly glittering in royalty's array.

But she that with the dark hair watch'd by the cold slumberer's side,
On *her* wan cheek no beauty dwelt, and in her garb no pride;   10
Only her full impassion'd eyes as o'er that clay she bent,
A wildness and a tenderness in strange resplendence blent.

And as the swift thoughts cross'd her soul, like shadows of a cloud,
Amidst the silent room of death, the dreamer spoke aloud;

She spoke to him who could not hear, and cried, "Thou yet wilt wake,
And learn my watchings and my tears, belov'd one! for thy sake.

"They told me this was death, but well I knew it could not be;
Fairest and stateliest of the earth! who spoke of death for *thee*?
They would have wrapt the funeral shroud thy gallant form around,
But I forbade—and there thou art, a monarch, rob'd and crown'd!   20

"With all thy bright locks gleaming still, their coronal beneath,
And thy brow so proudly beautiful—who said that this was death?
Silence hath been upon thy lips, and stillness round thee long,
But the hopeful spirit in my breast is all undimm'd and strong.

"I know thou hast not lov'd me yet; I am not fair like thee,
The very glance of whose clear eye threw round a light of glee!
A frail and drooping form is mine—a cold unsmiling cheek,
Oh! I have but a woman's heart, wherewith *thy* heart to seek.

"But when thou wak'st, my prince, my lord! and hear'st how I have kept
A lonely vigil by thy side, and o'er thee pray'd and wept;   30
How in one long deep dream of thee my nights and days have past,
Surely that humble, patient love *must* win back love at last!

"And thou wilt smile—my own, my own, shall be the sunny smile,
Which brightly fell, and joyously, on all *but* me erewhile!
No more in vain affection's thirst my weary soul shall pine—
Oh! years of hope deferr'd were paid by one fond glance of thine!

"Thou'lt meet me with that radiant look when thou comest from the chase,
For me, for me, in festal halls it shall kindle o'er thy face!
Thou'lt reck no more tho' beauty's gift mine aspect may not bless;
In thy kind eyes this deep, deep love, shall give me loveliness.   40

"But wake! my heart within me burns, yet once more to rejoice
In the sound to which it ever leap'd, the music of thy voice:

Awake! I sit in solitude, that thy first look and tone,
And the gladness of thine opening eyes may all be mine alone."

In the still chambers of the dust, thus pour'd forth day by day,
The passion of that loving dream from a troubled soul found way,
Until the shadows of the grave had swept o'er every grace,
Left midst the awfulness of death on the princely form and face.

And slowly broke the fearful truth upon the watcher's breast,
And they bore away the royal dead with requiems to his rest,   50
With banners and with knightly plumes all waving in the wind—
But a woman's broken heart was left in its lone despair behind.

THE AMERICAN FOREST GIRL

A fearful gift upon thy heart is laid,
Woman!—a power to suffer and to love,
Therefore thou so canst pity.

Wildly and mournfully the Indian drum
    On the deep hush of moonlight forests broke;—
"Sing us a death-song, for thine hour is come,"—
    So the red warriors to their captive spoke.
Still, and amidst those dusky forms alone,
    A youth, a fair-hair'd youth of England stood,
Like a king's son; tho' from his cheek had flown
    The mantling crimson of the island-blood,
And his press'd lips look'd marble.—Fiercely bright,
And high around him, blaz'd the fires of night,   10
Rocking beneath the cedars to and fro,
As the wind pass'd, and with a fitful glow
Lighting the victim's face:—But who could tell
Of what within his secret heart befell,
Known but to heaven that hour?—Perchance a thought

Of his far home then so intensely wrought,
That its full image, pictured to his eye
On the dark ground of mortal agony,
Rose clear as day!—and he might *see* the band,
Of his young sisters wandering hand in hand,   20
Where the laburnums droop'd; or haply binding
The jasmine, up the door's low pillars winding;
Or, as day clos'd upon their gentle mirth,
Gathering with braided hair, around the hearth
Where sat their mother;—and that mother's face
Its grave sweet smile yet wearing in the place
Where so it ever smiled!—Perchance the prayer
Learn'd at her knee came back on his despair;
The blessing from her voice, the very tone
Of her "*Good-night*" might breathe from boyhood gone!—   30
He started and look'd up:—thick cypress boughs
      Full of strange sound, wav'd o'er him, darkly red
In the broad stormy firelight;—savage brows,
      With tall plumes crested and wild hues o'erspread,
Girt him like feverish phantoms; and pale stars
Look'd thro' the branches as thro' dungeon bars,
Shedding no hope.—He knew, he felt his doom—
Oh! what a tale to shadow with its gloom
That happy hall in England!—Idle fear!
Would the winds tell it?—Who might dream or hear   40
The secret of the forests?—To the stake
      They bound him; and that proud young soldier strove
His father's spirit in his breast to wake,
      Trusting to die in silence! He, the love
Of many hearts!—the fondly rear'd,—the fair,
Gladdening all eyes to see!—And fetter'd there
He stood beside his death-pyre, and the brand
Flamed up to light it, in the chieftain's hand.
He thought upon his God.—Hush! hark!—a cry
Breaks on the stern and dread solemnity,—   50
A step hath pierc'd the ring!—Who dares intrude
On the dark hunters in their vengeful mood?—
A girl—a young slight girl—a fawn-like child

Of green savannas and the leafy wild,
Springing unmark'd till then, as some lone flower,
Happy because the sunshine is its dower;
Yet one that knew how early tears are shed,—
For *hers* had mourn'd a playmate brother dead.

She had sat gazing on the victim long,
Until the pity of her soul grew strong;   60
And, by its passion's deepening fervour sway'd,
Ev'n to the stake she rush'd, and gently laid
His bright head on her bosom, and around
His form her slender arms to shield it wound
Like close Liannes; then rais'd her glittering eye
And clear-toned voice that said, "He shall not die!"

"He shall not die!"—the gloomy forest thrill'd
    To that sweet sound. A sudden wonder fell
On the fierce throng; and heart and hand were still'd,
    Struck down, as by the whisper of a spell.   70
They gaz'd,—their dark souls bow'd before the maid,
She of the dancing step in wood and glade!
And, as her cheek flush'd thro' its olive hue,
As her black tresses to the night-wind flew,
Something o'ermaster'd them from that young mien—
Something of heaven, in silence felt and seen;
And seeming, to their child-like faith, a token
That the Great Spirit by her voice had spoken.

They loos'd the bonds that held their captive's breath;
From his pale lips they took the cup of death;   80
They quench'd the brand beneath the cypress tree;
"Away," they cried, "young stranger, thou art free!"

COSTANZA

———Art thou then desolate?
Of friends, of hopes forsaken?—Come to me!
I am thine own.—Have trusted hearts prov'd false?
Flatterers deceiv'd thee? Wanderer, come to me!
Why didst thou ever leave me? Know'st thou all
I would have borne, and call'd it joy to bear,
For thy sake? Know'st thou that thy voice had power
To shake me with a thrill of happiness
By one kind tone?—to fill mine eyes with tears
Of yearning love? And thou—oh! thou didst throw
That crush'd affection back upon my heart;—
Yet come to me!—it died not.

She knelt in prayer. A stream of sunset fell
Thro' the stain'd window of her lonely cell,
And with its rich, deep, melancholy glow
Flushing her cheek and pale Madonna-brow,
While o'er her long hair's flowing jet it threw
Bright waves of gold—the autumn forest's hue—
Seem'd all a vision's mist of glory, spread
By painting's touch around some holy head,
Virgin's or fairest martyr's. In her eye,
Which glanced as dark clear water to the sky,   10
What solemn fervour lived! And yet what woe,
Lay like some buried thing, still seen below
The glassy tide! Oh! he that could reveal
What life had taught that chasten'd heart to feel,
Might speak indeed of woman's blighted years,
And wasted love, and vainly bitter tears!
But she had told her griefs to heaven alone,
And of the gentle saint no more was known,
Than that she fled the world's cold breath, and made
A temple of the pine and chestnut shade,   20
Filling its depths with soul, whene'er her hymn
Rose thro' each murmur of the green, and dim,

‹ 72 ›

And ancient solitude; where hidden streams
Went moaning thro' the grass, like sounds in dreams,
Music for weary hearts! Midst leaves and flowers
She dwelt, and knew all secrets of their powers,
All nature's balms, wherewith her gliding tread
To the sick peasant on his lowly bed,
Came, and brought hope; while scarce of mortal birth
He decm'd the pale fair form, that held on earth   30
Communion but with grief.

            Ere long a cell,
   A rock-hewn chapel rose, a cross of stone
Gleam'd thro' the dark trees o'er a sparkling well,
   And a sweet voice, of rich, yet mournful tone,
Told the Calabrian wilds, that duly there
Costanza lifted her sad heart in prayer.
And now 'twas prayer's own hour. That voice again
Thro' the dim foliage sent its heavenly strain,
That made the cypress quiver where it stood   40
In day's last crimson soaring from the wood
Like spiry flame. But as the bright sun set,
Other and wilder sounds in tumult met
The floating song. Strange sounds!—the trumpet's peal,
Made hollow by the rocks; the clash of steel,
The rallying war-cry.—In the mountain-pass,
There had been combat; blood was on the grass,
Banners had strewn the waters; chiefs lay dying,
And the pine-branches crash'd before the flying.

And all was chang'd within the still retreat,   50
Costanza's home:—there enter'd hurrying feet,
   Dark looks of shame and sorrow; mail-clad men,
   Stern fugitives from that wild battle-glen,
Scaring the ringdoves from the porch-roof, bore
A wounded warrior in: the rocky floor
Gave back deep echoes to his clanging sword,
As there they laid their leader, and implor'd
The sweet saint's prayers to heal him; then for flight,

Thro' the wide forest and the mantling night,
Sped breathlessly again.—They pass'd—but he,   60
The stateliest of a host—alas! to see
What mother's eyes have watch'd in rosy sleep
Till joy, for very fulness, turn'd to weep,
Thus changed!—a fearful thing! His golden crest
Was shiver'd, and the bright scarf on his breast—
Some costly love-gift—rent:—but what of these?
There were the clustering raven-locks—the breeze
As it came in thro' lime and myrtle flowers,
Might scarcely lift them—steep'd in bloody showers
So heavily upon the pallid clay   70
Of the damp cheek they hung! the eyes' dark ray—
Where was it?—and the lips!—they gasp'd apart,
With their light curve, as from the chisel's art,
Still proudly beautiful! but that white hue—
Was it not death's?—that stillness—that cold dew
On the scarr'd forehead? No! his spirit broke
From its deep trance ere long, yet but awoke
To wander in wild dreams; and there he lay,
By the fierce fever as a green reed shaken,
The haughty chief of thousands—the forsaken   80
Of all save one!—*She* fled not. Day by day—
Such hours are woman's birthright—she, unknown,
Kept watch beside him, fearless and alone;
Binding his wounds, and oft in silence laving
His brow with tears that mourn'd the strong man's raving.
He felt them not, nor mark'd the light veil'd form
Still hovering nigh; yet sometimes, when that storm
    Of frenzy sank, her voice, in tones as low
As a young mother's by the cradle singing,
Would sooth him with sweet *aves,* gently bringing   90
    Moments of slumber, when the fiery glow
Ebb'd from his hollow cheek.

                    At last faint gleams
Of memory dawn'd upon the cloud of dreams,
And feebly lifting, as a child, his head,

And gazing round him from his leafy bed,
He murmur'd forth, "Where am I? What soft strain
Pass'd, like a breeze, across my burning brain?
Back from my youth it floated, with a tone
Of life's first music, and a thought of one—   100
Where is she now? and where the gauds of pride
Whose hollow splendour lured me from her side?
All lost!   and this is death!—I *cannot* die
Without forgiveness from that mournful eye!
Away! the earth hath lost her. Was *she* born
To brook abandonment, to strive with scorn?
My first, my holiest love!—her broken heart
Lies low, and I—unpardon'd I depart."

But then Costanza rais'd the shadowy veil
From her dark locks and features brightly pale,   110
And stood before him with a smile—oh! ne'er
Did aught that *smiled* so much of sadness wear—
And said, "Cesario! look on me; I live
To say my heart hath bled, and can forgive.
I loved thee with such worship, such deep trust
As should be Heaven's alone—and Heaven is just!
I bless thee—be at peace!"

            But o'er his frame
Too fast the strong tide rush'd—the sudden shame,
The joy, th' amaze!—he bow'd his head—it fell   120
On the wrong'd bosom which had lov'd so well;
And love still perfect, gave him refuge there,—
His last faint breath just wav'd her floating hair.

MADELINE,
a Domestic Tale

Who should it be?—Where shouldst thou look for kindness?
When we are sick where can we turn for succour,

"There was woman's fearless eye, / Lit by her deep love's truth." Illustration by L.B. Humphrey to Hemans's "The Pilgrim Fathers in New England" in *The Breaking Waves Dashed High* (Boston: Lee and Shepard; New York: Charles T. Dillingham, 1879).

When we are wretched where can we complain;
And when the world looks cold and surly on us,
Where can we go to meet a warmer eye
With such sure confidence as to a mother?

Joanna Baillie

"My child, my child, thou leav'st me!—I shall hear
The gentle voice no more that blest mine ear
With its first utterance; I shall miss the sound
Of thy light step amidst the flowers around,
And thy soft-breathing hymn at twilight's close,
And thy "Good-night" at parting for repose.
Under the vine-leaves I shall sit alone,
And the low breeze will have a mournful tone
Amidst their tendrils, while I think of thee,
My child! and thou, along the moonlight sea,   10
With a soft sadness haply in thy glance,
Shalt watch thine own, thy pleasant land of France,
Fading to air.—Yet blessings with thee go!
Love guard thee, gentlest! and the exile's woe
From thy young heart be far!—And sorrow not
For me, sweet daughter! in my lonely lot,
God shall be with me.—Now farewell, farewell!
Thou that hast been what words may never tell
Unto thy mother's bosom, since the days
When thou wert pillow'd there, and wont to raise   20
In sudden laughter thence thy loving eye
That still sought mine:—those moments are gone by,
Thou too must go, my flower!—Yet with thee dwell
The peace of God!—One, one more gaze—farewell!"

This was a mother's parting with her child,
A young meek Bride on whom fair fortune smil'd,
And wooed her with a voice of love away
From childhood's home; yet there, with fond delay
She linger'd on the threshold, heard the note
Of her caged bird thro' trellis'd rose-leaves float,   30
And fell upon her mother's neck, and wept,

Whilst old remembrances, that long had slept,
Gush'd o'er her soul, and many a vanish'd day,
As in one picture traced, before her lay.

But the farewell was said; and on the deep,
When its breast heav'd in sunset's golden sleep,
With a calm'd heart, young Madeline ere long
Pour'd forth her own sweet solemn vesper-song,
Breathing of home: thro' stillness heard afar,
And duly rising with the first pale star,   40
That voice was on the waters; till at last
The sounding ocean-solitudes were pass'd,
And the bright land was reach'd, the youthful world
That glows along the West: the sails were furl'd
In its clear sunshine, and the gentle bride
Look'd on the home that promis'd hearts untried
A bower of bliss to come.—Alas! we trace
The map of our own paths, and long ere years
With their dull steps the brilliant lines efface,
On sweeps the storm, and blots them out with tears.   50
That home was darken'd soon: the summer breeze
Welcom'd with death the wanderers from the seas,
Death unto one, and anguish how forlorn!
To her, that widow'd in her marriage-morn,
Sat in her voiceless dwelling, whence with him,
    Her bosom's first belov'd, her friend and guide,
Joy had gone forth, and left the green earth dim,
    As from the sun shut out on every side,
By the close veil of misery!—Oh! but ill,
    When with rich hopes o'erfraught, the young high heart   60
    Bears its first blow!—it knows not yet the part
Which life will teach—to suffer and be still,
And with submissive love to count the flowers
Which yet are spared, and thro' the future hours
To send no busy dream!—*She* had not learn'd
Of sorrow till that hour, and therefore turn'd,
In weariness from life: then came th' unrest,
The heart-sick yearning of the exile's breast,

The haunting sounds of voices far away,
And household steps; until at last she lay   70
On her lone couch of sickness, lost in dreams
Of the gay vineyards and blue-rushing streams
In her own sunny land, and murmuring oft
Familiar names, in accents wild, yet soft,
To strangers round that bed, who knew not aught
Of the deep spells wherewith each word was fraught.
To strangers?—Oh! could strangers raise the head
Gently as *hers* was rais'd?—did strangers shed
The kindly tears which bath'd that feverish brow
And wasted cheek with half unconscious flow?   80
Something was there, that thro' the lingering night
Outwatches patiently the taper's light,
Something that faints not thro' the day's distress,
That fears not toil, that knows not weariness;
Love, true and perfect love!—Whence came that power,
Uprearing thro' the storm the drooping flower?
Whence?—who can ask?—the wild delirium pass'd,
And from her eyes the spirit look'd at last
Into her *mother's* face, and wakening knew
The brow's calm grace, the hair's dear silvery hue,   90
The kind sweet smile of old!—and had *she* come,
Thus in life's evening, from her distant home,
To save her child?—Ev'n so—nor yet in vain:
In that young heart a light sprung up again,
And lovely still, with so much love to give,
Seem'd this fair world, tho' faded; still to live
Was not to pine forsaken. On the breast
That rock'd her childhood, sinking in soft rest,
"Sweet mother, gentlest mother! can it be?"
The lorn one cried, "and do I look on thee?   100
Take back thy wanderer from this fatal shore,
Peace shall be ours beneath our vines once more."

THE QUEEN OF PRUSSIA'S TOMB

"This tomb is in the garden of Charlottenburgh, near Berlin. It was not without surprise that I came suddenly, among trees, upon a fair white Doric temple. I might, and should have deemed it a mere adornment of the grounds, but the cypress and the willow declare it a habitation of the dead. Upon a sarcophagus of white marble lay a sheet, and the outline of the human form was plainly visible beneath its folds. The person with me reverently turned it back, and displayed the statue of his Queen. It is a portrait-statue recumbent, said to be a perfect resemblance—not as in death, but when she lived to bless and be blessed. Nothing can be more calm and kind than the expression of her features. The hands are folded on the bosom; the limbs are sufficiently crossed to show the repose of life.—Here the King brings her children annually, to offer garlands at her grave. These hang in withered mournfulness above this living image of their departed mother."

Sherer's *Notes and Reflections during a Ramble in Germany*

In sweet pride upon that insult keen
She smiled; then drooping mute and broken-hearted,
To the cold comfort of the grave departed.

Milman

It stands where northern willows weep,
      A temple fair and lone;
Soft shadows o'er its marble sweep,
      From cypress-branches thrown;
While silently around it spread,
Thou feel'st the presence of the dead.

And what within is richly shrined?
      A sculptur'd woman's form,
Lovely in perfect rest reclined,
      As one beyond the storm:
Yet not of death, but slumber, lies
The solemn sweetness on those eyes.

The folded hands, the calm pure face,
      The mantle's quiet flow,

10

The gentle, yet majestic grace,
    Throned on the matron brow;
These, in that scene of tender gloom,
With a still glory robe the tomb.

There stands an eagle, at the feet
    Of the fair image wrought;
A kingly emblem—nor unmeet
    To wake yet deeper thought:
She whose high heart finds rest below,
Was royal in her birth and woe.

There are pale garlands hung above,
    Of dying scent and hue;—
She was a mother—in her love
    How sorrowfully true!
Oh! hallow'd long be every leaf,
The record of her children's grief!

She saw their birthright's warrior-crown
    Of olden glory spoil'd,
The standard of their sires borne down,
    The shield's bright blazon soiled:
She met the tempest meekly brave,
Then turn'd, o'erwearied, to the grave.

She slumber'd; but it came—it came,
    Her land's redeeming hour,
With the glad shout, and signal-flame,
    Sent on from tower to tower!
Fast thro' the realm a spirit moved—
'Twas hers, the lofty and the loved.

Then was her name a note that rung
    To rouse bold hearts from sleep,
Her memory, as a banner flung
    Forth by the Baltic deep;
Her grief, a bitter vial pour'd
To sanctify th' avenger's sword.

20

30

40

And the crown'd eagle spread again
    His pinion to the sun;   50
And the strong land shook off its chain—
    So was the triumph won!
But woe for earth, where sorrow's tone
Still blends with victory's!—*She* was gone!

THE MEMORIAL PILLAR

On the road-side between Penrith and Appleby, stands a small pillar, with this inscription:—"This pillar was erected in the year 1656, by Ann, Countess Dowager of Pembroke, for a memorial of her last parting, in this place, with her good and pious mother, Margaret, Countess Dowager of Cumberland, on the 2d April, 1616."—See Notes to the *Pleasures of Memory.*

Hast thou, thro' Eden's wild-wood vales pursued
Each mountain-scene, magnificently rude,
Nor with attention's lifted eye, revered
That modest stone, by pious Pembroke rear'd,
Which still records, beyond the pencil's power,
The silent sorrows of a parting hour?
                                   Rogers

Mother and child! whose blending tears
    Have sanctified the place,
Where, to the love of many years,
    Was given one last embrace;
Oh! ye have shrin'd a spell of power,
Deep in your record of that hour!

A spell to waken solemn thought,
    A still, small under-tone,
That calls back days of childhood, fraught
    With many a treasure gone;   10
And smites, perchance, the hidden source,
Tho' long untroubled—of remorse.

For who, that gazes on the stone
    Which marks your parting spot,
Who but a mother's love hath known,
    The *one* love changing not?
Alas! and haply learn'd its worth
First with the sound of "Earth to earth?"

But thou, high-hearted daughter! thou,
    O'er whose bright, honour'd head,   20
Blessings and tears of holiest flow,
    Ev'n here were fondly shed,
Thou from the passion of thy grief,
In its full burst, couldst draw relief.

For oh! tho' painful be th' excess,
    The might wherewith it swells,
In nature's fount no bitterness
    Of nature's mingling, dwells;
And thou hadst not, by wrong or pride,
Poison'd the free and healthful tide.   30

But didst thou meet the face no more,
    Which thy young heart first knew?
And all—was all in this world o'er,
    With ties thus close and true?
It was!—On earth no other eye
Could give thee back thine infancy.

No other voice could pierce the maze
    Where deep within thy breast,
The sounds and dreams of other days,
    With memory lay at rest;   40
No other smile to thee could bring
A gladd'ning, like the breath of spring.

Yet, while thy place of weeping still
    Its lone memorial keeps,
While on thy name, midst wood and hill,
    The quiet sunshine sleeps,

And touches, in each graven line,
Of reverential thought a sign;

Can I, while yet these tokens wear
   The impress of the dead,   50
Think of the love embodied there,
   As of a vision fled?
A perish'd thing, the joy and flower
And glory of one earthly hour?

Not so!—I will not bow me so,
   To thoughts that breathe despair!
A loftier faith we need below,
   Life's farewell words to bear.
Mother and child!—Your tears are past—
Surely your hearts have met at last!   60

THE GRAVE OF A POETESS

"Ne me plaignez pas—si vous saviez
Combien de peines ce tombeau m'a épargnées!"

I stood beside thy lowly grave;—
   Spring-odours breath'd around,
And music, in the river-wave,
   Pass'd with a lulling sound.

All happy things that love the sun
   In the bright air glanc'd by,
And a glad murmur seem'd to run
   Thro' the soft azure sky.

Fresh leaves were on the ivy-bough
   That fring'd the ruins near;   10
Young voices were abroad—but thou
   Their sweetness couldst not hear.

And mournful grew my heart for thee,
　　Thou in whose woman's mind
The ray that brightens earth and sea,
　　The light of song was shrined.

Mournful, that thou wert slumbering low,
　　With a dread curtain drawn
Between thee and the golden glow
　　Of this world's vernal dawn.　　　　　　　　　20

Parted from all the song and bloom
　　Thou wouldst have lov'd so well,
To thee the sunshine round thy tomb
　　Was but a broken spell.

The bird, the insect on the wing,
　　In their bright reckless play,
Might feel the flush and life of spring,—
　　And thou wert pass'd away!

But then, ev'n then, a nobler thought
　　O'er my vain sadness came;　　　　　　　　　30
Th' immortal spirit woke, and wrought
　　Within my thrilling frame.

Surely on lovelier things, I said,
　　Thou must have look'd ere now,
Than all that round our pathway shed
　　Odours and hues below.

The shadows of the tomb are here,
　　Yet beautiful is earth!
What seest thou then where no dim fear,
　　No haunting dream hath birth?　　　　　　　　40

Here a vain love to passing flowers
　　Thou gav'st—but where thou art,
The sway is not with changeful hours,
　　There love and death must part.

Thou hast left sorrow in thy song,
    A voice not loud, but deep!
The glorious bowers of earth among,
    How often didst thou weep!

Where couldst thou fix on mortal ground
    Thy tender thoughts and high?—   50
Now peace the woman's heart hath found,
    And joy the poet's eye.

MISCELLANEOUS PIECES

THE HOMES OF ENGLAND

Where's the coward that would not dare
To fight for such a land?

Marmion

The stately Homes of England,
    How beautiful they stand!
Amidst their tall ancestral trees,
    O'er all the pleasant land.
The deer across their greensward bound
    Thro' shade and sunny gleam,
And the swan glides past them with the sound
    Of some rejoicing stream.

The merry Homes of England!
    Around their hearths by night,   10
What gladsome looks of household love
    Meet, in the ruddy light!
There woman's voice flows forth in song,
    Or childhood's tale is told,
Or lips move tunefully along
    Some glorious page of old.

The blessed Homes of England!
    How softly on their bowers
Is laid the holy quietness
    That breathes from Sabbath-hours!   20
Solemn, yet sweet, the church-bell's chime
    Floats thro' their woods at morn;
All other sounds, in that still time,
    Of breeze and leaf are born.

The Cottage Homes of England!
    By thousands on her plains,
They are smiling o'er the silvery brooks,

And round the hamlet-fanes.
Thro' glowing orchards forth they peep,
    Each from its nook of leaves,   30
And fearless there the lowly sleep,
    As the bird beneath their eaves.

The free, fair Homes of England!
    Long, long, in hut and hall,
May hearts of native proof be rear'd
    To guard each hallow'd wall!
And green for ever be the groves,
    And bright the flowery sod,
Where first the child's glad spirit loves
    Its country and its God!   40

THE SICILIAN CAPTIVE

————I have dreamt thou wert
A captive in thy hopelessness; afar
From the sweet home of thy young infancy,
Whose image unto thee is as a dream
Of fire and slaughter; I can see thee wasting,
Sick for thy native air.

                         L. E. L.

The champions had come from their fields of war,
Over the crests of the billows far,
They had brought back the spoils of a hundred shores,
Where the deep had foam'd to their flashing oars.

They sat at their feast round the Norse-king's board,
By the glare of the torch-light the mead was pour'd,
The hearth was heap'd with the pine-boughs high,
And it flung a red radiance on shields thrown by.

"The Sicilian Captive." Frontispiece illustration to *The Poetical Works of Mrs. Felicia Hemans* (New York: The American News Company, [ca. 1888]).

The Scalds had chaunted in Runic rhyme,
Their songs of the sword and the olden time,   10
And a solemn thrill, as the harp-chords rung,
Had breath'd from the walls where the bright spears hung.

But the swell was gone from the quivering string,
They had summon'd a softer voice to sing,
And a captive girl, at the warriors' call,
Stood forth in the midst of that frowning hall.

Lonely she stood:—in her mournful eyes
Lay the clear midnight of southern skies,
And the drooping fringe of their lashes low,
Half veil'd a depth of unfathom'd woe.   20

Stately she stood—tho' her fragile frame
Seem'd struck with the blight of some inward flame,
And her proud pale brow had a shade of scorn,
Under the waves of her dark hair worn.

And a deep flush pass'd, like a crimson haze,
O'er her marble cheek by the pine-fire's blaze;
No soft hue caught from the south-wind's breath,
But a token of fever, at strife with death.

She had been torn from her home away,
With her long locks crown'd for her bridal day,   30
And brought to die of the burning dreams
That haunt the exile by foreign streams.

They bade her sing of her distant land—
She held its lyre with a trembling hand,
Till the spirit its blue skies had given her, woke,
And the stream of her voice into music broke.

Faint was the strain, in its first wild flow,
Troubled its murmur, and sad, and low;
But it swell'd into deeper power ere long,
As the breeze that swept over her soul grew strong.   40

*   *   *   *   *   *   *   *   *   *   *

"They bid me sing of thee, mine own, my sunny land! of thee!
Am I not parted from thy shores by the mournful-sounding sea?
Doth not thy shadow wrap my soul?—in silence let me die,
In a voiceless dream of thy silvery founts, and thy pure deep
    sapphire sky;
How should thy lyre give *here* its wealth of buried sweetness forth?
Its tones, of summer's breathings born, to the wild winds of the
    north?

"Yet thus it shall be once, once more!—my spirit shall awake,
And thro' the mists of death shine out, my country! for thy sake!
That I may make *thee* known, with all the beauty and the light,
And the glory never more to bless thy daughter's yearning sight!   50
Thy woods shall whisper in my song, thy bright streams warble by,
Thy soul flow o'er my lips again—yet once, my Sicily!

"There are blue heavens—far hence, far hence! but oh! their
    glorious blue!
Its very night is beautiful, with the hyacinth's deep hue!
It is above my own fair land, and round my laughing home,
And arching o'er my vintage-hills, they hang their cloudless dome,
And making all the waves as gems, that melt along the shore,
And steeping happy hearts in joy—that now is mine no more.

"And there are haunts in that green land—oh! who may dream
    or tell,
Of all the shaded loveliness it hides in grot and dell!   60
By fountains flinging rainbow-spray on dark and glossy leaves,
And bowers wherein the forest-dove her nest untroubled weaves;
The myrtle dwells there, sending round the richness of its breath,
And the violets gleam like amethysts, from the dewy moss beneath.

"And there are floating sounds that fill the skies thro' night and day,
Sweet sounds! the soul to hear them faints in dreams of heaven
    away!
They wander thro' the olive-woods, and o'er the shining seas,
They mingle with the orange-scents that load the sleepy breeze;
Lute, voice, and bird, are blending there;—it were a bliss to die,
As dies a leaf, thy groves among, my flowery Sicily!   70

"*I* may not thus depart—farewell! yet no, my country! no!
Is not love stronger than the grave? I feel it must be so!
My fleeting spirit shall o'ersweep the mountains and the main,
And in thy tender starlight rove, and thro' thy woods again.
Its passion deepens—it prevails!—I break my chain—I come
To dwell a viewless thing, yet blest—in thy sweet air, my home!"

*   *   *   *   *   *   *   *   *   *   *

And her pale arms dropp'd the ringing lyre,
There came a mist o'er her eye's wild fire,
And her dark rich tresses, in many a fold,
Loos'd from their braids, down her bosom roll'd.   80

For her head sank back on the rugged wall,—
A silence fell o'er the warrior's hall;
She had pour'd out her soul with her song's last tone;
The lyre was broken, the minstrel gone!

IVAN THE CZAR

"Ivan le Terrible, étant déjà devenu vieux, assiégeait Novogorod. Les Boyards, le voyant affaibli, lui démandèrent s'il ne voulait pas donner le commandement de l'assaut à son fils. Sa fureur fut si grande à cette proposition, que rien ne pût l'appaiser; son fils se prosterna à ses pieds; il le repoussa avec un coup d'une telle violence, que deux jours après le malheureux en mourut. Le père, alors au désespoir, devint indifférent à la guerre comme au pouvoir, et ne survécut que peu de mois à son fils."

Dix années d'exil, par Madame de Staël

*Gib diesen Toten mir heraus. Ich muss
Ihn wieder haben! . . .
. . . Trostlose Allmacht,
Die nicht einmal in Gräber ihren Arm
Verlängern, eine kleine Übereilung
Mit Menschenleben nicht verbessern kann!*

Schiller

He sat in silence on the ground,
    The old and haughty Czar;
Lonely, tho' princes girt him round,
    And leaders of the war:
He had cast his jewell'd sabre,
    That many a field had won,
To the earth beside his youthful dead,
    His fair and first-born son.

With a robe of ermine for its bed,
    Was laid that form of clay,   10
Where the light a stormy sunset shed,
    Thro' the rich tent made way:
And a sad and solemn beauty
    On the pallid face came down,
Which the Lord of nations mutely watch'd,
    In the dust, with his renown.

Low tones at last of woe and fear
    From his full bosom broke;—
A mournful thing it was to hear
    How then the proud man spoke!   20
The voice that thro' the combat
    Had shouted far and high,
Came forth in strange, dull, hollow tones,
    Burden'd with agony.

"There is no crimson on thy cheek,
    And on thy lip no breath,
I call thee, and thou dost not speak—
    They tell me this is death!
And fearful things are whispering
    That I the deed have done—   30
For the honour of thy father's name,
    Look up, look up, my son!

"Well might I know death's hue and mien,
    But on *thine* aspect, boy!

What, till this moment, have I seen,
  Save pride and tameless joy?
Swiftest thou wert to battle,
  And bravest there of all—
How could I think a warrior's frame
  Thus like a flower should fall?   40

"I will not bear that still, cold look—
  Rise up, thou fierce and free!
Wake as the storm wakes! I will brook
  All, save this calm, from thee!
Lift brightly up, and proudly,
  Once more thy kindling eyes!
Hath my word lost its power on earth?
  I say to thee, arise!

"Didst thou not know I lov'd thee well?
  Thou didst not! and art gone   50
In bitterness of soul, to dwell
  Where man must dwell alone.
Come back, young fiery spirit!
  If but one hour, to learn
The secrets of the folded heart,
  That seem'd to thee so stern.

"Thou wert the first, the first fair child,
  That in mine arms I press'd;
Thou wert the bright one, that hast smil'd
  Like summer on my breast!   60
I reared thee as an eagle,
  To the chase thy steps I led,
I bore thee on my battle-horse,
  I look upon thee—dead!

"Lay down my warlike banners here,
  Never again to wave,
And bury my red sword and spear,
  Chiefs! in my first-born's grave!

And leave me!—I have conquer'd,
    I have slain—my work is done!   70
Whom have I slain?—ye answer not—
    Thou too art mute, my son!"

And thus his wild lament was pour'd
    Thro' the dark resounding night,
And the battle knew no more his sword,
    Nor the foaming steed his might.
He heard strange voices moaning
    In every wind that sigh'd;
From the searching stars of heaven he shrank—
    Humbly the conqueror died.   80

CAROLAN'S PROPHECY

Thy cheek too swiftly flushes; o'er thine eye
The lights and shadows come and go too fast,
Thy tears gush forth too soon, and in thy voice
Are sounds of tenderness too passionate
For peace on earth; oh! therefore, child of song!
'Tis well thou shouldst depart.

A sound of music, from amidst the hills,
Came suddenly, and died; a fitful sound
Of mirth, soon lost in wail.—Again it rose,
And sank in mournfulness.—There sat a bard,
By a blue stream of Erin, where it swept
Flashing thro' rock and wood; the sunset's light
Was on his wavy silver-gleaming hair,
And the wind's whisper in the mountain-ash,
Whose clusters droop'd above. His head was bow'd
His hand was on his harp, yet thence its touch   10
Had drawn but broken strains; and many stood,
Waiting around, in silent earnestness,
Th' unchaining of his soul, the gush of song:
Many, and graceful forms! yet one alone,

Seem'd present to his dream; and she indeed,
With her pale virgin brow, and changeful cheek,
And the clear starlight of her serious eyes,
Lovely amidst the flowing of dark locks
And pallid braiding flowers, was beautiful,
Ev'n painfully!—a creature to behold   20
With trembling midst our joy, lest aught unseen
Should waft the vision from us, leaving earth
Too dim without its brightness!—Did such fear
O'ershadow, in that hour, the gifted one,
By his own rushing stream?—Once more he gaz'd
Upon the radiant girl, and yet once more
From the deep chords his wandering hand brought out
A few short festive notes, an opening strain
Of bridal melody, soon dashed with grief,
As if some wailing spirit in the strings   30
Met and o'ermaster'd him: but yielding then
To the strong prophet-impulse, mournfully,
Like moaning waters, o'er the harp he pour'd
The trouble of his haunted soul, and sang—

            Voice of the grave!
        I hear thy thrilling call;
    It comes in the dash of the foaming wave,
        In the sear leaf's trembling fall!
    In the shiver of the tree,
        I hear thee, O thou voice!   40
    And I would thy warning were but for me,
        That my spirit might rejoice.

            But thou art sent
        For the sad earth's young and fair,
    For the graceful heads that have not bent
        To the wintry hand of care!
    They hear the wind's low sigh,
        And the river sweeping free,
    And the green reeds murmuring heavily,
        And the woods—but they hear not thee!   50

Long have I striven
    With my deep foreboding soul,
But the full tide now its bounds hath riven,
    And darkly on must roll.
There's a young brow smiling near,
    With a bridal white-rose wreath,—
Unto *me* it smiles from a flowery bier,
    Touch'd solemnly by death!

    Fair art thou, Morna!
    The sadness of thine eye   60
Is beautiful as silvery clouds
    On the dark-blue summer sky!
And thy voice comes like the sound
    Of a sweet and hidden rill,
That makes the dim woods tuneful round—
    But soon it must be still!

    Silence and dust
    On thy sunny lips must lie,
Make not the strength of love thy trust,
    A stronger yet is nigh!   70
No strain of festal flow
    That my hand for thee hath tried,
But into dirge-notes wild and low,
    Its ringing tones have died.

    Young art thou, Morna!
    Yet on thy gentle head,
Like heavy dew on the lily's leaves,
    A spirit hath been shed!
And the glance is thine which sees
    Thro' nature's awful heart—   80
But bright things go with the summer-breeze,
    And thou too, must depart!

    Yet shall I weep?
    I know that in thy breast
There swells a fount of song too deep,

Too powerful for thy rest!
And the bitterness I know,
      And the chill of this world's breath—
Go, all undimm'd, in thy glory go!
      Young and crown'd bride of death!   90

      Take hence to heaven
      Thy holy thoughts and bright,
And soaring hopes, that were not given
      For the touch of mortal blight!
Might we follow in thy track,
      This parting should not be!
But the spring shall give us violets back,
      And every flower but thee!

There was a burst of tears around the bard:
All wept but one, and she serenely stood,   100
With her clear brow and dark religious eye,
Rais'd to the first faint star above the hills,
And cloudless; though it might be that her cheek
Was paler than before.—So Morna heard
The minstrel's prophecy.
                        And spring return'd,
Bringing the earth her lovely things again,
All, save the loveliest far! A voice, a smile,
A young sweet spirit gone.

THE LADY OF THE CASTLE

From the "Portrait Gallery," an unfinished Poem.

If there be but one spot upon thy name,
One eye thou fear'st to meet, one human voice
Whose tones thou shrink'st from—Woman! veil thy face,
And bow thy head—and die!

Thou seest her pictured with her shining hair,
   (Famed were those tresses in Provençal song,)
Half braided, half o'er cheek and bosom fair
   Let loose, and pouring sunny waves along
Her gorgeous vest. A child's light hand is roving
Midst the rich curls, and oh! how meekly loving
Its earnest looks are lifted to the face,
Which bends to meet its lip in laughing grace!
Yet that bright lady's eye methinks hath less
Of deep, and still, and pensive tenderness,   10
Than might beseem a mother's;—on her brow
   Something too much there sits of native scorn,
And her smile kindles with a conscious glow,
   As from the thought of sovereign beauty born.
—These may be dreams—but how shall woman tell
Of woman's shame, and not with tears?—She fell!
That mother left that child!—went hurrying by
Its cradle—haply, not without a sigh,
Haply one moment o'er its rest serene
She hung—but no! it could not thus have been,   20
For *she went on!*—forsook her home, her hearth,
All pure affection, all sweet household mirth,
To live a gaudy and dishonour'd thing,
Sharing in guilt the splendours of a king.

Her lord, in very weariness of life,
Girt on his sword for scenes of distant strife;
He reck'd no more of glory—grief and shame
Crush'd out his fiery nature, and his name
Died silently. A shadow o'er his halls
Crept year by year; the minstrel pass'd their walls;   30
The warder's horn hung mute;—meantime the child,
On whose first flowering thoughts no parent smiled,
A gentle girl, and yet deep-hearted, grew
Into sad youth; for well, too well, she knew
Her mother's tale! Its memory made the sky
Seem all too joyous for her shrinking eye;
Check'd on her lip the flow of song, which fain

Would there have linger'd; flush'd her cheek to pain,
If met by sudden glance; and gave a tone
Of sorrow, as for something lovely gone,   40
Ev'n to the spring's glad voice. Her own was low,
And plaintive—oh! there lie such depths of woe
In a *young* blighted spirit! Manhood rears
A haughty brow, and age has done with tears;
But youth bows down to misery, in amaze
At the dark cloud o'ermantling its fresh days,—
And thus it was with her. A mournful sight
    In one so fair—for she indeed was fair—
Not with her mother's dazzling eyes of light,
    Hers were more shadowy, full of thought and prayer,   50
And with long lashes o'er a white-rose cheek,
Drooping in gloom, yet tender still and meek,
Still that fond child's—and oh! the brow above,
So pale and pure! so form'd for holy love
To gaze upon in silence!—but she felt
That love was not for her, tho' hearts would melt
Where'er she mov'd, and reverence mutely given
Went with her; and low prayers, that call'd on Heaven
To bless the young Isaure.

              One sunny morn,   60
    With alms before her castle gate she stood,
Midst peasant-groups; when breathless and o'erworn,
    And shrouded in long weeds of widowhood,
A stranger thro' them broke:—the orphan maid
With her sweet voice, and proffer'd hand of aid,
Turn'd to give welcome; but a wild sad look
Met hers; a gaze that all her spirit shook;
And that pale woman, suddenly subdued
By some strong passion in its gushing mood,
Knelt at her feet, and bath'd them with such tears   70
As rain the hoarded agonies of years
From the heart's urn; and with her white lips press'd
The ground they trod; then, burying in her vest
Her brow's deep flush, sobb'd out—"Oh! undefiled!
I am thy mother—spurn me not, my child!"

Isaure had pray'd for that lost mother; wept
O'er her stain'd memory, while the happy slept
In the hush'd midnight; stood with mournful gaze
Before yon picture's smile of other days,
But never breath'd in human ear the name   80
Which weigh'd her being to the earth with shame.
What marvel if the anguish, the surprise,
The dark remembrances, the alter'd guise,
Awhile o'erpower'd her?—from the weeper's touch
She shrank—'twas but a moment—yet too much
For that all humbled one; its mortal stroke
Came down like lightning, and her full heart broke
At once in silence. Heavily and prone
She sank, while, o'er her castle's threshold-stone,
Those long fair tresses—*they* still brightly wore   90
Their early pride, tho' bound with pearls no more—
Bursting their fillet, in sad beauty roll'd,
And swept the dust with coils of wavy gold.

Her child bent o'er her—call'd her—'twas too late—
Dead lay the wanderer at her own proud gate!
The joy of Courts, the star of knight and bard,—
How didst thou fall, O bright-hair'd Ermengarde!

THE MOURNER FOR
THE BARMECIDES

O good old man! how well in thee appears
The constant service of the antique world!
Thou art not for the fashion of these times.
As You Like It

Fall'n was the House of Giafar; and its name,
The high romantic name of Barmecide,
A sound forbidden on its own bright shores,

< 103 >

By the swift Tygris' wave. Stern Haroun's wrath,
Sweeping the mighty with their fame away,
Had so pass'd sentence: but man's chainless heart
Hides that within its depths, which never yet
Th' oppressor's thought could reach.

           'Twas desolate
Where Giafar's halls, beneath the burning sun,   10
Spread out in ruin lay. The songs had ceas'd;
The lights, the perfumes, and the genii-tales,
Had ceas'd; the guests were gone. Yet still one voice
Was there—the fountain's; thro' those eastern courts,
Over the broken marble and the grass,
Its low clear music shedding mournfully.

And still another voice!—an aged man,
Yet with a dark and fervent eye beneath
His silvery hair, came, day by day, and sate
On a white column's fragment; and drew forth,   20
From the forsaken walls and dim arcades,
A tone that shook them with its answering thrill
To his deep accents. Many a glorious tale
He told that sad yet stately solitude,
Pouring his memory's fulness o'er its gloom,
Like waters in the waste; and calling up,
By song or high recital of their deeds,
Bright solemn shadows of its vanish'd race
To people their own halls: with these alone,
In all this rich and breathing world, his thoughts   30
Held still unbroken converse. He had been
Rear'd in this lordly dwelling, and was now
The ivy of its ruins; unto which
His fading life seem'd bound. Day roll'd on day,
And from that scene the loneliness was fled;
For crowds around the grey-hair'd chronicler
Met as men meet, within whose anxious hearts
Fear with deep feeling strives; till, as a breeze
Wanders thro' forest-branches, and is met

By one quick sound and shiver of the leaves,   40
The spirit of his passionate lament,
As thro' their stricken souls it pass'd, awoke
One echoing murmur.—But this might not be
Under a despot's rule, and summon'd thence,
The dreamer stood before the Caliph's throne:
Sentenced to death he stood, and deeply pale,
And with his white lips rigidly compress'd;
Till, in submissive tones, he ask'd to speak
Once more, ere thrust from earth's fair sunshine forth.
Was it to sue for grace?—his burning heart   50
Sprang, with a sudden lightning, to his eye,
And he was changed!—and thus, in rapid words,
Th' o'ermastering thoughts, more strong than death, found way.

"And shall I not rejoice to go, when the noble and the brave,
With the glory on their brows, are gone before me to the grave?
What is there left to look on now, what brightness in the land?—
I hold in scorn the faded world, that wants their princely band!

"My chiefs! my chiefs! the old man comes, that in your halls was
    nurs'd,
That follow'd you to many a fight, where flash'd your sabres
    first;
That bore your children in his arms, your name upon his heart—   60
Oh! must the music of that name with him from earth depart?

"It shall not be!—a thousand tongues, tho' human voice were still,
With that high sound the living air triumphantly shall fill;
The wind's free flight shall bear it on, as wandering seeds are sown,
And the starry midnight whisper it, with a deep and thrilling tone.

"For it is not as a flower whose scent with the dropping leaves
    expires,
And it is not as a household lamp, that a breath should quench
    its fires;
It is written on our battle-fields with the writing of the sword,
It hath left upon our desert-sands a light in blessings pour'd.

"The founts, the many gushing founts, which to the wild ye gave,   70
Of you, my chiefs, shall sing aloud, as they pour a joyous wave;
And the groves, with whose deep lovely gloom ye hung the
   pilgrim's way,
Shall send from all their sighing leaves your praises on the day.

"The very walls your bounty rear'd, for the stranger's homeless
   head,
Shall find a murmur to record your tale, my glorious dead!
Tho' the grass be where ye feasted once, where lute and cittern
   rung,
And the serpent in your palaces lies coil'd amidst its young.

"It is enough! mine eye no more of joy or splendour sees,
I leave your name in lofty faith, to the skies and to the breeze!
I go, since earth her flower hath lost, to join the bright and
   fair,   80
And call the grave a kingly house, for ye, my chiefs, are there!"

But while the old man sang, a mist of tears
O'er Haroun's eyes had gathered, and a thought—
Oh! many a sudden and remorseful thought
Of his youth's once-lov'd friends, the martyr'd race,
O'erflowed his softening heart.—"Live, live!" he cried,
"Thou faithful unto death! live on, and still
Speak of thy lords; they *were* a princely band!"

THE SPANISH CHAPEL

Weep not for those whom the veil of the tomb,
   In life's early morning, hath hid from our eyes,
Ere sin threw a veil o'er the spirit's young bloom,
   Or earth had profan'd what was born for the skies.
                                                            Moore

I made a mountain-brook my guide,
    Thro' a wild Spanish glen,
And wandered, on its grassy side,
    Far from the homes of men.

It lured me with a singing tone,
    And many a sunny glance,
To a green spot of beauty lone,
    A haunt for old romance.

A dim and deeply-bosom'd grove
    Of many an aged tree,   10
Such as the shadowy violets love,
    The fawn and forest-bee.

The darkness of the chestnut bough
    There on the waters lay,
The bright stream reverently below,
    Check'd its exulting play;

And bore a music all subdued,
    And led a silvery sheen,
On thro' the breathing solitude
    Of that rich leafy scene.   20

For something viewlessly around
    Of solemn influence dwelt,
In the soft gloom, and whispery sound,
    Not to be told, but felt;

While sending forth a quiet gleam
    Across the wood's repose,
And o'er the twilight of the stream,
    A lowly chapel rose.

A pathway to that still retreat
    Thro' many a myrtle wound,   30
And there a sight—how strangely sweet!
    My steps in wonder bound.

For on a brilliant bed of flowers,
    Even at the threshold made,
As if to sleep thro' sultry hours,
    A young fair child was laid.

To sleep?—oh! ne'er on childhood's eye,
    And silken lashes press'd,
Did the warm *living* slumber lie,
    With such a weight of rest!   40

Yet still a tender crimson glow
    Its cheek's pure marble dyed—
'Twas but the light's faint streaming flow
    Thro' roses heap'd beside.

I stoop'd—the smooth round arm was chill,
    The soft lip's breath was fled,
And the bright ringlets hung so still—
    The lovely child was dead!

"Alas!" I cried, "fair faded thing!
    Thou hast wrung bitter tears,   50
And thou hast left a woe, to cling
    Round yearning hearts for years!"

But then a voice came sweet and low—
    I turn'd, and near me sate
A woman with a mourner's brow,
    Pale, yet not desolate.

And in her still, clear, matron face,
    All solemnly serene,
A shadow'd image I could trace
    Of that young slumberer's mien.   60

"Stranger! thou pitiest me," she said,
    With lips that faintly smiled,
"As here I watch beside my dead,
    My fair and precious child.

"But know, the time-worn heart may be
    By pangs in this world riven,
Keener than theirs who yield, like me,
    An angel thus to Heaven!"

THE CAPTIVE KNIGHT

The prisoned thrush may brook the cage,
The captive eagle dies for rage.
                    Lady of the Lake

    'Twas a trumpet's pealing sound!
And the knight look'd down from the Paynim's tower,
And a Christian host, in its pride and power,
    Thro' the pass beneath him wound.
Cease awhile, clarion! Clarion, wild and shrill,
Cease! let them hear the captive's voice—be still!

    "I knew 'twas a trumpet's note!
And I see my brethren's lances gleam,
And their pennons wave by the mountain stream,
    And their plumes to the glad wind float!   10
Cease awhile, clarion! Clarion, wild and shrill,
Cease! let them hear the captive's voice—be still!

    "I am here, with my heavy chain!
And I look on a torrent sweeping by,
And an eagle rushing to the sky,
    And a host, to its battle-plain!
Cease awhile, clarion! Clarion, wild and shrill,
Cease! let them hear the captive's voice—be still!

    "Must I pine in my fetters here?
With the wild wave's foam, and the free bird's flight,   20
And the tall spears glancing on my sight,
    And the trumpet in mine ear?

Cease awhile, clarion! Clarion, wild and shrill,
Cease! let them hear the captive's voice—be still!

    "They are gone! they have all pass'd by!
They in whose wars I had borne my part,
They that I lov'd with a brother's heart,
    They have left me here to die!
Sound again, clarion! Clarion pour thy blast!
Sound! for the captive's dream of hope is past."   30

THE KAISER'S FEAST

 Louis, Emperor of Germany, having put his brother, the Palsgrave
Rodolphus, under the ban of the empire, (in the 12th century,) that unfor-
tunate Prince fled to England, where he died in neglect and poverty. "Af-
ter his decease, his mother, Matilda, privately invited his children to return
to Germany; and by her mediation, during a season of festivity, when
Louis kept wassail in the Castle of Heidelberg, the family of his brother
presented themselves before him in the garb of suppliants, imploring pity
and forgiveness. To this appeal the victor softened."
          Miss Benger's *Memoirs of the Queen of Bohemia*

The Kaiser feasted in his hall,
    The red wine mantled high;
Banners were trembling on the wall,
    To the peals of minstrelsy:
And many a gleam and sparkle came
    From the armour hung around,
As it caught the glance of the torch's flame,
    Or the hearth with pine-boughs crown'd.

Why fell there silence on the chord
    Beneath the harper's hand?   10
And suddenly, from that rich board,
    Why rose the wassail-band?
The strings were hush'd—the knights made way
    For the queenly mother's tread,

As up the hall, in dark array,
    Two fair-hair'd boys she led.

She led them ev'n to the Kaiser's place,
    And still before him stood;
Till, with strange wonder, o'er his face
    Flush'd the proud warrior-blood: 20
And "Speak, my mother! speak!" he cried,
    "Wherefore this mourning vest?
And the clinging children by thy side,
    In weeds of sadness drest?"

"Well may a mourning vest be mine,
    And theirs, my son, my son!
Look on the features of thy line
    In each fair little one!
Tho' grief awhile within their eyes
    Hath tamed the dancing glee,   30
Yet there thine own quick spirit lies—
    Thy brother's children see!

"And where is he, thy brother, where?
    He, in thy home that grew,
And smiling, with his sunny hair,
    Ever to greet thee flew?
How would his arms thy neck entwine,
    His fond lips press thy brow!
My son! oh, call these orphans thine—
    Thou hast no brother now!   40

"What! from their gentle eyes doth nought
    Speak of thy childhood's hours,
And smite thee with a tender thought
    Of thy dead father's towers?
Kind was thy boyish heart and true,
    When rear'd together there,
Thro' the old woods like fawns ye flew—
    Where is thy brother—where?

"Well didst thou love him then, and he
    Still at thy side was seen! 50
How is it that such things can be,
    As tho' they ne'er had been?
Evil was this world's breath, which came
    Between the good and brave!
Now must the tears of grief and shame
    Be offer'd to the grave.

"And let them, let them there be pour'd!
    Tho' all unfelt below,
Thine own wrung heart, to love restor'd,
    Shall soften as they flow. 60
Oh! death is mighty to make peace;
    Now bid his work be done!
So many an inward strife shall cease—
    Take, take these babes, my son!"

His eye was dimm'd—the strong man shook
    With feelings long suppress'd;
Up in his arms the boys he took,
    And strain'd them to his breast.
And a shout from all in the royal hall
    Burst forth to hail the sight; 70
And eyes were wet, midst the brave that met
    At the Kaiser's feast that night.

TASSO AND HIS SISTER

"Devant vous est Sorrente; là démeuroit la soeur de Tasse, quand il vint en pélérin demander à cette obscure amie, un asile contre l'injustice des princes,—Ses longues douleurs avaient presque égaré sa raison; il ne lui restoit plus que son génie."

                                                      Corinne

She sat, where on each wind that sigh'd,
    The citron's breath went by,

While the red gold of eventide
    Burn'd in th' Italian sky.
Her bower was one where daylight's close
    Full oft sweet laughter found,
As thence the voice of childhood rose
    To the high vineyards round.

But still and thoughtful, at her knee,
    Her children stood that hour,   10
Their bursts of song and dancing glee,
    Hush'd as by words of power.
With bright, fix'd, wondering eyes, that gaz'd
    Up to their mother's face,
With brows thro' parted ringlets rais'd,
    They stood in silent grace.

While she—yet something o'er her look
    Of mournfulness was spread—
Forth from a poet's magic book,
    The glorious numbers read;   20
The proud undying lay, which pour'd
    Its light on evil years;
His of the gifted pen and sword,
    The triumph—and the tears.

She read of fair Erminia's flight,
    Which Venice once might hear
Sung on her glittering seas at night,
    By many a Gondolier;
Of him she read, who broke the charm
    That wrapt the myrtle grove;   30
Of Godfrey's deeds, of Tancred's arm,
    That slew his Paynim love.

Young cheeks around that bright page glow'd,
    Young holy hearts were stirr'd;
And the meek tears of woman flow'd
    Fast o'er each burning word.

And sounds of breeze, and fount, and leaf,
 Came sweet, each pause between;
When a strange voice of sudden grief
 Burst on the gentle scene.   40

The mother turn'd—a way-worn man,
 In pilgrim-garb stood nigh,
Of stately mien, yet wild and wan,
 Of proud yet mournful eye.
But drops which would not stay for pride,
 From that dark eye gush'd free,
As pressing his pale brow, he cried,
 "Forgotten! ev'n by thee!

"Am I so changed?—and yet we two
 Oft hand in hand have play'd;—   50
This brow hath been all bath'd in dew,
 From wreaths which thou hast made;
We have knelt down and said one prayer,
 And sung one vesper-strain;
My soul is dim with clouds of care—
 Tell me those words again!

"Life hath been heavy on my head,
 I come a stricken deer,
Bearing the heart, midst crowds that bled,
 To bleed in stillness here."—   60
She gaz'd—till thoughts that long had slept,
 Shook all her thrilling frame—
She fell upon his neck and wept,
 Murmuring her brother's name.

Her *brother*'s name!—and who was he,
 The weary one, th' unknown,
That came, the bitter world to flee,
 A stranger to his own?—
He was the bard of gifts divine
 To sway the souls of men;   70
He of the song for Salem's shrine,
 He of the sword and pen!

ULLA, OR THE ADJURATION

Yet speak to me! I have outwatch'd the stars,
And gaz'd o'er heaven in vain, in search of thee.
Speak to me! I have wander'd o'er the earth,
And never found thy likeness.—Speak to me!
This once—once more!

Manfred

"Thou'rt gone!—thou'rt slumbering low,
   With the sounding seas above thee;
It is but a restless woe,
   But a haunting dream to love thee!
Thrice the glad swan has sung,
   To greet the spring-time hours,
Since thine oar at parting flung
   The white spray up in showers.

There's a shadow of the grave on thy hearth and round thy home;
Come to me from the ocean's dead!—thou'rt surely of them—
   come!"   10

    'Twas Ulla's voice—alone she stood
       In the Iceland summer night,
    Far gazing o'er a glassy flood,
       From a dark rock's beetling height.

"I know thou hast thy bed
   Where the sea-weed's coil hath bound thee;
The storm sweeps o'er thy head,
   But the depths are hush'd around thee.
What wind shall point the way
   To the chambers where thou'rt lying?   20
Come to me thence, and say
   If thou thought'st on me in dying?

I will not shrink to see thee with a bloodless lip and cheek—
Come to me from the ocean's dead!—thou'rt surely of them—
    speak!"

    She listened—'twas the wind's low moan,
        'Twas the ripple of the wave,
    'Twas the wakening ospray's cry alone,
        As it started from its cave.

   "I know each fearful spell
     Of the ancient Runic lay,   30
Whose mutter'd words compel
     The tempest to obey.
But I adjure not *thee*
     By magic sign or song,
My voice shall stir the sea
     By love,—the deep, the strong!

By the might of woman's tears, by the passion of her sighs,
Come to me from the ocean's dead—by the vows we pledg'd—
    arise!"

    Again she gaz'd with an eager glance,
        Wandering and wildly bright;—   40
    She saw but the sparkling waters dance
        To the arrowy northern light.

   "By the slow and struggling death
     Of hope that loath'd to part,
By the fierce and withering breath
     Of despair on youth's high heart;
By the weight of gloom which clings
     To the mantle of the night,
By the heavy dawn which brings
     Nought lovely to the sight,   50

By all that from my weary soul thou hast wrung of grief and fear,
Come to me from the ocean's dead—awake, arise, appear!"

Was it her yearning spirit's dream,
    Or did a pale form rise,
And o'er the hush'd wave glide and gleam,
    With bright, still, mournful eyes?

"Have the depths heard?—they have!
    My voice prevails—thou'rt there,
Dim from thy watery grave,
    Oh! thou that wert so fair!   60
Yet take me to thy rest!
    There dwells no fear with love;
Let me slumber on thy breast,
    While the billow rolls above!

Where the long-lost things lie hid, where the bright ones have
    their home,
We will sleep among the ocean's dead—stay for me, stay!—I come!"

    There was a sullen plunge below,
        A flashing on the main,
    And the wave shut o'er that wild heart's woe,
        Shut—and grew still again.   70

To Wordsworth

Thine is a strain to read among the hills,
    The old and full of voices;—by the source
Of some free stream, whose gladdening presence fills
    The solitude with sound; for in its course
Even such is thy deep song, that seems a part
Of those high scenes, a fountain from their heart.

Or its calm spirit fitly may be taken
    To the still breast, in sunny garden-bowers,
Where vernal winds each tree's low tones awaken,
    And bud and bell with changes mark the hours.   10

There let thy thoughts be with me, while the day
Sinks with a golden and serene decay.

Or by some hearth where happy faces meet,
    When night hath hush'd the woods, with all their birds,
There, from some gentle voice, that lay were sweet
    As antique music, link'd with household words.
While, in pleased murmurs, woman's lip might move,
And the rais'd eye of childhood shine in love.

Or where the shadows of dark solemn yews
    Brood silently o'er some lone burial-ground,   20
Thy verse hath power that brightly might diffuse
    A breath, a kindling, as of spring, around;
From its own glow of hope and courage high,
And steadfast faith's victorious constancy.

True bard, and holy!—thou art ev'n as one
    Who, by some secret gift of soul or eye,
In every spot beneath the smiling sun,
    Sees where the springs of living waters lie:
Unseen awhile they sleep—till, touch'd by thee,
Bright healthful waves flow forth to each glad wanderer free.   30

A MONARCH'S DEATH-BED

The Emperor Albert of Hapsburgh, who was assassinated by his
nephew, afterwards called John the Parricide, was left to die by the way-
side, and only supported in his last moments by a female peasant, who
happened to be passing.

A Monarch on his death-bed lay—
    Did censers waft perfume,
And soft lamps pour their silvery ray,
    Thro' his proud chamber's gloom?

He lay upon a greensward bed,
    Beneath a darkening sky—
A lone tree waving o'er his head,
    A swift stream rolling by.

Had he then fall'n as warriors fall,
    Where spear strikes fire with spear?   10
Was there a banner for his pall,
    A buckler for his bier?
Not so;—nor cloven shields nor helms
    Had strewn the bloody sod,
Where he, the helpless lord of realms,
    Yielded his soul to God.

Were there not friends with words of cheer,
    And princely vassals nigh?
And priests, the crucifix to rear
    Before the glazing eye?   20
A peasant girl that royal head
    Upon her bosom laid,
And, shrinking not for woman's dread,
    The face of death survey'd.

Alone she sat:—from hill and wood
    Red sank the mournful sun;
Fast gush'd the fount of noble blood,
    Treason its worst had done!
With her long hair she vainly press'd
    The wounds to staunch their tide—   30
Unknown, on that meek humble breast,
    Imperial Albert died!

To the Memory of Heber

Umile in tanta gloria.

Petrarch

If it be sad to speak of treasures gone,
    Of sainted genius called too soon away,
Of light, from this world taken, while it shone
    Yet kindling onward to the perfect day;
How shall our grief, if mournful these things be,
Flow forth, oh, Thou of many gifts! for thee?

Hath not thy voice been here amongst us heard?
    And that deep soul of gentleness and power,
Have we not felt its breath in every word,
    Wont from thy lip, as Hermon's dew, to shower?   10
Yes! in our hearts thy fervent thoughts have burn'd,
Of Heaven they were, and thither have return'd.

How shall we mourn thee?—With a lofty trust,
    Our life's immortal birthright from above!
With a glad faith, whose eye, to track the just,
    Thro' shades and mysteries lifts a glance of love,
And yet can weep!—for nature thus deplores
The friend that leaves us, tho' for happier shores.

And one high tone of triumph o'er thy bier,
    One strain of solemn rapture be allow'd!   20
Thou, that rejoicing on thy mid career,
    Not to decay, but unto death, hast bow'd;
In those bright regions of the rising sun,
Where victory ne'er a crown like thine had won.

Praise! for yet one more name with power endow'd,
    To cheer and guide us, onward as we press;
Yet one more image, on the heart bestow'd,
    To dwell there, beautiful in holiness!

Thine, Heber, thine! whose memory from the dead,
Shines as the star which to the Saviour led.   30
St. Asaph, Sept. 1826

THE ADOPTED CHILD

"Why wouldst thou leave me, oh! gentle child?
Thy home on the mountain is bleak and wild,
A straw-roof'd cabin with lowly wall—
Mine is a fair and a pillar'd hall,
Where many an image of marble gleams,
And the sunshine of picture for ever streams."

"Oh! green is the turf where my brothers play,
Thro' the long bright hours of the summer-day,
They find the red cup-moss where they climb,
And they chase the bee o'er the scented thyme,   10
And the rocks where the heath-flower blooms they know—
Lady, kind lady! oh! let me go."

"Content thee, boy! in my bower to dwell,
Here are sweet sounds which thou lovest well;
Flutes on the air in the stilly noon,
Harps which the wandering breezes tune;
And the silvery wood-note of many a bird,
Whose voice was ne'er in thy mountains heard."

"Oh! my mother sings, at the twilight's fall,
A song of the hills far more sweet than all;   20
She sings it under our own green tree,
To the babe half slumbering on her knee;
I dreamt last night of that music low—
Lady, kind lady! oh! let me go."

"Thy mother is gone from her cares to rest,

She hath taken the babe on her quiet breast;
Thou wouldst meet her footstep, my boy, no more,
Nor hear her song at the cabin door.
Come thou with me to the vineyards nigh,
And we'll pluck the grapes of the richest dye."   30

"Is my mother gone from her home away?—
But I know that my brothers are there at play.
I know they are gathering the fox-glove's bell,
Or the long fern-leaves by the sparkling well,
Or they launch their boats where the bright streams flow,—
Lady, kind lady! oh! let me go."

"Fair child, thy brothers are wanderers now,
They sport no more on the mountain's brow,
They have left the fern by the spring's green side,
And the streams where the fairy barks were tried.   40
Be thou at peace in thy brighter lot,
For thy cabin-home is a lonely spot."

"Are they gone, all gone from the sunny hill?—
But the bird and the blue-fly rove o'er it still;
And the red-deer bound in their gladness free,
And the heath is bent by the singing bee,
And the waters leap, and the fresh winds blow,—
Lady, kind lady! oh! let me go."

INVOCATION

I called on dreams and visions, to disclose
That which is veil'd from waking thought; conjured
Eternity, as men constrain a ghost
To appear and answer.

Wordsworth

Answer me, burning stars of night!
    Where is the spirit gone,
That past the reach of human sight,
    As a swift breeze hath flown?—
And the stars answer'd me—"We roll
    In light and power on high;
But, of the never-dying soul,
    Ask that which cannot die."

Oh! many-toned and chainless wind!
    Thou art a wanderer free;   10
Tell me if *thou* its place canst find,
    Far over mount and sea?—
And the wind murmur'd in reply,
    "The blue deep I have cross'd,
And met its barks and billows high,
    But not what thou hast lost."

Ye clouds that gorgeously repose
    Around the setting sun,
Answer! have ye a home for those
    Whose earthly race is run?   20
The bright clouds answer'd—"We depart,
    We vanish from the sky;
Ask what is deathless in thy heart,
    For that which cannot die."

Speak then, thou voice of God within,
    Thou of the deep low tone!
Answer me, thro' life's restless din,
    Where is the spirit flown?—
And the voice answered—"Be thou still!
    Enough to know is given;   30
Clouds, winds, and stars *their* part fulfil,
    Thine is to trust in Heaven."

Körner and his Sister

Charles Theodore Körner, the celebrated young German poet and soldier, was killed in a skirmish with a detachment of French troops, on the 20th of August, 1813, a few hours after the composition of his popular piece, "The Sword-song." He was buried at the village of Wöbbelin in Mecklenburgh, under a beautiful oak, in a recess of which he had frequently deposited verses composed by him while campaigning in its vicinity. The monument erected to his memory is of cast iron, and the upper part is wrought into a lyre and sword, a favourite emblem of Körner's, from which one of his works had been entitled. Near the grave of the poet is that of his only sister, who died of grief for his loss, having only survived him long enough to complete his portrait, and a drawing of his burial-place. Over the gate of the cemetery is engraved one of his own lines:

"Vergiss die treuen Tödten nicht."
Forget not the faithful dead.

See Richardson's translation of Körner's *Life and Works,* and Downes's *Letters from Mecklenburgh*

Green wave the oak for ever o'er thy rest,
    Thou that beneath its crowning foliage sleepest,
And, in the stillness of thy country's breast,
    Thy place of memory, as an altar keepest;
Brightly thy spirit o'er her hills was pour'd,
        Thou of the Lyre and Sword!

Rest, bard! rest, soldier!—by the father's hand
    Here shall the child of after-years be led,
With his wreath-offering silently to stand,
    In the hush'd presence of the glorious dead.   10
Soldier and bard! for thou thy path hast trod
        With freedom and with God.

The oak wav'd proudly o'er thy burial-rite,
    On thy crown'd bier to slumber warriors bore thee,
And with true hearts thy brethren of the fight

"Thekla at her Lover's Grave" from *The Poetical Works of Mrs. Felicia Hemans* (New York: The American News Company, [ca. 1888]).

Wept as they vail'd their drooping banners o'er thee.
And the deep guns with rolling peal gave token,
      That Lyre and Sword were broken.

Thou hast a hero's tomb:—a lowlier bed
    Is hers, the gentle girl beside thee lying,   20
The gentle girl, that bow'd her fair young head,
    When thou wert gone, in silent sorrow dying.
Brother, true friend! the tender and the brave—
      She pined to share thy grave.

Fame was thy gift from others;—but for *her*,
    To whom the wide world held that only spot,
She lov'd thee!—lovely in your lives ye were,
    And in your early deaths divided not.
Thou hast thine oak, thy trophy:—what hath she?—
      Her own blest place by thee!   30

It was thy spirit, brother! which had made
    The bright earth glorious to her thoughtful eye,
Since first in childhood midst the vines ye play'd,
    And sent glad singing thro' the free blue sky.
Ye were but two—and when that spirit pass'd,
      Woe to the one, the last!

Woe, yet not long!—She linger'd but to trace
    Thine image from the image in her breast,
Once, once again to see that buried face
    But smile upon her, ere she went to rest.   40
Too sad a smile! its living light was o'er,
      It answer'd hers no more.

The earth grew silent when thy voice departed,
    The home too lonely whence thy step had fled;
What then was left for her, the faithful-hearted?
    Death, death, to still the yearning for the dead!
Softly she perish'd:—be the Flower deplor'd
      Here with the Lyre and Sword!

Have ye not met ere now?—so let those trust
    That meet for moments but to part for years,   50
That weep, watch, pray, to hold back dust from dust,
    That love, where love is but a fount of tears.
Brother, sweet sister! peace around ye dwell—
        Lyre, Sword, and Flower, farewell!

An Hour of Romance

                        ——*I come*
To this sweet place for quiet. Every tree,
And bush, and fragrant flower, and hilly path,
And thymy mound that flings unto the winds
Its morning incense, is my friend.
                        Barry Cornwall

There were thick leaves above me and around,
    And low sweet sighs, like those of childhood's sleep,
Amidst their dimness, and a fitful sound
    As of soft showers on water;—dark and deep
Lay the oak shadows o'er the turf, so still,
They seem'd but pictur'd glooms: a hidden rill
Made music, such as haunts us in a dream,
Under the fern-tufts; and a tender gleam
Of soft green light, as by the glow-worm shed,
    Came pouring thro' the woven beech-boughs down,   10
And steep'd the magic page wherein I read
    Of royal chivalry and old renown,
A tale of Palestine.—Meanwhile the bee
    Swept past me with a tone of summer hours,
    A drowsy bugle, wafting thoughts of flowers,
Blue skies and amber sunshine: brightly free,
On filmy wings the purple dragon-fly
Shot glancing like a fairy javelin by;

And a sweet voice of sorrow told the dell
  Where sat the lone wood-pigeon: 20
         But ere long,
All sense of these things faded, as the spell
  Breathing from that high gorgeous tale grew strong
On my chain'd soul:—'twas not the leaves I heard—
A Syrian wind the Lion-banner stirr'd,
Thro' its proud floating folds:—'twas not the brook,
  Singing in secret thro' its grassy glen—
  A wild shrill trumpet of the Saracen
Peal'd from the desert's lonely heart, and shook
The burning air.—Like clouds when winds are high, 30
O'er glittering sands flew steeds of Araby,
And tents rose up, and sudden lance and spear
Flash'd where a fountain's diamond wave lay clear,
Shadow'd by graceful palm-trees. Then the shout
Of merry England's joy swell'd freely out,
Sent thro' an Eastern heaven, whose glorious hue
Made shields dark mirrors to its depths of blue;
And harps were there—I heard their sounding strings,
As the waste echoed to the mirth of kings.—
The bright masque faded.—Unto life's worn track, 40
What call'd me from its flood of glory, back?
A voice of happy childhood!—and they pass'd,
Banner, and harp, and Paynim trumpet's blast;
Yet might I scarce bewail the splendours gone,
My heart so leap'd to that sweet laughter's tone.

A Voyager's Dream of Land

   His very heart athirst
To gaze at nature in her green array,
Upon the ship's tall side he stands, possess'd
With visions prompted by intense desire;
Fair fields appear below, such as he left

Far distant, such as he would die to find—
He seeks them headlong, and is seen no more.
Cowper

The hollow dash of waves!—the ceaseless roar!—
Silence, ye billows!—vex my soul no more.

There's a spring in the woods by my sunny home,
Afar from the dark sea's tossing foam;
Oh! the fall of that fountain is sweet to hear,
As a song from the shore to the sailor's ear!
And the sparkle which up to the sun it throws,
Thro' the feathery fern and the olive boughs,
And the gleam on its path as it steals away
Into deeper shades from the sultry day,   10
And the large water lilies that o'er its bed
Their pearly leaves to the soft light spread,
They haunt me! I dream of that bright spring's flow,
I thirst for its rills, like a wounded roe!

Be still thou sea-bird, with thy clanging cry!
My spirit sickens, as thy wing sweeps by.

Know ye my home, with the lulling sound
Of leaves from the lime and the chestnut round?
Know ye it, brethren! where bower'd it lies,
Under the purple of southern skies?   20
With the streamy gold of the sun that shines
In thro' the cloud of its clustering vines,
And the summer-breath of the myrtle-flowers;
Borne from the mountains in dewy hours,
And the fire-fly's glance thro' the darkening shades,
Like shooting stars in the forest-glades,
And the scent of the citron at eve's dim fall—
Speak! have ye known, have ye felt them all?

The heavy rolling surge! the rocking mast!
Hush! give my dream's deep music way, thou blast!   30

Oh! the glad sounds of the joyous earth!
The notes of the singing cicala's mirth,
The murmurs that live in the mountain pines,
The sighing of reeds as the day declines,
The wings flitting home thro' the crimson glow
That steeps the woods when the sun is low,
The voice of the night-bird that sends a thrill
To the heart of the leaves when the winds are still—
I hear them!—around me they rise, they swell,
They call back my spirit with Hope to dwell,   40
They come with a breath from the fresh spring-time,
And waken my youth in its hour of prime.

The white foam dashes high—away, away!
Shroud my green land no more, thou blinding spray!

It is there!—down the mountains I see the sweep
Of the chestnut forests, the rich and deep,
With the burden and glory of flowers that they bear,
Floating upborne on the blue summer-air,
And the light pouring thro' them in tender gleams,
And the flashing forth of a thousand streams!—   50
Hold me not, brethren! I go, I go,
To the hills of my youth, where the myrtles blow,
To the depths of the woods, where the shadows rest,
Massy and still, on the greensward's breast,
To the rocks that resound with the water's play—
I hear the sweet laugh of my fount—give way!

Give way!—the booming surge, the tempest's roar,
The sea-bird's wail, shall vex my soul no more.

THE EFFIGIES

Der rasche Kampf verewigt einen Mann:
Er falle gleich, so preiset ihn das Lied.
Allein die Thränen, die unendlichen,
Der überbliebnen, der verlass'nen Frau,
Zählt keine Nachwelt.

Goethe

Warrior! whose image on thy tomb,
    With shield and crested head,
Sleeps proudly in the purple gloom
    By the stain'd window shed;
The records of thy name and race
    Have faded from the stone,
Yet, thro' a cloud of years I trace
    What thou hast been and done.

A banner, from its flashing spear
    Flung out o'er many a fight,   10
A war-cry ringing far and clear,
    And strong to turn the flight;
An arm that bravely bore the lance
    On for the holy shrine;
A haughty heart and a kingly glance—
    Chief! were not these things thine:

A lofty place where leaders sate
    Around the council-board;
In festive halls a chair of state
    When the blood-red wine was pour'd;   20
A name that drew a prouder tone
    From herald, harp, and bard;—
Surely these things were all thine own,
    So hadst thou thy reward.

Woman! whose sculptur'd form at rest
    By the armed knight is laid,

With meek hands folded o'er a breast
    In matron robes array'd;
What was *thy* tale?—Oh! gentle mate
    Of him, the bold and free,   30
Bound unto his victorious fate,
    What bard hath sung of *thee?*

He wooed a bright and burning star—
    Thine was the void, the gloom,
The straining eye that follow'd far
    His fast receding plume;
The heart-sick listening while his steed
    Sent echoes on the breeze;
The pang—but when did *Fame* take heed
    Of griefs obscure as these?   40

Thy silent and secluded hours
    Thro' many a lonely day,
While bending o'er thy broider'd flowers,
    With spirit far away;
Thy weeping midnight prayers for him
    Who fought on Syrian plains,
Thy watchings till the torch grew dim—
    These fill no minstrel strains.

A still, sad life was thine!—long years
    With tasks unguerdon'd fraught,   50
Deep, quiet love, submissive tears,
    Vigils of anxious thought;
Prayer at the cross in fervour pour'd,
    Alms to the pilgrim given—
Oh! happy, happier than thy lord,
    In that lone path to heaven!

THE LANDING OF THE PILGRIM
FATHERS IN NEW ENGLAND

Look now abroad—another race has fill'd
  Those populous borders—wide the wood recedes,
And towns shoot up, and fertile realms are till'd;
  The land is full of harvests and green meads.
Bryant

The breaking waves dash'd high
  On a stern and rock-bound coast,
And the woods against a stormy sky
  Their giant branches toss'd;

And the heavy night hung dark,
  The hills and waters o'er,
When a band of exiles moor'd their bark
  On the wild New-England shore.

Not as the conqueror comes,
  They, the true-hearted came;   10
Not with the roll of the stirring drums,
  And the trumpet that sings of fame:

Not as the flying come,
  In silence and in fear;—
They shook the depths of the desert gloom
  With their hymns of lofty cheer.

Amidst the storm they sang,
  And the stars heard and the sea!
And the sounding aisles of the dim woods rang
  To the anthem of the free.   20

The ocean-eagle soar'd
  From his nest by the white wave's foam,

"Freedom to Worship God." Illustration by L.B. Humphrey to Hemans's "The Pilgrim Fathers in New England" in *The Breaking Waves Dashed High* (Boston: Lee and Shephard; New York: Charles T. Dillingham, 1879).

And the rocking pines of the forest roar'd—
    This was their welcome home!

There were men with hoary hair,
    Amidst that pilgrim band;—
Why had *they* come to wither there,
    Away from their childhood's land?

There was woman's fearless eye,
    Lit by her deep love's truth;   30
There was manhood's brow serenely high,
    And the fiery heart of youth.

What sought they thus afar?
    Bright jewels of the mine?
The wealth of seas, the spoils of war?—
    They sought a faith's pure shrine!

Ay, call it holy ground,
    The soil where first they trod!
They have left unstain'd what there they found—
    Freedom to worship God.   40

THE SPIRIT'S MYSTERIES

And slight, withal, may be the things which bring
Back on the heart the weight which it would fling
    Aside for ever;—it may be a sound—
A tone of music—summer's breath, or spring—
    A flower—a leaf—the ocean—which may wound—
Striking th' electric chain wherewith we are darkly bound.
                         Childe Harold

The power that dwelleth in sweet sounds to waken
    Vague yearnings, like the sailor's for the shore,

And dim remembrances, whose hue seems taken
    From some bright former state, our own no more;
Is not this all a mystery?—Who shall say
Whence are those thoughts, and whither tends their way?

The sudden images of vanish'd things,
    That o'er the spirit flash, we know not why;
Tones from some broken harp's deserted strings,
    Warm sunset hues of summers long gone by,   10
A rippling wave—the dashing of an oar—
A flower scent floating past our parents' door;

A word—scarce noted in its hour perchance,
    Yet back returning with a plaintive tone;
A smile—a sunny or a mournful glance,
    Full of sweet meanings now from this world flown;
Are not these mysteries when to life they start,
And press vain tears in gushes from the heart?

And the far wanderings of the soul in dreams,
    Calling up shrouded faces from the dead,   20
And with them bringing soft or solemn gleams,
    Familiar objects brightly to o'erspread;
And wakening buried love, or joy, or fear,—
These are night's mysteries—who shall make them clear?

And the strange inborn sense of coming ill,
    That ofttimes whispers to the haunted breast,
In a low tone which nought can drown or still,
    Midst feasts and melodies a secret guest;
Whence doth that murmur wake, that shadow fall?
Why shakes the spirit thus?—'tis mystery all!   30

Darkly we move—we press upon the brink
    Haply of viewless worlds, and know it not;
Yes! it may be, that nearer than we think,
    Are those whom death has parted from our lot!
Fearfully, wondrously, our souls are made—
Let us walk humbly on, but undismay'd!

Humbly—for knowledge strives in vain to feel
    Her way amidst these marvels of the mind;
Yet undismay'd—for do they not reveal
    Th' immortal being with our dust entwin'd?—   40
So let us deem! and e'en the tears they wake
Shall then be blest, for that high nature's sake.

THE DEPARTED

Thou shalt lie down
With patriarchs of the infant world—with kings,
The powerful of the earth—the wise—the good,
Fair forms, and hoary seers of ages past,
All in one mighty sepulchre.

                        Bryant

And shrink ye from the way
    To the spirit's distant shore?—
Earth's mightiest men, in arm'd array,
    Are thither gone before.

The warrior kings, whose banner
    Flew far as eagles fly,
They are gone where swords avail them not,
    From the feast of victory.

And the seers who sat of yore
    By orient palm or wave,   10
They have pass'd with all their starry lore—
    Can *ye* still fear the grave?

We fear! we fear!—the sunshine
    Is joyous to behold,
And we reck not of the buried kings,
    Nor the awful seers of old.

Ye shrink!—the bards whose lays
    Have made your deep hearts burn,
They have left the sun, and the voice of praise,
    For the land whence none return.   20

And the beautiful, whose record
    Is the verse that cannot die,
They too are gone, with their glorious bloom,
    From the love of human eye.

Would ye not join that throng
    Of the earth's departed flowers,
And the masters of the mighty song
    In their far and fadeless bowers?

Those songs are high and holy,
    But they vanquish not our fear;   30
Not from *our* path those flowers are gone—
    We fain would linger here!

Linger then yet awhile,
    As the last leaves on the bough!—
Ye have lov'd the light of many a smile,
    That is taken from you now.

There have been sweet singing voices
    In your walks that now are still,
There are seats left void in your earthly homes,
    Which none again may fill.   40

Soft eyes are seen no more,
    That made spring-time in your heart;
Kindred and friends are gone before—
    And *ye* still fear to part?

We fear not now, we fear not!
    Though the way thro' darkness bends;

Our souls are strong to follow *them,*
  Our own familiar friends!

The Palm-Tree

It wav'd not thro' an Eastern sky,
Beside a fount of Araby;
It was not fann'd by southern breeze
In some green isle of Indian seas,
Nor did its graceful shadow sleep
O'er stream of Afric, lone and deep.

But fair the exil'd Palm-tree grew
Midst foliage of no kindred hue;
Thro' the laburnum's dropping gold
Rose the light shaft of orient mould,   10
And Europe's violets, faintly sweet,
Purpled the moss-beds at its feet.

Strange look'd it there!—the willow stream'd
Where silvery waters near it gleam'd;
The lime-bough lured the honey-bee
To murmur by the Desert's Tree,
And showers of snowy roses made
A lustre in its fan-like shade.

There came an eve of festal hours—
Rich music fill'd that garden's bowers: 20
Lamps, that from flowering branches hung,
On sparks of dew soft colours flung,
And bright forms glanc'd—a fairy show—
Under the blossoms to and fro.

But one, a lone one, midst the throng,
Seem'd reckless all of dance or song:
He was a youth of dusky mien,
Whereon the Indian sun had been,

Of crested brow, and long black hair—
A stranger, like the Palm-tree there.   30

And slowly, sadly, mov'd his plumes,
Glittering athwart the leafy glooms:
He pass'd the pale green olives by,
Nor won the chestnut-flowers his eye;
But when to that sole Palm he came,
Then shot a rapture through his frame!

To him, to him, its rustling spoke,
The silence of his soul it broke!
It whisper'd of his own bright isle,
That lit the ocean with a smile;   40
Aye, to his ear that native tone
Had something of the sea-wave's moan!

His mother's cabin home, that lay
Where feathery cocoas fring'd the bay;
The dashing of his brethren's oar,
The conch-note heard along the shore;—
All thro' his wakening bosom swept:
He clasp'd his country's Tree and wept!

Oh! scorn him not!—the strength, whereby
The patriot girds himself to die,   50
Th' unconqucrable power, which fills
The freeman battling on his hills,
These have one fountain deep and clear—
The same whence gush'd that child-like tear!

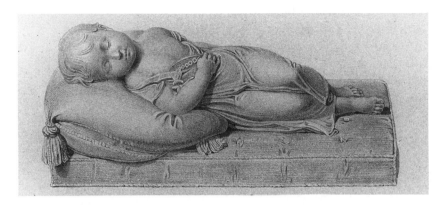

"Sleeping Child, after Chantrey." Engraving by W.T. Fry, after a drawing by H. Corbould, published in *Friendship's Offering* (1826) opposite "The Child's Last Sleep."

THE CHILD'S LAST SLEEP

Suggested by a monument of Chantrey's

Thou sleepest—but when wilt thou wake, fair child?—
When the fawn awakes in the forest wild?
When the lark's wing mounts with the breeze of morn?
When the first rich breath of the rose is born?—
Lovely thou sleepest, yet something lies
Too deep and still on thy soft-seal'd eyes,
Mournful, tho' sweet, is thy rest to see—
When will the hour of thy rising be?

Not when the fawn wakes, not when the lark
On the crimson cloud of the morn floats dark—   10
Grief with vain passionate tears hath wet
Thy hair, shedding gleams from thy pale brow yet;
Love with sad kisses, unfelt, hath press'd
Thy meek-dropt eyelids and quiet breast;
And the glad spring, calling out bird and bee,
Shall colour all blossoms, fair child! but thee.

Thou'rt gone from us, bright one!—that *thou* shouldst die,
And life be left to the butterfly!
Thou'rt gone, as a dew-drop is swept from the bough—
Oh! for the world where thy home is now!　　　　　20
How may we love but in doubt and fear,
How may we anchor our fond hearts here,
How should e'en joy but a trembler be,
Beautiful dust! when we look on thee?

THE SUNBEAM

Thou art no lingerer in monarch's hall,
A joy thou art, and a wealth to all!
A bearer of hope unto land and sea—
Sunbeam! what gift hath the world like thee?

Thou art walking the billows, and ocean smiles—
Thou hast touch'd with glory his thousand isles;
Thou hast lit up the ships, and the feathery foam,
And gladden'd the sailor, like words from home.

To the solemn depths of the forest shades,
Thou art streaming on thro' their green arcades,　　10
And the quivering leaves that have caught thy glow,
Like fire-flies glance to the pools below.

I look'd on the mountains—a vapour lay
Folding their heights in its dark array:
Thou brakest forth—and the mist became
A crown and a mantle of living flame.

I look'd on the peasant's lowly cot—
Something of sadness had wrapt the spot;—
But a gleam of *thee* on its lattice fell,
And it laugh'd into beauty at that bright spell.　　　20

To the earth's wild places a guest thou art,
Flushing the waste like the rose's heart;
And thou scornest not from thy pomp to shed
A tender smile on the ruin's head.

Thou tak'st thro' the dim church-aisle thy way,
And its pillars from twilight flash forth to day,
And its high pale tombs, with their trophies old,
Are bath'd in a flood as of molten gold.

And thou turnest not from the humblest grave,
Where a flower to the sighing winds may wave;   30
Thou scatterest its gloom like the dreams of rest,
Thou sleepest in love on its grassy breast.

Sunbeam of summer! oh! what is like thee?
Hope of the wilderness, joy of the sea!—
One thing is like thee to mortals given,
The faith touching all things with hues of Heaven!

BREATHINGS OF SPRING

Thou giv'st me flowers, thou giv'st me songs;—bring back
The love that I have lost!

What wak'st thou, Spring?—sweet voices in the woods,
    And reed-like echoes, that have long been mute;
Thou bringest back, to fill the solitudes,
    The lark's clear pipe, the cuckoo's viewless flute,
Whose tone seems breathing mournfulness or glee,
        Ev'n as our hearts may be.

And the leaves greet thee, Spring!—the joyous leaves,
    Whose tremblings gladden many a copse and glade,
Where each young spray a rosy flush receives,
    When thy south-wind hath pierc'd the whispery shade,   10

And happy murmurs, running thro' the grass,
    Tell that thy footsteps pass.

And the bright waters—they too hear thy call,
    Spring, the awakener! thou hast burst their sleep!
Amidst the hollows of the rocks their fall
    Makes melody, and in the forests deep,
Where sudden sparkles and blue gleams betray
    Their windings to the day.

And flowers—the fairy-peopled world of flowers!
    Thou from the dust hast set that glory free,   20
Colouring the cowslip with the sunny hours,
    And pencilling the wood-anemone;
Silent they seem—yet each to thoughtful eye
    Glows with mute poesy.

But what awak'st thou in the *heart*, O, Spring!
    The human heart, with all its dreams and sighs?
Thou that giv'st back so many a buried thing,
    Restorer of forgotten harmonies!
Fresh songs and scents break forth where'er thou art,
    What wak'st thou in the heart?   30

Too much, oh! there too much!—we know not well
    Wherefore it should be thus, yet rous'd by thee,
What fond strange yearnings, from the soul's deep cell,
    Gush for the faces we no more may see!
How are we haunted, in thy wind's low tone,
    By voices that are gone!

Looks of familiar love, that never more,
    Never on earth, our aching eyes shall meet,
Past words of welcome to our household door,
    And vanish'd smiles, and sounds of parted feet—   40
Spring! midst the murmurs of thy flowering trees,
    Why, why reviv'st thou these?

Vain longings for the dead!—why come they back
　　With thy young birds, and leaves, and living blooms?
Oh! is it not, that from thine earthly track
　　Hope to thy world may look beyond the tombs?
Yes! gentle spring; no sorrow dims thine air,
　　　　Breath'd by our lov'd ones *there!*

THE ILLUMINATED CITY

The hills all glow'd with a festive light,
For the royal city rejoic'd by night:
There were lamps hung forth upon tower and tree,
Banners were lifted and streaming free;
Every tall pillar was wreath'd with fire,
Like a shooting meteor was every spire;
And the outline of many a dome on high
Was traced, as in stars, on the clear dark sky.

I pass'd thro' the streets; there were throngs on throngs—
Like sounds of the deep were their mingled songs;　　　10
There was music forth from each palace borne—
A peal of the cymbal, the harp, and horn;
The forests heard it, the mountains rang,
The hamlets woke to its haughty clang;
Rich and victorious was every tone,
Telling the land of her foes o'erthrown.

Didst thou meet not a mourner for all the slain?
Thousands lie dead on their battle-plain!
Gallant and true were the hearts that fell—
Grief in the homes they have left must dwell;　　　20
Grief o'er the aspect of childhood spread,
And bowing the beauty of woman's head:
Didst thou hear, midst the songs, not one tender moan,
For the many brave to their slumbers gone?

I saw not the face of a weeper there—
Too strong, perchance, was the bright lamp's glare!
I heard not a wail midst the joyous crowd—
The music of victory was all too loud!
Mighty it roll'd on the winds afar,
Shaking the streets like a conqueror's car;   30
Thro' torches and streamers its flood swept by—
How could I listen for moan or sigh?

Turn then away from life's pageants, turn,
If its deep story thy heart would learn!
Ever too bright is that outward show,
Dazzling the eyes till they see not woe.
But lift the proud mantle which hides from thy view
The things thou shouldst gaze on, the sad and true;
Nor fear to survey what its folds conceal—
So must thy spirit be taught to feel!   40

THE SPELLS OF HOME

There blend the ties that strengthen
*   Our hearts in hours of grief,*
The silver links that lengthen
*   Joy's visits when most brief.*
                                        Bernard Barton

By the soft green light in the woody glade,
On the banks of moss where thy childhood play'd;
By the household tree thro' which thine eye
First look'd in love to the summer-sky;
By the dewy gleam, by the very breath
Of the primrose tufts in the grass beneath,
Upon thy heart there is laid a spell,
Holy and precious—oh! guard it well!

By the sleepy ripple of the stream,
Which hath lull'd thee into many a dream;   10
By the shiver of the ivy-leaves
To the wind of morn at thy casement-eaves,
By the bees' deep murmur in the limes,
By the music of the Sabbath-chimes,
By every sound of thy native shade,
Stronger and dearer the spell is made.

By the gathering round the winter hearth,
When twilight call'd unto household mirth;
By the fairy tale or the legend old
In that ring of happy faces told;   20
By the quiet hour when hearts unite
In the parting prayer and the kind "Good-night;"
By the smiling eye and the loving tone,
Over thy life has the spell been thrown.

And bless that gift!—it hath gentle might,
A guardian power and a guiding light.
It hath led the freeman forth to stand
In the mountain-battles of his land;
It hath brought the wanderer o'er the seas
To die on the hills of his own fresh breeze;   30
And back to the gates of his father's hall,
It hath led the weeping prodigal.

Yes! when thy heart in its pride would stray
From the pure first loves of its youth away;
When the sullying breath of the world would come
O'er the flowers it brought from its childhood's home;
Think thou again of the woody glade,
And the sound by the rustling ivy made,
Think of the tree at thy father's door,
And the kindly spell shall have power once more!   40

ROMAN GIRL'S SONG

Roma, Roma, Roma!
Non è più come era prima.

Rome, Rome! thou art no more
    As thou hast been!
On thy seven hills of yore
    Thou satst a queen.

Thou hadst thy triumphs then
    Purpling the street,
Leaders and sceptred men
    Bow'd at thy feet.

They that thy mantle wore,
    As gods were seen—   10
Rome, Rome! thou art no more
    As thou hast been!

Rome! thine imperial brow
    Never shall rise:
What hast thou left thee now?—
    Thou hast thy skies!

Blue, deeply blue, they are,
    Gloriously bright!
Veiling thy wastes afar
    With colour'd light.   20

Thou hast the sunset's glow,
    Rome, for thy dower,
Flushing tall cypress-bough,
    Temple and tower!

And all sweet sounds are thine,
    Lovely to hear,

While night, o'er tomb and shrine,
    Rests darkly clear.

Many a solemn hymn,
    By starlight sung,   30
Sweeps thro' the arches dim,
    Thy wrecks among.

Many a flute's low swell,
    On thy soft air
Lingers, and loves to dwell
    With summer there.

Thou hast the South's rich gift
    Of sudden song,
A charmed fountain, swift,
    Joyous, and strong.   40

Thou hast fair forms that move
    With queenly tread;
Thou hast proud fanes above
    Thy mighty dead.

Yet wears thy Tiber's shore
    A mournful mien:—
Rome, Rome! Thou art no more
    As thou hast been!

THE DISTANT SHIP

The sea-bird's wing, o'er ocean's breast
    Shoots like a glancing star,
While the red radiance of the west
    Spreads kindling fast and far;
And yet that splendour wins thee not,—
    Thy still and thoughtful eye

Dwells but on one dark distant spot
    Of all the main and sky.

Look round thee!—o'er the slumbering deep
    A solemn glory broods;   10
A fire hath touch'd the beacon-steep,
    And all the golden woods;
A thousand gorgeous clouds on high
    Burn with the amber light;—
What spell, from that rich pageantry,
    Chains down thy gazing sight?

A softening thought of human cares,
    A feeling link'd to earth!
Is not yon speck a bark, which bears
    The lov'd of many a hearth?   20
Oh! do not Hope, and Grief, and Fear,
    Crowd her frail world even now,
And manhood's prayer and woman's tear,
    Follow her venturous prow?

Bright are the floating clouds above,
    The glittering seas below;
But we are bound by cords of love
    To kindred weal and woe.
Therefore, amidst this wide array
    Of glorious things and fair,   30
My soul is on that bark's lone way
    For human hearts are there.

THE BIRDS OF PASSAGE

Birds, joyous birds of the wandering wing!
Whence is it ye come with the flowers of spring?
—"We come from the shores of the green old Nile,
From the land where the roses of Sharon smile,

From the palms that wave thro' the Indian sky,
From the myrrh-trees of glowing Araby.

"We have swept o'er cities in song renown'd—
Silent they lie, with the deserts round!
We have cross'd proud rivers, whose tide hath roll'd
All dark with the warrior-blood of old; 10
And each worn wing hath regain'd its home,
Under peasant's roof-tree, or monarch's dome."

And what have ye found in the monarch's dome,
Since last ye travers'd the blue sea's foam?
—"We have found a change, we have found a pall,
And a gloom o'ershadowing the banquet's hall,
And a mark on the floor as of life-drops spilt,—
Nought looks the same save the nest we built!"

Oh! joyous birds, it hath still been so;
Thro' the halls of kings doth the tempest go! 20
But the huts of the hamlet lie still and deep,
And the hills o'er their quiet a vigil keep.
Say what have ye found in the peasant's cot,
Since last ye parted from that sweet spot?

"A change we have found there—and many a change!
Faces and footsteps and all things strange!
Gone are the heads of the silvery hair,
And the young that were, have a brow of care,
And the place is hush'd where the children play'd,—
Nought looks the same, save the nest we made!" 30

Sad is your tale of the beautiful earth,
Birds that o'ersweep it in power and mirth!
Yet thro' the wastes of the trackless air,
Ye have a Guide, and shall *we* despair?
Ye over desert and deep have pass'd,—
So may *we* reach our bright home at last!

"The Graves of a Household." Frontispiece illustration to Hemans's *Poems* (London and New York: George Routledge and Sons [ca. 1877]).

THE GRAVES OF A HOUSEHOLD

They grew in beauty, side by side,
    They fill'd one home with glee;—
Their graves are sever'd, far and wide,
    By mount, and stream, and sea.

The same fond mother bent at night
    O'er each fair sleeping brow;
She had each folded flower in sight,—
    Where are those dreamers now?

One, midst the forests of the west,
    By a dark stream is laid—   10
The Indian knows his place of rest,
    Far in the cedar shade.

The sea, the blue lone sea, hath one,
    He lies where pearls lie deep;
He was the lov'd of all, yet none
    O'er his low bed may weep.

One sleeps where southern vines are drest
    Above the noble slain:
He wrapt his colours round his breast,
    On a blood-red field of Spain.   20

And one—o'er *her* the myrtle showers
    Its leaves, by soft winds fann'd;
She faded midst Italian flowers,—
    The last of that bright band.

And parted thus they rest, who play'd
    Beneath the same green tree;
Whose voices mingled as they pray'd
    Around one parent knee!

They that with smiles lit up the hall,
    And cheer'd with song the hearth,—   30
Alas! for love, if *thou* wert all,
    And nought beyond, oh, earth!

"The Graves of a Household" as sheet music. Published by Oliver Ditson, Boston, in 1850 with music by C.H.M.

MOZART'S REQUIEM

A short time before the death of Mozart, a stranger of remarkable appearance, and dressed in deep mourning, called at his house, and requested him to prepare a requiem, in his best style, for the funeral of a distinguished person. The sensitive imagination of the composer immediately seized upon the circumstance as an omen of his own fate; and the nervous anxiety with which he laboured to fulfil the task, had the effect of realizing his impression. He died within a few days after completing this magnificent piece of music, which was performed at his interment.

These birds of Paradise but long to flee
Back to their native mansion.
                                    Prophecy of Dante

       A requiem!—and for whom?
       For beauty in its bloom?
For valour fall'n—a broken rose or sword?
       A dirge for king or chief,
       With pomp of stately grief,
Banner, and torch, and waving plume deplor'd?

       Not so, it is not so!
       The warning voice I know,
From other worlds a strange mysterious tone;
       A solemn funeral air   10
       It call'd me to prepare,
And my heart answer'd secretly—my own!

       One more then, one more strain,
       In links of joy and pain
Mighty the troubled spirit to inthral!
       And let me breathe my dower
       Of passion and of power
Full into that deep lay—the last of all!

       The last!—and I must go
       From this bright world below,   20
This realm of sunshine, ringing with sweet sound!
       Must leave its festal skies,
       With all their melodies,
That ever in my breast glad echoes found!

       Yet have I known it long:
       Too restless and too strong
Within this clay hath been th' o'ermastering flame;
       Swift thoughts, that came and went,
       Like torrents o'er me sent,
Have shaken, as a reed, my thrilling frame.   30

Like perfumes on the wind,
Which none may stay or bind,
The beautiful comes floating thro' my soul;
I strive with yearnings vain,
The spirit to detain
Of the deep harmonies that past me roll!

Therefore disturbing dreams
Trouble the secret streams
And founts of music that o'erflow my breast;
Something far more divine   40
Than may on earth be mine,
Haunts my worn heart, and will not let me rest.

Shall I then *fear* the tone
That breathes from worlds unknown?—
Surely these feverish aspirations *there*
Shall grasp their full desire,
And this unsettled fire,
Burn calmly, brightly, in immortal air.

One more then, one more strain,
To earthly joy and pain   50
A rich, and deep, and passionate farewell!
I pour each fervent thought
With fear, hope, trembling, fraught,
Into the notes that o'er my dust shall swell.

THE IMAGE IN LAVA

Thou thing of years departed!
    What ages have gone by,
Since here the mournful seal was set
    By love and agony!

Temple and tower have moulder'd,
   Empires from earth have pass'd,—
And woman's heart hath left a trace
   Those glories to outlast!

And childhood's fragile image
   Thus fearfully enshrin'd,   10
Survives the proud memorials rear'd
   By conquerors of mankind.

Babe! wert thou brightly slumbering
   Upon thy mother's breast,
When suddenly the fiery tomb
   Shut round each gentle guest?

A strange dark fate o'ertook you,
   Fair babe and loving heart!
One moment of a thousand pangs—
   Yet better than to part!   20

Haply of that fond bosom,
   On ashes here impress'd,
Thou wert the only treasure, child!
   Whereon a hope might rest.

Perchance all vainly lavish'd,
   Its other love had been,
And where it trusted, nought remain'd
   But thorns on which to lean.

Far better then to perish,
   Thy form within its clasp,   30
Than live and lose thee, precious one!
   From that impassion'd grasp.

Oh! I could pass all relics
   Left by the pomps of old,
To gaze on this rude monument,
   Cast in affection's mould.

Love, human love! what art thou?
    Thy print upon the dust
Outlives the cities of renown
    Wherein the mighty trust!   40

Immortal, oh! immortal
    Thou art, whose earthly glow
Hath given these ashes holiness—
    It must, it *must* be so!

THE LAST WISH

*"Well may I weep to leave this world—thee—all these beautiful woods,
and plains, and hills."*

                                            Lights and Shadows

        Go to the forest-shade,
        Seek thou the well-known glade,
Where, heavy with sweet dew, the violets lie,
        Gleaming thro' moss-tufts deep,
        Like dark eyes fill'd with sleep,
And bath'd in hues of summer's midnight sky.

        Bring me their buds, to shed
        Around my dying bed,
A breath of May, and of the wood's repose;
        For I in sooth depart,   10
        With a reluctant heart,
That fain would linger where the bright sun glows.

        Fain would I stay with thee—
        Alas! this may not be;
Yet bring me still the gifts of happier hours!
        Go where the fountain's breast
        Catches in glassy rest
The dim green light that pours thro' laurel bowers.

I know how softly bright,
   Steep'd in that tender light,   20
The water-lilies tremble there ev'n now;
   Go to the pure stream's edge,
   And from its whisp'ring sedge,
Bring me those flowers to cool my fever'd brow!

   Then, as in Hope's young days,
   Track thou the antique maze
Of the rich garden to its grassy mound;
   There is a lone white rose,
   Shedding, in sudden snows,
Its faint leaves o'er the emerald turf around.   30

   Well know'st thou that fair tree—
   A murmur of the bee
Dwells ever in the honey'd lime above;
   Bring me one pearly flower
   Of all its clustering shower—
For on that spot we first reveal'd our love.

   Gather one woodbine bough,
   Then, from the lattice low,
Of the bower'd cottage which I bade thee mark,
   When by the hamlet last,   40
   Thro' dim wood-lanes we pass'd,
While dews were glancing to the glow-worm's spark.

   Haste! to my pillow bear
   Those fragrant things and fair;
My hand no more may bind them up at eve,
   Yet shall their odour soft
   One bright dream round me waft
Of life, youth, summer,—all that I must leave!

   And oh! if thou would'st ask
   Wherefore thy steps I task,   50
The grove, the stream, the hamlet-vale to trace;

'Tis that some thought of me,
When I am gone, may be
The spirit bound to each familiar place.

I bid mine image dwell,
(Oh! break not thou the spell!)
In the deep wood, and by the fountain-side;
Thou must not, my belov'd!
Rove where we two have rov'd,
Forgetting her that in her spring-time died!   60

FAIRY FAVOURS

————Give me but
Something whereunto I may bind my heart;
Something to love, to rest upon, to clasp
Affection's tendrils round.

Wouldst thou wear the gift of immortal bloom?
Wouldst thou smile in scorn at the shadowy tomb?
Drink of this cup! it is richly fraught
With balm from the gardens of genii brought;
Drink, and the spoiler shall pass thee by,
When the young all scatter'd like rose-leaves lie.

And would not the youth of my soul be gone,
If the lov'd had left me, one by one?
Take back the cup that may never bless,
The gift that would make me brotherless!   10
How should I live, with no kindred eye
To reflect mine immortality?

Wouldst thou have empire, by sign or spell,
Over the mighty in air that dwell?
Wouldst thou call the spirits of shore and steep
To fetch thee jewels from ocean's deep?

Wave but this rod, and a viewless band
Slaves to thy will, shall around thee stand.

And would not fear, at my coming then,
Hush every voice in the homes of men?   20
Would not bright eyes in my presence quail?
Young cheeks with a nameless thrill turn pale?
No gift be mine that aside would turn
The human love for whose founts I yearn!

Wouldst thou then read thro' the hearts of those
Upon whose faith thou hast sought repose?
Wear this rich gem! it is charm'd to show
When a change comes over affection's glow;
Look on its flushing or fading hue,
And learn if the trusted be false or true!   30

Keep, keep the gem, that I still may trust,
Tho' my heart's wealth be but pour'd on dust!
Let not a doubt in my soul have place,
To dim the light of a lov'd one's face;
Leave to the earth its warm sunny smile—
That glory would pass could I look on guile!

Say then what boon of my power shall be
Favour'd of spirits! pour'd forth on thee?
Thou scornest the treasures of wave and mine,
Thou wilt not drink of the cup divine,   40
Thou art fain with a mortal's lot to rest—
Answer me! how may I grace it best?

Oh! give me no sway o'er the powers unseen,
But a human heart where my own may lean!
A friend, one tender and faithful friend,
Whose thoughts' free current with mine may blend,
And leaving not either on earth alone,
Bid the bright calm close of our lives be one!

A PARTING SONG

"Oh! mes Amis, rappelez–vous quelquefois mes vers; mon âme y est empreinte."

Corinne

When will ye think of me, my friends?
      When will ye think of me?—
When the last red light, the farewell of day,
From the rock and the river is passing away,
When the air with a deep'ning hush is fraught,
And the heart grows burden'd with tender thought—
      Then let it be!

When will ye think of me, kind friends?
      When will ye think of me?—
When the rose of the rich midsummer time   10
Is fill'd with the hues of its glorious prime;
When ye gather its bloom, as in bright hours fled,
From the walks where my footsteps no more may tread;
      Then let it be!

When will ye think of me, sweet friends?
      When will ye think of me?
When the sudden tears o'erflow your eye
At the sound of some olden melody;
When ye hear the voice of a mountain stream,
When ye feel the charm of a poet's dream;   20
      Then let it be!

Thus let my memory be with you, friends!
      Thus ever think of me!
Kindly and gently, but as of one
For whom 'tis well to be fled and gone;
As of a bird from a chain unbound,
As of a wanderer whose home is found;—
      So let it be.

NOTES TO THE POEMS

VOLUME EPIGRAPHS

Wordsworth] William Wordsworth (1770–1850), "Laodamia" (1815), ll. 86–90. In this work, Laodamia convinces Jove to allow her to see her beloved husband, Protesilaus, who had been killed in battle. The phantom of Protesilaus appears but soon speaks of going; she protests that merciful gods might relent and let him stay with her. In support of this hope, she utters this passage about the power and the agony of love. See also Hemans's "To Wordsworth" and the accompanying note.

Schiller] "That is the lot of the beautiful on earth," from Thekla's last monologue in *Wallenstein* (act 4, sc. 12), by Friedrich von Schiller (1759–1805), German poet, philosopher, dramatist, and historian. Thekla has just learned that her lover, Max Piccolomini, has been killed in battle and insists upon going to see his grave. When Lady Neubrunn objects that the mission is too dangerous, Thekla replies with a twenty-six-line speech. Samuel Taylor Coleridge's translation of the play, which Hemans admired, takes some liberties with Thekla's monologue; he concludes it as follows (reference is to act, scene, and lines):

> Life is an empty casket:
> I throw it from me. O! my only hope;—
> To die beneath the hoofs of trampling steeds—
> That is the lot of heroes upon earth!
>   (*The Death of Wallenstein* (1800), 4.6.8–11)

In June 1830 at Rydal Mount, Hemans introduced William Wordsworth to the works of Schiller. She told a friend, "I hope . . . to read with him some of my own *first loves* in Schiller—'The Song of the Bell,' 'Cassandra,' or 'Thekla's Spirit-voice,' with none of which he is acquainted. Indeed, I think he is inclined to undervalue German literature from not knowing its best and purest masterpieces. . . . However, I shall try to bring him into a better way of thinking, if only out of my own deep love for what has been to me a source of intellectual joy so cheering and elevating" (Henry Fothergill Chorley, *Memorials of Mrs. Hemans, with Illustrations of Her Literary Character from Her Private Correspondence,* 2 vols. [London: Saunders and Otley, 1836], 2:145–46).

DEDICATION PAGE

Joanna Baillie] leading British playwright (1762–1851). Her *Ethwald* (1802) and *The Family Legend* (1810) were early favorites of Hemans, who said of Baillie's heroines, "Nothing in all her writings delights me so much as her general idea of what is beautiful in the female character. There is so much gentle fortitude, and deep self-devoting affection in the women whom she portrays, and they are so perfectly different from the pretty *'un-idea'd girls,'* who seem to form the *beau ideal* of our whole sex in the works of some modern poets" (Chorley, *Memorials* 1:96; Harriet Hughes, "Memoir of The Life and Writings of Mrs Hemans," in *The Works of Mrs Hemans; with a Memoir of Her Life, by Her Sister,* 7 vols. [Edinburgh: William Blackwood & Sons, 1839], 1:69). Baillie asked Hemans to contribute to her edited anthology, *A Collection of Poems, Chiefly Manuscript and from Living Authors* (1823), for the benefit of a financially troubled friend. Hemans sent "Belshazzar's Feast," and the two poets then began an active correspondence. When Hemans's five-act tragedy, *The Vespers of Palermo,* closed after only one night in London in December 1823, Baillie enlisted Walter Scott to persuade Sarah Siddons to stage the play in Edinburgh the following April, where it enjoyed a successful run. On 31 May 1827, Hemans wrote to Baillie, "I have another favour to request; it is the permission to dedicate to you, of whose name my whole sex may be proud, a work which I shall probably publish in the course of this present year, and which is to be called 'Records of Woman.' If you do not object to this, I will promise that the inscription shall be as simple as you could desire. . . . I hope you will allow me to offer you, whether in your own country [Scotland] or mine [Wales], this little token of unfeigned respect" (Chorley, *Memorials* 1:146). For more on the Hemans-Baillie friendship, see Hughes, "Memoir," 74.

ARABELLA STUART

Arabella Stuart] Shortly before she died, Queen Elizabeth I subjected Arbella (or Arabella) Stuart (1575–1615), niece of Mary, Queen of Scots, to house arrest because of her liaison with Edward Seymour; but Stuart was released upon the ascension of James I to the throne. On 22 June 1610, against the king's wishes, Arbella Stuart secretly married William Seymour, Edward Seymour's younger brother. A little more than two weeks later, on 8 and 9 July, both were interrogated and arrested. Seymour was imprisoned in the Tower of London and Stuart was placed in private custody. On 3 June 1611, disguised as a man, Stuart walked away from her captors. Seymour escaped the same day and landed safely at Ostend on 7 June, while Stuart was recaptured and then imprisoned in the Tower of London. Sympathy for Stuart was widespread, and various literary works, including John Webster's *Duchess of Malfi* (1623) and William Shakespeare's *Cymbeline* (1623), drew on the public's interest in the case. Although in Hemans's time it was accepted that Stuart went mad in prison, recent evidence suggests that she kept her sanity and that she participated in several plots to escape. Stuart spent the last year of her life bedridden, probably from the effects of porphyria, and died in the Tower of London on 25 September 1615. See Sara Jayne Steen, ed., *The Letters of Lady Arbella Stuart* (New York: Oxford University Press, 1994), 81–97.

D'Israeli's *Curiosities of Literature*] Isaac D'Israeli, *Curiosities of Literature*, 2d ser. (London, 1823), from the literary anecdote entitled "The Loves of 'The Lady Arabella.'" D'Israeli (1766–1848) was the father of Benjamin Disraeli (1804–81), novelist and prime minister of England (1868, 1874–80).

epigraphs]

Byron] George Gordon, Lord Byron (1788–1824), "The Prophecy of Dante" (1821), canto 3, ll. 147–48. The full passage reads, "Perhaps he'll *love,*—and is not love in vain / Torture enough without a living tomb?" (See also Hemans's "Mozart's Requiem" and "The Dying Improvisatore" for other epigraphs taken from "The Prophecy of Dante.") One of Hemans's favorite accessories at this time was a brooch containing a small lock of Byron's hair. She quotes liberally from Byron's works in *Records of Woman* as she had earlier in her career, but two years later she was dismayed to learn of the contents of Thomas Moore's *Life* of Byron (1830). She told a friend, "Some *Quarterly Reviews* have lately been sent to me, one of which contains an article on Byron, by which I have been deeply and sorrowfully impressed. His character, as there portrayed, reminded me of some of those old Eastern cities, where travellers constantly find a squalid mud hovel built against the ruins of a gorgeous temple; for alas! the best part of that fearfully mingled character is but ruin—the wreck of what might have been" (Hughes, "Memoir," 227). "From this time forth," according to Chorley, "she never wore the relic" (*Memorials* 2:22–23). The Countess of Blessington reported that Byron admired Hemans's poetry and paid "homage . . . to the genius of Mrs. Hemans" (*Conversations of Lord Byron*, [1834]).

Pindemonte] from "Clizia" (l. 55), by Ippolito Pindemonte (1753–1828), an Italian poet best known for his translation of the *Odyssey*. He was also the author of *Field Prose* (1784) and *Field Poems* (1788). Hemans translated and published one of his sonnets in *Translations from Camoëns, and Other Poets* (1818). This passage, which Hemans had earlier used as an epigraph for canto 3 of "The Abencerrage" in *Tales, and Historic Scenes* (1819), may be translated, "The heart that beat so strongly stopped at last" and occurs when Clizia, a nymph suffering from unrequited love, is transformed into a heliotrope. Anne Louise Germaine (Necker) de Staël (1766–1817) also quotes this passage in *Corinne ou L'Italie* (1807) at the end of chapter 5.

l. 12 plumes] feathers (in their hats).

l. 52 beautiful!] "Wheresoever you are, or in what state soever you be, it sufficeth me you are mine. *Rachel wept, and would not be comforted, because her children were no more.* And that, indeed, is the remediless sorrow, and none else!"—From a letter of Arabella Stuart's to her husband.—See *Curiosities of Literature.* (*Hemans's note.*) As Isaac D'Israeli gives it in *Curiosities of Literature* (2d ser.), from "The Loves of 'The Lady Arabella'" section, the letter continues, "And therefore God bless us from that, and I will hope well of the rest, though I see no apparent hope. But I am sure God's book mentioneth many of his children in as great distress, that have done well after, even in this world!" The full document, circa 1610, is printed in Steen, *Letters of Lady Arbella Stuart,* 241–42.

l. 85 lattice] window.

l. 113 What boots it] what good is it.

1.138 stricken deer] Compare this image to that of line 1, in which "the stag leap[s] free." See also Percy Bysshe Shelley's *Adonais*, l. 297.

l. 145 Heaven's eye] the sky.

l. 160 car] chariot.

l. 163 prov'd] tested.

l. 182 bark] small ship.

l. 204 swords of fire] "And if you remember of old, *I dare die.*—Consider what the world would conceive, if I should be violently enforced to do it."—*Fragments of Her Letters.* (*Hemans's note.*) The first of these two sentences comes from a letter c. March 1611 to Thomas Erskine. The latter sentence comes from a letter to the Privy Council c. March 1611. For the full texts, see Steen, *Letters of Lady Arbella Stuart,* 257–59.

The Bride of the Greek Isle

Founded on a circumstance related in the Second Series of the *Curiosities of Literature*, and forming part of a picture in the "Painted Biography" there described. Originally published, as well as several other of these Records, in the *New Monthly Magazine.* (*Hemans's note.*) When "The Bride of the Greek Isle" was first printed in the *New Monthly Magazine* [NMM], 14 (October 1825): 370–74, the epigraph was absent, and the footnote included an additional sentence: "The scene of the catastrophe is, however, transferred from Cyprus to the Greek Isles." "Of a Biography Painted" in Isaac D'Israeli's *Curiosities of Literature* describes the eighteen-page account of the sixteenth-century adventures and travels of Charles Magius, a noble Venetian, painted in a series of unique miniatures on vellum. According to D'Israeli, "The Turks are seen landing with their pillage and their slaves.—In one of the pictures are seen two ships on fire; a young lady of Cyprus preferring death to the loss of her honour and the miseries of slavery, determined to set fire to the vessel in which she was carried; she succeeded, and the flames communicated to another." epigraph]

Sardanapalus] George Gordon, Lord Byron, *Sardanapalus* (1821), act 1, sc. 2, ll. 527–28, 676. Myrrha, Sardanapalus's Greek slave and lover, speaks the first two lines, vowing to die with the Assyrian King if his enemies defeat him. The last line belongs to Sardanapalus, who chooses suicide over living in captivity or exile. His full statement reads: "Fate made me what I am—may make me nothing—/ But either that or nothing must I be; / I will not live degraded." Myrrha and Sardanapalus die together in a fire.

l. 3 Scio] Greek island, now called Chios, in the Aegean Sea near the western shore of Turkey. Homer was said to have been born there. The island was subject to severe earthquakes and over the centuries had been a much-fought-over commercial center. In 1822, during the Greek war for independence, the Turks attacked Chios, making slaves of forty-five thousand inhabitants and massacring twenty thousand more, an event which aroused great indignation in England and which Eugene Delacroix (1798–1863) depicted in an 1824 painting titled "Scenes from the Chios Massacres." See Hemans's poems "The Voice of Scio," which speaks of "ruin'd hearths, . . . burning fanes, / . . . kindred blood on yon red plains, / From desolated homes!" (30–32) and "The Sisters of Scio," about which John Wilson commented in an 1829 review, "But who are they that sit, mourning in their loveliness, beneath the shadow of a rock on the surf-beaten shore? The Sisters of Scio. . . . Die—rather let them die in famine amongst sea-sand shells, than ere their virgin charms be polluted in the harem of the barbarian who has desolated their native isle! Bowed down and half dead, beneath what a load of anguish hangs the orphan's dishevelled head on the knee of a sister, in pensive resignation, and holy faith triumphant over despair, as Felicia [Hemans] happily singeth." (*Blackwood's Edinburgh Magazine* 26 [December 1829]:956). Hemans also published "Greek Song: the Voice of Scio" in the *New Monthly Magazine* 7 (April 1823): 352.

l. 31 song] lyre [NMM]

l. 42 plaintive lay.] A Greek Bride, on leaving her father's house, takes leave of her friends and relatives frequently in extemporaneous verse.— See *Fauriel's Chants populaires de la Grèce moderne.* (*Hemans's note.*) Claude Charles Fauriel (1772–1844) published *Chants populaires de la*

Grèce moderne recueillis et publiés, avec une traduction française, des éclaircissements et des notes (Popular songs of modern Greece) in two volumes (Paris, 1824). When "The Bride of the Greek Isle" was first published (*New Monthly Magazine*, [October 1825]: 370–74), rather than paraphrasing Fauriel, Hemans notes that "a Greek bride, before she quits her father's house, 'fait de tendres adieux à son père, à sa mère, à ses proches, à ses amies, à tout son voisinage, et aux lieux où se sont passés les jours de son enfance.—En certains endroits, la douleur de la fiancée s'exprime par une formule d'usage.'" Hemans also cites Fauriel's *Chants populaires* as a source for her "Greek Parting Song" and "Greek Funeral Chant."

l. 92 gliding tread] floating tread [NMM].

l. 99 glow] rays [NMM].

l. 105 rays] sheen [NMM].

l. 111 fane] temple.

l. 119 chaplet] wreath; coronal.

l. 124 wavy] whispery [NMM].

l. 144 a gathering film in] the gathering film o'er [NMM].

l. 158 Sciote hill] hill of Scio.

l. 176 pennon] long, pointed streamer of a ship.

l. 193 brake] thicket.

l. 204 brand] torch.

l. 217 On the pyre] The ritual of suttee in India required a new widow to perform self-immolation on her husband's funeral pyre in what was regarded as a second marriage.

THE SWITZER'S WIFE

The legendary tale of Werner Stauffacher and his unnamed wife appears in the early "White Book of Sarnen." According to this account, "There was a man in Swiz called Stoupacher [Stauffacher] who lived at Steinen . . . [in] a pretty stone house. Now at that time a Gesler was bailiff there, in the name of the empire; he came one day, and rode by there, and called to Stoupacher, and asked him, whose the pretty dwelling was. Stoupacher answered him and spake sadly: 'Gracious lord, it is yours and mine in fief,' and dared not say it was his, so greatly did he fear the lord. The lord rode away. Now Stoupacher was a wise man and well to do. He had also a wise wife, and thought over the matter, and had great grief, and was full of fear before the lord, lest he should take his life and his goods from him. His wife, she noticed it and did as women do, and would like to have known what was the matter with him, or why he was sad; but he denied her that. At last she overwhelmed him with great entreaty, that he might let her know his matter, and spake: 'Be so good and tell me thy need; although it is said, women give cold counsels, who knows what God will do?' She begged him so often in her trusting way, that he told her

what his grief was. She went and strengthened him with words and spake: 'There'll be some good plan,' and asked him if he knew any one in Ure [Uri] who was so trusted by him that he might confide his need to him, and told him of the family of Furst and of zer Fraowen [zur Frauen]. He answered her and spake: 'Yea, he knew them well, and thought about the counsel of his wife, and went to Ure, and stayed there, until he found one who had also a like grief. She had also bid him ask in Unterwalden; for she thought, there were people there also, who did not like such tyranny. . . . So there came three of them together, Stoupacher of Schwitz, and one of the Fursts of Ure, and he from Melche in Unterwalden, and each confided his need and grief to the other, and took counsel, and they took an oath together" (quoted in W. D. McCrackan, *The Rise of the Swiss Republic: A History*, 2d ed. [Geneva: Libraries-Editeurs, 1901], 106–7). "The Switzer's Wife" first appeared in the *New Monthly Magazine* 16 (January 1826): 23–25, in which Hemans appended the following note to line 35: "See the beautiful scene between Stauffacher and his wife in Schiller's *Wilhelm Tell*—'So ernst, mein Freund? Ich kenne dich nicht mehr,' &c." Hemans's poems "On a Flower from the Field of Grutli" and "The League of the Alps; or, the Meeting on the Field of Grutli" in *Tales, and Historic Scenes* (1819) and "The Cavern of the Three Tells" from *Lays of Many Lands* (1825) also take as their subject this fourteenth-century uprising by the Swiss against Albert I (1250?–1308) of Austria. Werner Stauffacher figures prominently in the latter poem. Hemans treats other dimensions of this historical event in "Gertrude, or Fidelity Till Death" and "A Monarch's Death Bed," both in *Records of Woman*.
title]
     Switzer] Swiss.
epigraph]
     M. J. J.] Maria Jane Jewsbury, "Arria," in *Phantasmagoria* (London, 1825), 1:122, ll. 5–8. Jewsbury (1800–1833) was a fiction writer, poet, essayist, and close friend of Hemans. William Wordsworth said of her, "In one quality, viz., quickness in the motions of the mind, she had, within the range of his acquaintance, no equal" (quoted in Hughes, "Memoir," 142 from Wordsworth's annotation to his poem "Liberty"). Jewsbury admired Hemans's poetry and initiated a correspondence sometime before 1827. She and her family spent the summer and fall of 1828 at St. Asaph, near where Hemans lived. Her *Lays of Leisure Hours* (1829) is dedicated to Hemans, and several poems, including "To an Absent One," are addressed to her. She also depicted Hemans as Egeria in *The Three Histories* (1830): "Egeria was totally different from any other woman I had ever seen, either in Italy or England. She did not dazzle—she subdued me. Other women might be more commanding, more versatile, more acute; but I never saw one so exquisitely feminine. She was lovely without being beautiful; her movements were features; and if a blind man had been privi-

leged to pass his hand over the silken length of hair, that when unbraided flowed round her like a veil, he would have been justified in expecting softness and a love of softness, beauty and a perception of beauty, to be distinctive traits of her mind. Nor would he have been deceived. Her birth, her education, but, above all, the genius with which she was gifted, combined to inspire a passion for the ethereal, the tender, the imaginative, the heroic,—in one word, the beautiful. It was in her a faculty divine, and yet of daily life;—it touched all things, but, like a sunbeam, touched them with 'a golden finger.' Any thing abstract or scientific was unintelligible and distasteful to her; her knowledge was extensive and various, but, true to the first principle of her nature, it was poetry that she sought in history, scenery, character, and religious belief,—poetry that guided all her studies, governed all her thoughts, colored all her conversation.—Her nature was at once simple and profound; there was no room in her mind for philosophy, or in her heart for ambition,—one was filled by imagination, the other engrossed by tenderness. Her strength and her weakness alike lay in her affections: these would sometimes make her weep at a word,— at others imbue her with courage;—so that she was alternately a 'falcon-hearted dove,' and 'a reed shaken with the wind.' Her voice was a sad, sweet melody, her spirits reminded me of an old poet's description of the orange-tree, with its 'Golden lamps hid in a night of green,' or of those Spanish gardens where the pomegranate grows beside the cypress. Her gladness was like a burst of sunlight; and if in her depression she resembled night, it was night wearing her stars. I might describe, and describe for ever, but I should never succeed in portraying Egeria; she was a muse, a grace, a variable child, a dependent woman—the Italy of human beings" (quoted in Chorley, *Memorials* 1:187–89). Jewsbury encouraged Hemans to read the poetry of her friend, William Wordsworth. For a discussion of Hemans's friendship with Jewsbury, see Hughes, "Memoir," 141–47.

Wilhelm Tell] Friedrich von Schiller, *Wilhelm Tell* (William Tell) (1804), 1.3.330–31. The passage may be translated "He who presses such a heart to his breast / Can fight for hearth and home with joy." This second epigraph was not present in the poem's first periodical printing. In the 1828 first edition, "Wilhelm" appeared as "Willholm," but this misspelling, along with several errors in capitalization, was corrected in later editions. These corrections have been adopted here.

l. 51 couch'd] concealed.

rill] small stream or brook.

l. 56 heritage] inheritance.

l. 64 frail] wild [NMM].

l. 92 chamois-paths] path used by a type of antelope inhabiting the Alps and other mountain ranges in Europe and Asia.

l. 98 clarion] trumpet.

l. 111 free] deep [NMM].

PROPERZIA ROSSI

title]
Properzia Rossi] Properzia de' Rossi (c. 1490–1530) of Bologna, Italy, was a highly accomplished musician and became a professional sculptor of some note, specializing in bas-relief in stone or wood. In 1524 she was invited to decorate the canopy of the high altar of Santa Maria del Baraccano and later created sculpture for part of the great west front of San Petronio. She was said to harbor an unrequited love for Anton Galeazzo di Napoleone Malvasia, who, in response to a lawsuit, publicly declared that she was not his mistress. Rossi was persecuted by the painter Amico Aspertini, who maligned her to the administrators of San Petronio. As a result, the price she could demand for her work fell, and she was forced to give up sculpture for engraving on copper. She died in poverty on 24 February 1530 at the Spedale della Morte on the same day and near the site of Charles V's coronation by Clement VII. It is said that after the coronation, Clement VII asked to have her presented to him but was told he was too late. See Giorgio Vasari, *Le vite de' più eccellenti pittori, scultori e architettori* (1568), translated as *Lives of the Most Eminent Painters, Sculptors, and Architects* (1878; reprint, London: Macmillan, 1912) and Laura Marie Roberts Ragg, *The Women Artists of Bologna* (London: Methuen, 1907), 167–87.
headnote]
Ducis] French painter Louis Ducis (1775–1847), who created a series entitled "Arts Under the Empire of Love," which allegorically represented poetry, sculpture, painting, and music. Hemans would have been especially interested in his compositions symbolizing poetry, "Tasso Reading His Verses to Eleonora d'Este," exhibited in the salon of 1814, and "Tasso in the House of his Sister Cornelia in Sorrento," exhibited in the salon of 1812. Ducis's "Properzia de' Rossi and Her Last Bas-relief" represented sculpture in the series.
Ariadne] In classical mythology, Ariadne, daughter of King Minos of Crete, loved the Greek prince Theseus and helped him to escape from the minotaur's labyrinth. She had his child, but Theseus abandoned her, eventually marrying her sister Phaedra; later Ariadne wed Dionysius, god of wine, who took the wreath from her head and placed it in the sky as a constellation (Corona Borealis) to make her famous.
l. 27 dower] dowry; the money or property a bride brings into a marriage.
l. 40 lineaments] distinctive features.
l. 50 lorn] forlorn.
l. 84 meed] reward; recompense.
l. 96 instinct] inspired.
l. 116 wert nigh] were near.

GERTRUDE, OR FIDELITY TILL DEATH

First published under the simpler title "Gertrude" in the *New Monthly Magazine,* 16 (May 1826): 469–70. Hemans included in this first printing a footnote that does not appear in subsequent printings: "The author was not aware, at the time this little poem was written, that the courage and affection of Gertrude Von der Wart had previously been celebrated by another writer in a yet unpublished poem."
headnote]

Baron Von Der Wart] Rudolph von Wart, one of four conspirators who assassinated the emperor Albert I (1250?–1308), king of Germany and ruler of the Holy Roman Empire, along the Reuss River near Brugg, Switzerland, on 1 May 1308. According to W. D. McCrackan, Rudolph von Wart was the only one of the four captured and was probably the least culpable. Still, he "was put to death amid frightful tortures upon the scene of the murder" (*Rise of the Swiss Republic,* 120). The book Hemans recalls is Johann Conrad Appenzeller's *Gertrud von Wart; oder Treue bis in den Tod* (Gertrude von Wart; or Fidelity unto Death) (Zurich, 1813). See "A Monarch's Death-Bed" for Hemans's portrayal of Albert I's death.

the wheel] an instrument of torture.
epigraph]

Joanna Baillie] *De Monfort, A Tragedy* (1798), 5.4.65–72. This speech, by the courageous Jane de Monfort, spoken to her brother shortly after he murders her lover, Rezenvelt, does not appear in the earliest editions of the play, but Baillie added it later. Hemans appended this epigraph after the first periodical printing of her poem.

l. 29 glazing] freezing [NMM].

l. 45 mantle] cloak.

l. 51 meed] reward.

IMELDA

The tale of Imelda is related in Sismondi's *Histoire des républiques italiennes.* Vol. iii, p. 443. (*Hemans's note.*) Jean-Charles-Léonard Simonde de Sismondi (1773–1842), Swiss economist and historian, produced *Histoire des républiques italiennes du moyen âge* (History of the Italian republics of the middle ages) (1809–18) in sixteen volumes. The tragedy of Imelda, which bears a strong resemblance to the story of Romeo and Juliet, took place, according to Sismondi, in Bologna, Italy, sometime around 1273, when the conflict between the Guelph and Ghibelline factions was at its height. The Gieremei family (who headed the Guelphs) and the Lambertazzi family (who headed the Ghibellines) harbored a violent hatred for one another. But Boniface Gieremei and Imelda Lambertazzi ignored their families' animosities and fell in love. One day Imelda re-

ceived a visit from Boniface in her home. A spy told her brothers, who burst into her apartment. Imelda escaped, but one of her brothers stabbed Boniface in the heart with a poison dagger. His body was hidden in a deserted courtyard but Imelda followed a trail of blood and found him. In hopes of reviving him, she sucked the poison from the wound. Her servants found her, Sismondi recounts, "à côté du cadavre de celui qu'elle avoit trop aimé" (beside the body of he whom she had loved too well). Hemans's "Night-Scene in Genoa," "The Death of Conradin," and "The Widow of Crescentius" in *Tales and Historic Scenes* (1819) also draw on Sismondi's *Histoire des républiques italiennes,* and "The Burial of William the Conqueror" draws on his *Histoire des Français.* In a letter to Maria Jane Jewsbury, Hemans writes, "I cannot help . . . mentioning, as works from which I have derived much clear and general information, those of Sismondi; in particular his 'Littérature du Midi,' and 'Républiques Italiennes'" (Chorley, *Memorials* 1:177). "Imelda" was first published in the *New Monthly Magazine* 13 (May 1825): 467–69.
epigraphs]

    Italy, a Poem] 1822–28, by Samuel Rogers (1763–1855). These lines come from the section entitled "The Campagna of Florence," ll. 234–36. Rogers says that his account, which calls Imelda's lover Paolo, relies upon Cherubino Ghiradacci's history of Bologna, from which Sismondi also drew. When *Italy* was reprinted in an edition illustrated by steel-plate engravings after paintings by J. M. W. Turner, Hemans wrote, "Have you seen Rogers's *Italy,* with its exquisite embellishments? The whole book seems to me quite a triumph of art and taste. Some of Turner's Italian scenes, with their moon-lit vestibules and pillared arcades, the shadows of which seem almost trembling on the ground as you look at them, really might be fit representations of Armida's enchanted gardens" (Hughes, "Memoir," 223).

    Tasso] Torquato Tasso (1544–95), Italian poet, best known for his epic written in ottava rima, *La Gerusalemme Liberata* (Jerusalem delivered) (1575), from which this passage is taken (canto 12, st. 69, l. 5). It may be translated "The beautiful lady dies and seems to sleep" and comes from the subplot in which Tancred, in combat, unwittingly slays his beloved Clorinda. In Ralph Nash's translation (*Jerusalem Delivered* [Detroit: Wayne State University Press, 1987]) the preceding lines read, "Repressing his grief he bent his efforts to giving her life with water whom with the sword he killed. While he released the sound of the holy words, she was with joy transfigured, and smiled: and through the act of her joyful and living death, she seemed to say: 'Heaven is opening; I depart in peace.' Her fair face is overspread with a lovely pallor, as would be violets intermixed with lilies, and she fixes her eyes on the heavens; and it seems that the sun and the heavens are bent toward her for pity. And lifting to the knight, in place of speech, her hand ungloved and cold, she gives him her pledge of peace" (269). It was only after the first periodical publication of "Imelda" that Hemans added this epigraph from Tasso. Hemans includes a translation of one of Tasso's sonnets in her *Translations from Camoëns, and Other Poets* (1818) and pays tribute to him in "Tasso's Coronation," "The Release of Tasso," and "Tasso and his Sister." One of the few prose pieces Hemans ever published was entitled "Scenes and Passages from the 'Tasso' of Goethe" with her translations and commentary on the poet (*New Monthly Magazine* 40 (January 1834): 1–8. Hemans told a friend on 10 April 1831, "I was compelled to choose between Tasso and Ariosto, and fear you will hardly approve my preference of the former, but there is much in the story of his sufferings which intensely interests me, and, perhaps, deepens my reverence for his poetry" (Chorley, *Memorials* 2:198).

l. 3 Naiad] in Roman mythology, a water nymph.
l. 19 dying] fainting [NMM].
l. 21 reck'd] thought.
l. 23 vernal] springlike.
l. 49 there were] there were those.
l. 55 mazy] wild.
l. 92 shiver'd] splintered.
l. 105 Appenines] mountain range extending the full length of Italy and continuing into Sicily.

EDITH, A TALE OF THE WOODS

Founded on incidents related in an American work, "Sketches of Connecticut." (*Hemans's note.*) Hemans draws her story from the last three chapters of Lydia Sigourney's *Sketch of Connecticut, Forty Years Since* (Hartford, 1824). There the Englishwoman Oriana Selden is adopted by Zachary and Martha, a kindly Mohegan Indian couple, after she witnesses the death of her husband, Edward, by an advance guard at Yorktown (1781). Sigourney's account includes a graphic description of the battle, an episode in which Oriana cross-dresses as a soldier to accompany her husband, and several emotional deathbed scenes. Sigourney would later become better known as a poet and was often referred to as the "American Hemans." "Edith, A Tale of the Woods" was first published, without the epigraph, under the title "Edith" in the *New Monthly Magazine* 20 (July 1827): 33–37.
epigraph]
Wallenstein] Friedrich von Schiller, *Die Piccolomini*, ll. 1764–66. This play is the second part of *Wallenstein* (1799). In his fairly literal translation (New York: H. Holt, 1901), W. H. Carruth gives this passage as "You Holy! Call your child back! / I have enjoyed earthly happiness, / I have lived and loved." But Samuel Taylor Coleridge translates

the passage "Thou Holy One, call thy child away! / I've lived and loved, and that was to-day—" (2.6.31–32). Hemans read *Wallenstein* in the original German as well as in Coleridge's translation. Her sister, Harriet Hughes, recalled Hemans's "almost actual, relation-like love for the characters of Max and Thekla, whom, like many other 'beings of the mind,' she had learned to consider as friends; and her constant quotations of certain passages from this noble tragedy, which peculiarly accorded with her own views and feelings" (Hughes, "Memoir," 54). Her poems "Thekla's Song; or, The Voice of a Spirit," "Thekla at her Lover's Grave," "Nature's Farewell," "The Streams," "The King of Arragon's Lament for his Brother," and "The Peasant Girl of the Rhone" all use passages from Coleridge's translation of *Wallenstein* for their epigraphs.

l. 1 boundless] mighty [NMM].

l. 8 might] gloom [NMM].

l. 14 bloody] dewy [NMM].

l. 20 of other days] of days [NMM].

l. 47 heard,—and] heard—there [NMM].

l. 60 Æolian lyre] a rectangular, stringed instrument popular in the nineteenth century; when placed in a casement window, the breeze vibrates the strings to make "music" without human intervention. Wind chimes are a modern-day equivalent. Hemans alludes here to S. T. Coleridge's poem "The Æolian Harp" and his question, "And what if all of animated nature / Be but organic harps diversely framed. . . ?" (ll. 44–45).

l. 69 'twere for something] missing somewhat [NMM].

l. 168 Then with a look where all her hope awoke,] Calmly she smiled, and, raising her faint head, [NMM].

l. 169 spoke—] said, [NMM].

l. 174 murmur'd in low tones;] murmur'd, but with pain; [NMM].

l. 196 time] days [NMM].

l. 203 whispering] lonely [NMM].

l. 219 strain] song.

THE INDIAN CITY

From a tale in Forbes's *Oriental Memoirs*. (*Hemans's note.*) James Forbes (1749–1819), *Oriental Memoirs. Selected and Abridged from a Series of Familiar Letters Written during Seventeen Years Residence in India including Observations on Parts of Africa and South America, and a Narrative of Occurrences in Four India Voyages*, 4 vols. (London, 1813), 2:337–38. As Forbes describes it, Sciad Ballah and his mother Mamah-Doocre, Muslims on a pilgrimage to Mecca, pass by the gates of Dhuboy, a Hindu city in Guzerat, in western India, which does not allow Muslims

within its gates. Sciad Ballah wanders in and bathes in Dhuboy's sacred lake, thereby "polluting" it. As punishment, his hands are cut off, and he dies just after reaching his mother. Mamah-Doocre returns home and appeals to her sovereign for revenge against Dhuboy. A seige lasting several years ensues, during which Mamah-Doocre dies, but at last the Hindus are driven out and the Muslims burn down most of Dhuboy's fortress and city. According to Forbes, Mamah-Doocre "was revered as a saint, and buried in a grove near the gate of diamonds, where her tomb still remains." "The Indian City" was first published in the *New Monthly Magazine* 14 (December 1825): 574–78.
epigraph]

Childe Harold] George Gordon, Lord Byron, *Childe Harold's Pilgrimage,* canto 3 (first published 1816), st. 84, ll. 1–3. This epigraph did not appear in the first periodical printing of "The Indian City."

l. 7 Banian] the banyan tree (*Ficus benghalensis*). Its branches drop shoots to the ground which root and support the parent branch and have the appearance of pillars. The tree produces figs and is sometimes an object of worship.

l. 9 plantain] plant of the genus *Plantago* with coarse, ribbed leaves and fruit resembling the banana.

l. 10 genii] in Arabian demonology, a goblin or sprite.

l. 11 lifted] pointed [NMM].

l. 21 roe] a type of small deer (*Capreolus capreolus*) indigenous to parts of Europe and Asia.

l. 23 plashing] splashing.

l. 26 Bramin] Brahmin; a member of the Hindu priestly caste.

l. 34 brake] thicket.

l. 57 Mecca's fane] This pilgrimage was undertaken from the interior parts of Hindostan. (*Hemans's note* in the *New Monthly Magazine* text; not present in the 1828 text.)

l. 66 in his lonely] on his lonely [NMM].

l. 79 wrongs] wrong [NMM].

l. 80 born] borne [NMM].

l. 107 we love so well] such woe can dwell [NMM].

l. 108 anguish like this can dwell!] we fear not to love so well! [NMM].

l. 129 midnight sky] morn's clear sky, [NMM].

l. 141 in the starlight] to the Orient [NMM].

l. 145 tambour] drum.

l. 147 leaguer'd] beleaguered.

l. 159 hot wind's blight] disease was thought to be spread by wind.

l. 167 begirt] surrounded.

l. 178 Sybil] woman prophet.

l. 210 When] Where [NMM].

l. 215 vanquish'd] conquer'd [NMM].

l. 218 glow'd] flow'd [NMM].

l. 221 begirt] spread round [NMM].

l. 222 Where the boy and his mother at rest were laid.] In the *New Monthly Magazine* text, Hemans included the following footnote here: "Their tombs are still remaining, according to Forbes, in a grove near the city."

THE PEASANT GIRL OF THE RHONE

First published in the *Literary Souvenir* for 1826 [81–84] without the epigraphs and under the title "Aymer's Tomb."
epigraphs]

Coleridge's *Wallenstein*] *The Death of Wallenstein* translated from the German of Friedrich von Schiller by Samuel Taylor Coleridge (4.5.5–6, 9–10). Thekla speaks these lines to Lady Neubrunn just after she learns of the death of her lover, Max Piccolomini, and the place he has been buried. See Hemans's poem "Thekla at Her Lover's Grave."

Childe Harold] George Gordon, Lord Byron, *Childe Harold's Pilgrimage, canto* 4 (first published 1818), st. 120, ll. 1–2. Hemans used *Childe Harold* for epigraphs in several other poems, including "The Spirit's Mysteries," "The Beings of the Mind," and the first periodical printing of "Mozart's Requiem."

l. 7 greensward] grassy turf.

l. 19 Stretch'd by its] Stretched by a [LS]

l. 26 De Couci's] The family of de Coucy was famed in feudal times and gave its name to the castle of Coucy in northern France. One of the early lords, Enguerrand VI, had his lands ravaged by the English in 1339. Enguerrand VII married Isabel, eldest daughter of British King Edward III, and fought in the crusades. Guy de Couci, castellan (governor or keeper) of the castle from 1186 to 1203, was a minstrel, with more than two dozen songs attributed to him, but was not related to the lords of de Couci.

l. 27 Aymer] possibly Aymer de Valence (d. 1324), earl of Pembroke, although he survived his father, William of Valence (d. 1296), who fought in Palestine. Aymer fought at Flanders and at Bannockburn. In 1317, on a journey from Rome to England, he was kidnapped in Germany and held prisoner until a ransom was paid. He died suddenly near Paris in 1324, and his body was brought back to London and buried near the high altar in Westminster Abbey, where his tomb is considered one of the finest. In his honor, his wife, Mary de Chatillon, founded Pembroke College, Cambridge, built a chantry, now part of the chapel of St. John, founded Denny Abbey in Cambridgeshire, and installed a memorial window in the church of the Grey Friars in London (J. R. S. Phillips, *Aymer de Valence, Earl of Pembroke, 1307–1324: Baronial Politics in the Reign of Edward II* [Oxford: Clarendon Press, 1972], 7, 233). These historical facts differ somewhat from Hemans's account. This is equally true of her play, *De Chatillon; or, the Crusaders* (1839), not published until after her death, which is set in Palestine and features a French baron, Rainier de Chatillon, and his brother Aymer.

l. 53 waving] wavings [LS].

l. 67 Thro' storied windows] From pictured windows [LS].

l. 77 coronals] circlets of gems for the head; coronets.

l. 80 summer's realm] sunshine's realm [LS].

l. 83 In lone devotedness!] With a sad constancy! [LS].

l. 93 For death] For night [LS].

INDIAN WOMAN'S DEATH SONG

epigraphs]

Long's *Expedition to the Source of St Peter's River*] William Hypolitus Keating (1799–1840) based a play entitled *Narrative of an Expedition to the Source of St. Peter's River* on the notes of Stephen H. Long (1784–1864), commander of the expedition (1819–20). By order of John C. Calhoun, then U.S. secretary of war, the play was first performed in 1823. It was published in two volumes the following year in Philadelphia and in London in 1825.

Bride of Messina] "No, I cannot live with a broken heart. I must find joy again and reunite myself with the free spirits of the air" (Friedrich von Schiller, *Die Braut von Messina* [1803]). Anne Louise Germaine (Necker) de Staël (1766–1817) summarizes the play in French in chapter 19 of *De l'Allemagne* (Germany) (Paris, 1810), 242. This same work includes her argument in favor of the translation of great writings and helped to encourage the translation of Schiller's work in 1821. See Gretchen Rous Besser, *Germaine de Staël, Revisited* (New York: Twayne, 1994), 107.

The Prairie] from chapter 26 of *The Prairie* (1827), one of James Fenimore Cooper's (1789–1851) Leatherstocking novels, featuring protagonist Natty Bumppo's final days as a trapper on the Great Plains. These lines are uttered by a Sioux chief's third wife who feels betrayed on learning that her husband plans to take a captured Mexican woman as his fourth wife. Hemans has altered the original passage, which reads, "Let him not be a girl, for very sad is the life of a woman."

l. 17 Father of ancient waters] "Father of waters," the Indian name for the Mississippi. (*Hemans's note.*)

l. 33 lave] wash.

Joan of Arc, in Rheims

Joan of Arc (ca. 1412–31) became a popular heroine and symbol of French national unity in 1429 after successfully leading troops against the English at the siege of Orléans during the Hundred Years' War and escorting the dauphin to Rheims Cathedral, where he was crowned King of France. She continued leading the war against the English but was taken prisoner in 1430. She was tried by the Inquisition in 1431 and condemned for resisting the authority of the church and for dressing in men's clothes. Before a large crowd in Rouen's Old Market, the English burned her at the stake.

Frances Jeffrey said that "'Joan of Arc in Rheims,' is in a loftier and more ambitious vein [than some of Hemans's other poems]; but sustained with equal grace, and as touching in its solemn tenderness" (*Edinburgh Review* 50 [October 1829]: 32–47). "Joan of Arc, in Rheims" was first published, without the epigraphs, in the *New Monthly Magazine* 17 (October 1826): 314–16.

epigraphs]

Vie de Joanno d'Arc] Possibly Jean Baptiste Prosper Jollois, *Histoire abrégée de la vie et des exploits de Jeanne d'Arc* (1821). Hemans would also have been familiar with Friedrich von Schiller's tragedy *Die Jungfrau von Orleans* (The Maid of Orleans), first staged in 1801 and published in Berlin in 1802. The passage may be translated, "Joan of Arc had the joy of seeing several of her childhood friends at Chalons. An even more inexpressible joy was awaiting her at Rheims, amidst her triumph: Jack of Arc, her father, arrived there as soon as the troops of Charles VII had entered the city; and as the two brothers of our heroine had accompanied him, she found herself for a moment in the midst of her family, in the arms of a virtuous father." In the *New Monthly Magazine* text, Hemans continues the quotation—"Auquel cette vertueuse fille se plut à renvoyer ces hommages d'estime dont elle étoit entourée"(to whom this virtuous daughter returned the veneration that embraced her)—and identifies as its source the periodical *Almanach de Gotha* (1822).

Thou hast a charmed cup . . . affection's spring] These six lines also served Hemans as the opening to "Woman and Fame," which appeared in the *Amulet* for 1829 (actually published in late 1828).

l. 6 listen'd at] listen'd to [NMM].

l. 8 pictured] storied [NMM].

l. 17 stoles] states [NMM].

l. 20 helm] helmet.

l. 27 its pure paleness] their pure paleness [NMM].

l. 29 votaress] a female religious devotee, often taking a special saint. In this case, Joan of Arc is votaress to the Virgin Mary.

l. 74 glade,] A beautiful fountain near Domremi, believed to be haunted by fairies, and a favourite resort of Jeanne d'Arc in her childhood. (*Hemans's note.*) Hemans here abbreviates her original note, which read in the poem's first periodical printing, "A tree and fountain near Domremi, the native village of Joanne d'Arc, were believed to be haunted by fairies and were much frequented by the young girls of the neighbouring hamlets, who often suspended wreaths of flowers from the branches of the tree, which was a beech of remarkable size and beauty." Joan of Arc was born in the village of Domremy La Pucelle.

PAULINE

"Pauline" was first published in the *New Monthly Magazine* 19 (February 1827): 155–57, with the following epigraph from William Wordsworth:

—One adequate support
For the calamities of mortal life
Exists, one only;—an assured belief
That the procession of our fate, howe'er
Sad or disturb'd, is order'd by a Being
Of infinite benevolence and power,
Whose everlasting purposes embrace
All accidents, converting them to good.
(*The Excursion,* bk. 4, ll. 11–18)

epigraph]
Tasso] Torquato Tasso, *La Gerusalemme Liberata,* canto 16, st. 15, ll. 1–2. Ralph Nash translates these lines, "So passes in the passing of a day the flower and leaf of mortal life" (*Jerusalem Delivered,* 342). Hemans substituted this epigraph, preceded by one of her own composition, for the Wordsworth epigraph that had appeared in the first periodical publication of "Pauline." See also the note to "Imelda."
l. 1 Seine] a river in northern France that flows through Paris north to the English Channel. Hemans alters the setting of the original story perhaps in part to play on the word "seine," a large fishing net.
l. 12 Danube-side] The Princess Pauline Schwartzenberg. The story of her fate is beautifully related in L'Allemagne. Vol. iii p. 336. (*Hemans's note [to NMM text only].*) Anne Louise Germaine (Necker) de Staël, *De l'Allemagne* (Paris, 1810) translated and published in London by John Murray as *Germany* (1813). The account appears in part 4, chapter 6, entitled "Of Pain," and includes, as well, the passage from Tasso that Hemans adopts as the second epigraph to this poem. Princess Paulina of Schwartzenberg, beautiful and the mother of eight, presided at a luxurious fête where a fire broke out. Though she had reached safety, she went

back into the inferno to rescue her daughter. According to the John Murray translation, "Her hand seized that of her daughter, her hand saved her daughter; and although the fatal blow then struck her, her last act was maternal; her last act preserved the object of her affection; it was at this sublime instant that she appeared before God; and it was impossible to recognise what remained of her upon earth except by the impression on a medal, given by her children, which also marked the place where this angel perished. . . . This generous Paulina will hereafter be the saint of mothers" (3:338–39). Hemans alters de Staël's story so that the daughter dies with her heroic mother, compounding the tragedy. The nightmare of a mother's futile efforts to protect a child caught in fire seems to have been a preoccupation of Hemans's. It appears in *Records of Woman* in both "The Bride of the Greek Isle" and in "The Image in Lava." But perhaps Hemans's most disturbing variation on this theme occurs in "Casabianca" (1829), in which the combination of a parent's commands and literal lack of consciousness detain a child in the killing inferno. Hemans also appears to have been intrigued by the notion of suttee, and dramatic evocations of this subject appear throughout her corpus. See also Hemans's "The Requiem of Genius," which takes its epigraph from *De l'Allemagne*.

l. 58 within] amidst [NMM].

l. 60 from the flame's] at the flame's [NMM].

l. 84 rest.] In the *New Monthly Magazine* text only, Hemans quotes in a footnote here from de Staël's original text, cited above in translation: "'L'on n'a pu reconnoître ce qui restoit d'elle sur la terre, qu'au chiffre de ses enfan[t]s, qui marquoit encore la place où cet ange avoit péri.' Madame De Staël."

JUANA

Juana] Juana of Aragon, Queen of Castile (1479–1555), was the daughter of King Ferdinand and Queen Isabella of Spain. In 1496 she was married to Philip (1478–1506), Duke of Burgundy, son of Mary of Burgundy and the Hapsburg Archduke Maximilian. Her marriage was part of her parents' plan to link the Spanish with the Austrian, Portuguese, and English royal houses in order to encircle France. Juana was unhappy in the marriage as a result of Philip's infidelity, neglect, and pro-French politics. When Queen Isabella died in 1504, Juana inherited from her the throne of Castile. Philip died of a fever on 25 September 1506; Juana refused to be separated from his body and was said to be insane. Her father assumed the regency. Now called "Juana la Loca," she was essentially imprisoned in Spain for the last forty-five years of her life. "Juana" was first published under the title "Joanna" in the *New Monthly Magazine* 20 (October 1827): 358–59.

Charles V] (1500–1558), emperor of the Holy Roman Empire from

1519 to 1556.
l. 21 coronal] circlet of gems for the head; coronet.

THE AMERICAN FOREST GIRL

In addition to the strong parallels between the narrative of "The American Forest Girl" and the Pocahontas–John Smith story, Hemans may have been drawing, too, from an episode in Lydia Sigourney's *Sketch of Connecticut, Forty Years Since* (1824) portraying the old Mohegan Indian warrior Arrowhamet (or Zachary) who saves Oriana Selden, cross-dressed as a soldier, just as she is about to be tortured and killed according to tribal ritual. "The American Forest Girl" was first published, without the epigraph, in the *New Monthly Magazine* 16 (April 1826): 407–8.
l. 21 laburnums] a small tree of the family *Leguminosae;* see note to "The Palm-Tree."
l. 23 clos'd upon] faded on [NMM].
l. 65 Liannes] or lianas, a tropical climbing plant.

COSTANZA

"Costanza" was first published, without the epigraph, in the *New Monthly Magazine* 14 (August 1825): 110–12.
l. 4 her cheek and pale Madonna-brow] the marble beauty of her brow [NMM].
l. 8 painting's] picture's [NMM].
l. 36 Calabrian] Calabria is a region of southern Italy.
l. 37 heart] soul [NMM].
l. 54 ringdoves] white doves [NMM].
l. 100 one—] *one.* [NMM].
l. 101 gauds] toys; in this case, military medals.
l. 109 shadowy] shadowing [NMM].

MADELINE, A DOMESTIC TALE

Published in the *Literary Souvenir* for 1828 [22–25]. (*Hemans's note.*) Hemans published five poems in the 1828 *Literary Souvenir* [LS], which actually came out in late 1827. "Madeline" appeared along with "The Wings of the Dove," "The Voice of Home," "Ancient Song of Victory," and "The Memory of the Dead." The poem appeared without the epigraph and with no subtitle. Contributors to this volume include S.T. Coleridge, L.E.L., William Howitt, Maria Jane Jewsbury, Mary Russell Mitford, Thomas Hood, Robert Southey, Caroline Bowles, John Clare, and Mary Howitt.
Joanna Baillie] *Rayner: A Tragedy,* 4.2.15–20; first published in *Mis-*

cellaneous Plays (1804). The Countess Zaterloo is addressing her ailing son just after she has removed her mask and allowed him to discover her identity. She replies to his question, "Ha, mother! Is it you?" After the section Hemans quotes, Countess Zaterloo's speech continues,

> The world may scowl, acquaintance may forsake,
> Friends may neglect, and lovers know a change,
> But when a mother doth forsake her child,
> Men lift their hands and cry, "a prodigy!" (4.2.21–24)

l. 4 step amidst] footstep, midst [LS].
l. 5 twilight's] evening's [LS].
l. 17 God shall] God will [LS].
l. 30 rose-leaves] rose-trees [LS].
l. 33 Gush'd] Streamed [LS].
l. 37 calm'd] stilled [LS].
l. 38 sweet] low [LS].
l. 39 Breathing of home:] To chiming waves. [LS]
l. 47 to come.] to be. [LS].
l. 50 On sweeps the storm,] Comes the swift storm, [LS].
  with] in [LS].
l. 51 summer] summer's [LS].
l. 55 voiceless] lonely [LS].
l. 66 hour] blight [LS].
l. 68 heart-sick yearning] vague sad yearnings [LS].
l. 72 blue-rushing] blue glancing [LS].
l. 79 feverish] pale young [LS].
l. 80 wasted] feverish [LS].
l. 81 lingering] heavy [LS].
l. 83 faints not thro'] bows not to [LS].
l. 84 that fears not toil,] that knows not change, [LS].
l. 86 Uprearing] upbearing [LS].
  drooping] fragile [LS].
l. 87 wild] long [LS].
l. 98 sinking] falling [LS].
l. 100 look] gaze [LS].

THE QUEEN OF PRUSSIA'S TOMB

Originally published in the *Monthly Magazine. (Hemans's note.)* The poem appeared in the December 1826 issue [627-28].
  sarcophagus] stone coffin adorned with sculpture.
  Ramble in Germany] Moyle Sherer, *Notes and Reflections during a Ramble in Germany* (London, 1826), 392–94. Hemans has extracted seg-

ments from a much longer description by Sherer of a visit to the tomb of Queen Louise (1776–1810), who was widely respected for her courage and dignity in suffering during the Napoleonic Wars. She came to embody libertarian hopes and patriotic spirit. Queen Louise was thirty-five when she died of a heart ailment on 19 July 1810 at Strelitz. Her grave in the palace park at Charlottenburg almost immediately became a popular shrine to which thousands made pilgrimages. Sherer was a friend and correspondent of Hemans's (Rose Lawrence, *The Last Autumn at a Favorite Residence,* 309). Hemans's "Two Monuments" (1834) was inspired by Sherer's book, and her "Marshal Schwerin's Grave" also draws its epigraph from this work. See, too, the note for "The Spanish Chapel."

Milman] Henry Hart Milman (1791–1868), "Judicium Regale, an Ode" (ll. 74–76), which describes a dream about Napoleon, Queen Louise, and others facing judgment. Milman portrays Queen Louise as a deeply wronged and highly sympathetic figure. For Milman, she is "the beautiful, the delicate, / The queenly, but too gentle for a Queen" (ll. 72–73). Milman helped Hemans to revise her play, *The Vespers of Palermo* (1823), for production on the London stage. The epigraphs from Milman and Sherer replaced one from William Cartwright's *On the Queen's Return from the Low Countries* (1643) in the *Monthly Magazine* text:

> Courage was cast about her like a dress
>   Of solemn comeliness;
> A gathered mind and an untroubled face
>   Did give her dangers grace. (ll. 7-10)

1.12 eyes.] The character of this monumental statue is that of the deepest serenity; the repose, however, of sleep—not the grave.—See the description in Russell's "Germany." (*Hemans's note.*) John Russell, *A Tour in Germany, and some of the Southern Provinces of the Austrian Empire in the Years 1820, 1821 and 1822* (1824): 263-64.

1.33 borne] bore [MM].
l. 34 blazon] heraldic coat of arms.
1.41 realm] land [MM].
1.43 note] word [MM].
1.49 crown'd] proud [MM].
    crown'd eagle] symbol of Prussia.
l. 50 pinion] wing.

The Memorial Pillar

Pembroke] Anne, Countess of Pembroke (1590–1676) was a friend of the poet George Herbert, and her mother, Margaret Russell Clifford, Countess of Cumberland (1560–1616), was one of Queen Elizabeth I's pallbearers. Lady Anne's diary records that "for some 2 nights my Mother & I lay together & had much talk. . . . Upon the 2nd . . . she & I had a grevious & heavy Parting. . . . Upon the 17th my Mother sickened as she came from Prayers, being taken with a cold chillness in the manner of an Ague which after wards turned to great heats and pains in her side. . . . Upon the 29th [May 1616] Kendal came and brought me the heavy news of my Mother's death, which I held as the greatest & most lamentable Cross that could have befallen me." Forty years later, Lady Anne consecrated the spot where she and her mother parted with a memorial which became known as the "Countess's Pillar." It survives today, located on the Appleby road, not far from Brougham Castle (D. J. H. Clifford, ed., *The Diaries of Lady Anne Clifford* [Wolfeboro Falls, NH: Allan Sutton, 1990], 18, 31, 36). Lady Anne said of her mother, "She was naturally of an high spirit, though she tempered it well by grace, having a very well-favoured face, with sweet and quick grey eyes, and of a comely personage. She was of a graceful behaviour which she increased the more by her being civil and courteous to all sorts of people. . . . She had a great, sharp, natural wit. . . . Few books of worth translated into English but she read them. . . . [She] was a lover of the study and practice of alchemy, by which she found out excellent medicines that did much good to many. She delighted in distilling waters . . . for she had some knowledge in most kinds of minerals, herbs, flowers, and plants. . . . She had a kind of prophetic spirit in her in many things. . . . [She] knew well that all in this world is but vanity" (quoted in Wallace Notestein, *Four Worthies* [London: J. Cape, 1956], 125). See also George Williamson, *Lady Anne Clifford* (Kendal, UK: T. Wilson and Son, 1922). Vita Sackville-West was a descendant of Lady Anne's and published an edition of her diaries in 1923. "The Memorial Pillar" was first published in the *New Monthly Magazine* 19 (June 1827): 522–23.

epigraph]

Pleasures of Memory.] (1792), part 2, ll. 173–80, by Samuel Rogers (1763–1855). Hemans has modified Rogers's poetry from its original:

Hast thou thro' Eden's wild-wood vales pursued
Each mountain-scene, majestically rude;
To note the sweet simplicity of life,
Far from the din of Folly's idle strife;
Nor there awhile, with lifted eye, revered
That modest stone which pious Pembroke reared;
Which still records, beyond the pencil's power,
The silent sorrows of a parting hour;

Hemans uses verbatim, however, Rogers's note to this passage, the continuation to which she quotes in the *New Monthly Magazine* text: "In memory whereof she hath left an annuity of 4£. to be distributed to the poor of the parish of Brougham, every 2[n]d day of April for ever, upon the stone table placed hard by. Laus Deo!" Rogers also notes that "the Eden is the principal river of Cumberland, and rises in the wildest part of Westmoreland."

l. 5 shrin'd] set [NMM].
l. 19 high-hearted daughter] true-hearted Daughter [NMM].
l. 24 burst,] tide [NMM].
l. 54 one earthly hour?] an earthly hour? [NMM].

The Grave of a Poetess

Extrinsic interest has lately attached to the fine scenery of Woodstock, near Kilkenny, on account of its having been the last residence of the author of *Psyche* [Mary Tighe]. Her grave is one of many in the church-yard of the village. The river runs smoothly by. The ruins of an ancient abbey that have been partially converted into a church, reverently throw their mantle of tender shadow over it.—*Tales by the O'Hara Family.* (*Hemans's note.*) John and Michael Banim, *Tales, by the O'Hara Family* (London, 1825). When "The Grave of a Poetess" was first published in the *New Monthly Magazine* 20 (July 1827): 69–70, this footnote contin-ued with the line: "It is the very spot for the grave of a poetess." Hemans once said of Mary Tighe (1722–1810), author of *Psyche* (1805), "Her poetry has always touched me greatly, from a similarity which I imagine I discover between her destiny and my own" (Chorley, *Memorials* 2:212). Tighe's destiny included an unhappy marriage, recognition as a poetic genius during her lifetime by a small literary circle, and a losing battle with painful tuberculosis in her late thirties; she never lived to enjoy the widespread acclaim *Psyche* earned. In 1831, Hemans traveled to Woodstock and made a pilgrimage to Tighe's grave, which she had only imagined three years earlier in "The Grave of a Poetess." According to Hemans, "We went to the tomb . . . where there is a monument by Flaxman: it consists of a recumbent female figure, with much of the repose, the mysterious sweetness of happy death, which is to me so affecting in monu-mental sculpture. There is, however, a very small Titania-looking sort of figure with wings, sitting at the head of the sleeper, which I thought inter-fered with the singleness of effect which the tomb would have produced: unfortunately, too, the monument is carved in very rough stone, which allows no delicacy of touch. That place of rest made me very thoughtful; I could not but reflect on the many changes which had brought me to the spot I had commemorated three years since, without the slightest idea of ever visiting it; and, though surrounded by attention and the appearance of interest, my heart was envying the repose of her who slept there" (Hughes, "Memoir," 238–39). This experience inspired more poems: "I

Stood Where the Life of Song Lay Low" (published among her "National Lyrics") and "Written after Visiting a Tomb near Woodstock, in the County of Kilkenny." She saw the house in which Tighe died; there she was allowed to read a collection of Tighe's early poems in manuscript, which inspired Hemans's sonnet "On Records of Immature Genius," published in *Poetical Remains* (Chorley, *Memorials* 2:208–19). The poem "Lines for the Album at Rosanna," beginning "Where a sweet spirit once in beauty moved," was also as result of this visit. "The Grave of a Poetess" is the only poem in the "Records of Woman" series set in present-day England. epigraph]

Ne me plaignez . . . épargnées!] "Do not pity me—if you were to know from how many sorrows this tomb has saved me!" From Anne Louise Germaine (Necker) de Staël, *Corinne ou L'Italie* (1807), bk. 18, chap. 3, last par. Corinne is in Florence wandering through a graveyard. In Avriel H. Goldberger's translation (New Brunswick, N.J.: Rutgers University Press, 1987), the novel reads, "Yet another epitaph caught her attention: *Do not pity me,* said a man who had died young. *If you only knew how many sorrows this tomb has spared me!* 'What detachment from life those words inspire!' said Corinne through her tears" (367). Hemans uses *Corinne* for the epigraph of "The Hour of Death," "A Parting Song," and "Tasso and his Sister." See also Hemans's "Corinne at the Capitol."

l. 20 vernal] in springtime.

l. 41 vain love to passing flowers] Just before she died Tighe wrote "On Receiving a Branch of Mezereon which Flowered at Woodstock, December, 1809," in which she lamented that she would not live to see the blooms of May again. The poem was published posthumously in *Psyche, with Other Poems* (1811).

THE HOMES OF ENGLAND

Originally published in *Blackwood's Magazine.* (*Hemans's note.*) *Blackwood's Edinburgh Magazine* 21 (April 1827): 392. "The Homes of England" became one of Hemans's best known and most widely recited and reprinted poems, eventually taking its place as a standard nineteenth-century English lyric. But it was read out of context. Read within the volume as the poem immediately following the elegiac "Records of Woman," the celebratory "Homes of England" seems ironic. epigraph]

Marmion] Walter Scott, *Marmion, A Tale of Flodden Field* (1808), canto 4, st. 30, ll. 34–35. Just before battle, giving a spur to his charger, Fitz-Eustace utters these lines in the hearing of Lord Marmion and Lindesay as he surveys the Scottish vista. This epigraph from Scott replaced the one in the *Blackwood's Edinburgh Magazine* text from Joanna Baillie's *Ethwald: A Tragedy* (1802):

> ———A land of peace,
> Where yellow fields unspoiled, and pastures green,
> Mottled with herds and flocks, who crop secure
> Their native herbage, nor have ever known
> A stranger's stall, smile gladly.
> See through its tufted alleys to Heaven's roof
> The curling smoke of quiet dwellings rise.
>
> (pt. 2, 1.2.76-82)

Walter Scott had been responsible for one of Hemans's first publications. She sent him a poem inspired by *Waverley* (1814), and he published it in the *Edinburgh Annual Register* for 1815. When *The Vespers of Palermo* had a disappointing reception in London, Scott helped get it staged in Edinburgh in 1824. A year after the publication of *Records of Woman*, in the summer of 1829, Hemans visited Walter Scott on a trip to Scotland. Scott had once told Joanna Baillie that Hemans "is somewhat too poetical for my taste—too many flowers I mean, and too little fruit—but that may be the cynical criticism of an elderly gentleman" (letter of 11 July 1823, quoted in John Gibson Lockhart, *Memoirs of the Life of Sir Walter Scott,* 5 vols. [Boston, 1901], 4:126). He liked Hemans personally, however, and invited her to be his houseguest at Abbotsford; she saw this visit as one of the high points of her life. She reported "long walks [with him] over moor and woodland, . . . listening to song and legend of other times, until my mind quite forgets itself, and is carried wholly back to the days of the Slogan and the fiery cross, and the wild gatherings of border chivalry. I cannot say enough of his cordial kindness to me" (Chorley, *Memorials* 2:40). Her son reported, "She used to spend the mornings chiefly in taking long walks or drives with Sir Walter; in the evenings she used to play to him, principally her sister's music, and sometimes sing" (Chorley, *Memorials* 2:54–55). Scott told her at parting, "There are some whom we meet, and should like ever after to claim as kith and kin; and *you* are one of those" (Hughes, "Memoir," 191). See also Lawrence, *Last Autumn,* 320–29.

l. 31 the lowly] they lowly [Blackwoods].

THE SICILIAN CAPTIVE

"The Sicilian Captive" was first published, without the epigraph, in the *New Monthly Magazine* 14 (August 1825): 122–23.

epigraph]
L. E. L.] pen name of Letitia Elizabeth Landon (1802–38), "Unknown Female Head," ll. 14–19, first published in the *Literary Gazette* no. 316

(8 February 1823): 91 and later included in her volume *The Vow of the Peacock and Other Poems* (London, 1835).

l. 8 it] they [NMM].

l. 9 Scalds] Icelandic poets of the ninth to the thirteenth centuries.

Runic] A rune is a character or letter from the earliest Teutonic alphabet used by the Anglo-Saxons and Scandinavians.

l. 18 the southern skies,] southern skies, [NMM].

l. 19 fringe of their lashes low,] lids—oh! the world of woe, [NMM].

l. 20 Half veil'd a depth of unfathom'd woe.] The cloud of dreams, that sweet veil below! [NMM].

l. 48 shine out,] break out [NMM].

l. 49 beauty] glory [NMM].

l. 50 glory] beauty [NMM].

l. 56 my vintage] the vintage [NMM].

l. 60 dell!] dell? [NMM].

l. 64 from the dewy] in the dewy [NMM].

l. 71 thus depart] perish thus [NMM].

l. 73 o'ersweep] o'erpass [NMM]

l. 77 ringing] singing [NMM].

l. 78 eye's wild] wild-eye's [NMM].

IVAN THE CZAR

Originally published in the *Literary Souvenir* for 1827. (*Hemans's note.*) It appeared on pages 164–67 without the epigraph, and four additional poems by Hemans appeared in this volume, actually published in late 1826: "The Breeze from Shore," "The Better Land," "Corinna at the Capitol," and "The Distant Ship." Other contributors included Mary Russell Mitford, Mary Howitt, Thomas Hood, S.T. Coleridge, L.E.L., Robert Southey, Jane Porter, and John Clare. T.K. Hervey chose "Ivan the Czar" as an example of Hemans's "chivalric and other ballads," remarking, "That she should succeed in this style might have been safely predicted of her, by everyone familiar with the pomp and gorgeousness of her diction, and the occasionally stately sweep of her melody,—so peculiarly appropriate both to the chivalric lay, and to the battle song. Accordingly, she has produced some spirit-stirring examples of ballad" (*Dublin Review* 21 [December 1836]: 266).

epigraphs]

de Staël] "Ivan the Terrible, who was already old, was besieging Novgorod. Seeing how enfeebled he was, the boyars asked him if he would not turn over the command to his son. This proposal enraged him so that nothing could appease him; his son prostrated himself at his feet, but he repulsed him with a blow of such violence that two days later the unfortunate son died. Then the father, in despair, grew indifferent to the war and to power, and survived his son by only a few months. *Ten Years' Exile* by Madame de Staël." Anne Louise Germaine (Necker) De Staël's *Dix années d'exil; ou, Mémoires de l'époque la plus intéressante de la vie de Madame de Staël, écrits par elle-même dans les années 1810 à 1813* was published in London in 1821 as *Ten Years' Exile*. The translation above is by Doris Beik (New York: Saturday Review Press, 1972), 219. De Staël's historical facts regarding Ivan IV (1530–84), who was czar of Russia beginning in 1547 and made Moscow a major power, are not entirely accurate. In January 1570, believing that the authorities of the city were conspiring against him, he attacked Great Novgorod, the second wealthiest city in his czardom, massacring, burning, pillaging, and plundering. However, the incident in which he struck his eldest surviving son and heir, Ivan, in a fit of rage, took place not in connection with this event but a decade later, in November 1580. The blow killed the child, whom he dearly loved, and the czar was so filled with grief and remorse that he wished to abdicate. He survived his son, however, not by a few months but by three years. De Staël offers her version of the incident, she says, to demonstrate that "good society is the same in all countries, and nothing is less appropriate than that elegant world for furnishing subjects for tragedy. . . . This revolt of an aged despot against the passage of time has something grand and solemn in it. The tenderness that succeeds the fury in that ferocious soul represents man as he comes from the hands of nature, sometimes driven by egoism, sometimes restrained by affection" (*Ten Years' Exile,* trans. Doris Beik, 219–20).

Schiller] "Give me back this dead man. I must have him back! . . . Bleak omnipotence, that cannot even stretch its arm into the grave, cannot amend a little overhaste with human life" from Friedrich von Schiller's play, *Don Karlos* (1787), act 5, sc. 9, ll. 5016-17, 5036-39.

l. 23 tones,] sounds, [LS].

CAROLAN'S PROPHECY

Founded on a circumstance related of the Irish Bard, in the "Percy Anecdotes of Imagination." (*Hemans's note.*) Joseph Clinton Robertson and Thomas Byerley, *The Percy Anecdotes. Original and Select. By Sholto and Reuben Percy, [pseudonyms] Brothers of the Benedictine Monastery, Mont Benger* (London, 1820). The bard is Turlough Carolan (Toirdhealbhach Cearbhallain) (1670–1738), blind composer, harpist, and poet, who drew upon Irish folk traditions for his songs, laments, and dance tunes but was also influenced by Europeans such as Vivaldi and Corelli. He played for Jonathan Swift, who adapted one of his pieces. Several authors, including Oliver Goldsmith, portrayed him in a pathetic light, as the last exemplar of a lost culture. The 1839 edition of Hemans's *Works* adds to Hemans's footnote the following explanation, drawn almost verbatim from the entry on "Carolan, the Irish Bard" in the "Anecdotes of Imagination" section of the *Percy Anecdotes:* "It is somewhat remarkable that Carolan, the Irish bard, even in his gayest mood, never could compose a planxty for a Miss Brett, in the county of Sligo, whose father's house he frequented, and where he always met with a reception due to his exquisite taste and mental endowments. One day, after an unsuccessful attempt to compose something in a sprightly strain for this lady, he threw aside his harp with a mixture of rage and grief; and addressing himself in Irish to her mother, 'Madam,' said he, 'I have often, from my great respect to your family, attempted a planxty in order to celebrate your daughter's perfections, but to no purpose. Some evil genius hovers over me; there is not a string in my harp that does not vibrate a melancholy sound when I set about this task. I fear she is not doomed to remain long among us; 'nay,' said he, emphatically, 'she will not survive twelve months.' The event verified the prediction, and the young lady died within the period limited by the unconsciously prophetic bard" (238 n). "Carolan's Prophecy" was first published under the title "The Bard's Prophecy" in the *New Monthly Magazine* 14 (July 1825): 68–69. This earlier text had an epigraph from Charles Robert Maturin's tragedy, *Bertram; or, The Castle of St. Aldobrand* (1816): "Ne'er err'd the prophet heart that Grief inspired, / Though Joy's illusions mock their votarist" (act 4, sc. 2, ll. 139–40). The female lead, Imogine, delivers the lines in a farewell speech to her husband, Aldobrand. In her youth, Hemans composed a poem extolling the powers of a local blind harpist: "To Mr. Edwards, The Harper of Conway" (written 1811; published 1839 in Hughes, "Memoir," 18–19).

l. 1 from amidst the] o'er the deep green [NMM].
l. 37 foaming] foamy [NMM].
l. 38 sear] dry; withered.
1. 53 riven] split; slashed.
l. 71 festal] joyous.

THE LADY OF THE CASTLE

"The Lady of the Castle" was first published, without the epigraph, in the *New Monthly Magazine* 14 (September 1825): 207–8. Frances Jeffrey singled out this poem for praise. He noted, "This story . . . is told, we think, with great force and sweetness" (*Edinburgh Review* 50 [October 1829]: 32–47).
subtitle]
"*Portrait Gallery*"] H. F. Chorley reports that "many of the imaginations which floated through [Hemans's] brain . . . [at her home in Rhyllon] were lost in the more interrupted and responsible life, which followed . . . [her] departure from Wales; when the breaking up of her household, on the marriage of one of her family, and the removal of another into Ireland,

threw her exclusively upon her own resources, and compelled her to make acquaintance with an 'eating, drinking, buying, bargaining' world, with which, from her disposition and habits, she was ill fitted to cope. One of these unfinished works was the 'Portrait Gallery,' of which one episode, 'The Lady of the Castle,' is introduced in the 'Records'" (*Memorials* 1:131). Harriet Hughes, the poet's sister, includes in her memoir Hemans's plan for "The Picture Gallery:" "A young Bride leads her husband through the castle of her ancestors, an ancient chateau in Provence or Languedoc. Her favourite haunt is the Picture Gallery, where she passes hours with him every day, relating to him the stories of the sons and daughters of her house." Hemans outlined eight stories for "The Picture Gallery" in a manuscript notebook but completed only "The Lady of the Castle." The series was to conclude with the story of Constance, who "possesses a gift of sacred song, and the young bride, Azalais, concludes her tales with an evening hymn of Constance's. She then bids the portraits of her ancestors farewell, as the day is come on which she is to leave the dwelling of her father for that of her husband" (Hughes, "Memoir," 113–16; includes Hemans's outline).

l. 2 those] its [NMM].

l. 16 shame, and not with tears?—She fell!] shame?—that radiant creature fell! [NMM].

l. 21 *she went on!*] *she pass'd on!* [NMM].

  home, her hearth,] home and hearth, [NMM].

l. 26 sword] mail [NMM].

l. 31 warder] one who wards or guards.

1.42 And plaintive—oh!] As drooping bird's—[NMM].

1.59 sunny] laughing [NMM].

l. 92 fillet] headband or ribbon to bind or ornament the hair.

THE MOURNER FOR THE BARMECIDES

The Barmecides, or Barmakids, were a noble Persian family which became powerful under the Abbasid caliphs. The events in this poem relate to the reign of the caliph Harun al-Rashid (786–809). Barmak's son, Ja'far, the Giafar of the *Arabian Nights,* was a close friend of the caliph. Without warning, the caliph had Giafar seized and beheaded. "The Mourner for the Barmecides" was first published without the epigraph in the *New Monthly Magazine* 17 (August 1826): 163–65.

epigraph]

As You Like It] The lines are spoken by Orlando (2.3.56–57, 59). The line Hemans omits is "When service sweat for duty, not for meed!"

l. 4 Tygris] The Tigris River flows through Persia, present-day Iran.

l. 76 cittern] cithern; a guitarlike, stringed instrument popular in the sixteenth and seventeenth centuries.

The Spanish Chapel

Suggested by a scene beautifully described in the "Recollections of the Peninsula." (*Hemans's note.*) J. M. Sherer, *Recollections of the Peninsula* (London, 1823). The chapel was located near Alegrete, where Sherer's regiment was stationed. Sherer recounts, "In one of my walks here, after wandering along the rude and pathless banks of a clear mountain stream[,] . . . I arrived at a small romantic chapel, such a one as you often find in the Peninsula, a league or more from any human habitation. In the shade, near the door, I observed a small basket, apparently filled only with the most beautiful flowers; I approached to take one;—when stooping, I beheld a lovely infant about a year old; it was dressed prettily and tastefully; though pale, I thought it slept, for its paleness did not appear as of death; it was, however, cold and lifeless, yet it had nothing of the corpse, nothing of the grave about it. I kissed its delicate fair face, and thought, not without a sigh, on its parents. A voice startled me, and turning, I beheld a decent looking peasant woman, with an old man, and two or three children from ten to fifteen years of age.—'Are you the mother of this babe?' said I; 'Yes, Senhor.' 'I pity you from my heart.'—'How so, Senhor? To have borne and buried a Christian, without sin, I look on as a blessing, and I praise the Holy Virgin that she has vouchsafed to take him to herself.'—I gazed earnestly at the woman. Was this insensibility? or was it enthusiastic reverence for, and pious resignation to, the will of God?—I decided for the latter; for I saw her bend over her child with an expression of countenance rapturously affectionate. I knelt down, once more, to read its innocent features.—Yes, there was the charm: remorse, fear, and doubt, could not be traced there. All was innocence, and purity, and truth" (86–87). "The Spanish Chapel" was first published without the epigraph in the *New Monthly Magazine* 17 (November 1826): 474–75.
epigraph]

Moore] Thomas Moore, "Weep Not for Those," ll. 1–4, from *Sacred Songs,* no. 1 (1816). Hemans softens Moore's line 3, "Ere sin threw a blight" by substituting "veil" for "blight."

l. 14 waters] water [NMM].

l. 15 The bright stream reverently below,] While, as in reverent love below, [NMM].

l. 16 Check'd its exulting play;] The bright stream check'd its play; [NMM].

l. 68 thus to Heaven!"] unto Heaven!" [NMM].

The Captive Knight

Hemans sent a copy of this poem in a letter to Joanna Baillie dated 12 April 1828 and wrote, "I do not know whether you may have heard of the interest which Sir Walter Scott [a mutual friend] has latterly most kindly taken in some music of my sister's [Harriet Hughes's] composition, accompanying words of mine. One song in particular, 'The Captive Knight,' struck him as being '*si chevaleresque*,' [so chivalrous] to use his own word on the occasion, that he has been quite bent on its publication, and it will in consequence be brought out and dedicated to him" (Chorley, *Memorials* 1:150). Scott may have been responsible for helping to secure the publication of "The Captive Knight" with I. Willis and Company, of Lower Grosvenor Street, London. Eventually, the firm became the authorized publishers of at least ninety-nine of Hemans's poems, set to music by Harriet Hughes and sold individually as sheet music in the "Royal Musical Repository." "The Captive Knight" appears to have been the first and most popular of these publications. An undated advertisement for the series of *Songs, Duets, &c. by Mrs. Hemans and Sister* lists "The Captive Knight" in its seventieth edition.

epigraph]
Lady of the Lake] (1810) by Sir Walter Scott, canto 6, verse 22, ll. 627–28. Hemans slightly misquotes Scott's lines taken from Allan-Bane's lament at the death of Highland chief Roderick Dhu by transposing "captive" and "prisoned."

l. 2 Paynim] pagan.

THE KAISER'S FEAST

headnote]
Miss Benger's *Memoirs of the Queen of Bohemia*] Elizabeth Benger, *Memoirs of Elizabeth Stuart, Queen of Bohemia, Daughter of King James the First* (London, 1825). The passage continues, ". . . and not only consented to revoke the ban, but invested his eldest nephew with the Upper and Lower Palatinate, to which he superadded the electoral dignity; not, however, without annexing to the grant a condition, afterwards the source of mischievous dissensions—namely, that the electoral privilege should be alternately exercised by the Bavarian princes, and the Counts Palatine" (1:6). The Roman emperor and duke of upper Bavaria Louis IV (c. 1287–1347) declared war on his elder brother Rudolph in 1310 and again a few years later over their joint inheritance of upper Bavaria and the Palatinate; but in 1317, Rudolph accepted a yearly subsidy in exchange for renouncing his claims. "The Kaiser's Feast" was first published in the *New Monthly Magazine* 17 (December 1826) 553–54.

l. 12 wassail] riotous party.

Tasso and his Sister

Corinne] "Sorrento lies before you. Tasso's sister lived there when he came as a pilgrim to ask refuge from princely injustice of this humble friend. His mind was almost deranged by his long suffering. He had nothing left but genius." In the original, the passage continues, "Only his knowledge of things divine was left intact, all images of the earth were blurred." From Avriel H. Goldberger's 1987 translation of de Staël's *Corinne ou L'Italie* (1807), bk. 13, chap. 4, p. 244–45. For Hemans's opinion of de Staël's *Corinne,* see the note to "A Parting Song." The historical context for "Tasso and his Sister" is as follows. After the exhausting task of completing the composition of his epic poem, *La Gerusalemme Liberata* (Jerusalem delivered) in 1573, Torquato Tasso's (1544–95) health began to fail him. He suffered from headaches, fevers, and delusions as well as from the critics' response to his work. He imagined that he had been denounced by the Inquisition and feared that he would be poisoned or that his servants would betray him. In the summer of 1577, as he spoke to the princess Lucrezia d'Este, he imagined that a servant was eavesdropping and attacked him with a knife. He was incarcerated in a room in the palace and later placed in a Franciscan convent at Ferrara. Tasso escaped at the end of July, disguised himself as a peasant, and walked to Sorrento to see his only sister Cornelia, in whose company he found peace and healing for a year. In February 1579, he returned to the court at Ferrara, where his presence was not wanted. Eventually in 1579 he was institutionalized at St. Anna, where he remained for seven years.

l. 3 red] deep [LA].

l. 15 parted] parting [LA].

l. 23 pen and sword,] It is scarcely necessary to recall the well-known Italian saying, that Tasso with his sword and pen was superior to all men. (*Hemans's note.*)

l. 25 Erminia] In *Gerusalemme Liberata,* Erminia, daughter of a king, is in love with Tancred. She borrows armor and ventures outside the city walls in order to assist him in battle. But a night patrol discovers her; she flees but then, because of the horse's speed, loses her way. A band of shepherds takes her in. Eventually, she finds Tancred wounded, revives him with her tears, and binds his wounds.

l. 31 Godfrey's deeds, of Tancred's arm] Godfrey of Bouillon (1060–1100) was one of the leaders of the first crusade. He sullied his reputation for piety when he ordered a massacre of Muslims during the capture of Jerusalem in 1099. Even so, he was elected sovereign over the newly declared Christian kingdom of Jerusalem. Tancrède de Hauteville (d. 1112) played a prominent role in many of the major battles of the first crusade and became known as Prince of Galilee after the taking of Jerusalem. He made war on the Turks and the Byzantines for the rest of his life. In

Gerusalemme Liberata, Tasso celebrates both Godfrey's and Tancred's skill in warfare and heroism.

l. 44 mournful] restless [LA].

l. 55 soul is] thoughts are [LA].

l. 64 Murmuring] And breath'd [LA].

l. 70 souls] hearts [LA].

l. 71 song for Salem's shrine] *Gerusalemme Liberata,* a song for Jersualem's shrine—Christ's tomb. See especially the last canto.

ULLA, OR THE ADJURATION

First published without the epigraph in the *New Monthly Magazine* 14 (September 1825): 259–60.

Adjuration] an earnest plea.

Manfred] by Lord Byron (1817), 2.4.141–44, 149. Manfred makes this plea to the phantom of his beloved deceased sister Astarte, who has appeared to him but has so far remained silent. She responds with his name and the enigmatic assurance, "To-morrow ends thine earthly ills. Farewell!"

l. 6 spring-time] sunny [NMM].

l. 14 beetling] overhanging.

l. 27 ospray] osprey, *Pandion haliaetus,* or sea-eagle, a large bird of prey frequenting lakes and seashores and feeding on fish.

l. 38 dead—by the vows we pledg'd—arise!"] dead!—thou'rt surely of them—rise!" [NMM].

l. 42 To the arrowy] In the arrowy [NMM].

TO WORDSWORTH

Originally published under the title "To the Author of The Excursion and the Lyrical Ballads" in the *Literary Magnet* (LM), 1 new series (April 1826): 169–70 and in *The League of the Alps* (Boston, 1826): 100-101 as "To the Poet Wordsworth." Hemans enclosed this poem in a letter to Maria Jane Jewsbury which reads in part: "The inclosed lines, an effusion of deep and sincere admiration, will give you some idea of the enjoyment, and, I hope I may say, advantage, which you have been the means of imparting, by so kindly entrusting me with your precious copy of Wordsworth's Miscellaneous Poems. It has opened to me such a treasure of thought and feeling, that I shall always associate your name with some of my pleasantest recollections, as having introduced me to the knowledge of what I can only regret should have been so long a 'Yarrow unvisited.' I would not write to you sooner, because I wished to tell you that I had really *studied* these poems, and they have been the daily food of my mind ever since I borrowed them. . . . This author is the true *Poet of Home,* and of all the lofty feelings which have their root in the soil of home affections. His fine sonnets to Liberty, and indeed, all his pieces which have any reference to political interest, remind me of the spirit in which Schiller has conceived the character of William Tell, a calm, single hearted herdsman of the hills, breaking forth into fiery and indignant eloquence, when the sanctity of his hearth is invaded. Then, what power Wordsworth condenses into single lines, like Lord Byron's 'curdling a long life into one hour.'

> The still, sad music of humanity.—
> The river glideth at his own sweet will—
> Over his own sweet voice the stock-dove broods.—

And a thousand others, which we must sometime, (and I hope not a very distant one), talk over together. Many of these lines quite haunt me, and I have a strange feeling, as if I must have known them in my child-hood; they come over me so like old melodies. I can hardly speak of *favourites* among so many things that delight me, but I think 'The Nar-row Glen,' the lines on 'Corra Linn,' the 'Song for the Feast of Brougham Castle,' 'Yarrow Visited,' and 'The Cuckoo,' are among those which take hold of imagination the soonest, and recur most frequently to memory. . . . I know not how I can have so long omitted to mention the 'Ecclesiastical Sketches,' which I have read, and do constantly read with deep interest. Their beauty grows upon you and develops as you study it, like that of the old pictures by the Italian masters" (Chorley, *Memorials* 1:173–76; Hughes, "Memoir," 145–47). Wordsworth said of Hemans in his "Prefatory Note" to "Extempore Effusion upon the Death of James Hogg," (1836): "There was much sympathy between us, and, if opportunity had been allowed me to see more of her, I should have loved and valued her accordingly; as it is, I remember her with true affection. . . . ." For contemporary accounts of Hemans's visit with Wordsworth, see Hughes, "Memoir," 206–19, Chorley, *Memorials* 2:106–49, and Lawrence, *Last Autumn,* 330–33. Hemans later dedicated *Scenes and Hymns of Life* (1834) to Wordsworth. For the origi-nal, rejected dedication of this volume to Wordsworth, see Hughes, "Mem-oir," 270–72.

l. 1 strain] verse.
l. 7 calm] pure [LM].
l. 8 still] calm [LM].
   in sunny garden-bowers,] in some sweet Garden's bowers, [LM].
l. 9 vernal] summer [LM].
l. 15 There,] *There,* [LM].
l. 29 Unseen awhile they sleep—till,] Thou mov'st through nature's realm, and [LM].
l. 30 Bright] Clear [LM].

A MONARCH'S DEATH-BED

First published as the lead work in *Friendship's Offering. A Literary Album* for 1826, pp. 1–2.

The Emperor Albert of Hapsburgh] Albert I (1250?–1308), king of Germany and ruler of the Holy Roman Empire, was assassinated along the Reuss River near Brugg, Switzerland, on 1 May 1308. Hemans specifies in her original headnote that this took place "in the field afterwards called Königsfelden." See Hemans's "Gertrude, or Fidelity till Death" and "The Switzer's Wife," which concern themselves with other aspects of this event.

l. 1 on his death-bed] in his death-pangs [FO].

l. 2 censers] incense burners.

waft] breathe [FO].

l. 11 pall] dark cloth spread over a coffin.

l. 12 buckler] small round shield carried in battle.

l. 20 glazing] fading [FO].

TO THE MEMORY OF HEBER

Heber] Anglican bishop Reginald Heber (1783–1826). While a student at Brasenose College, he wrote "Palestine," considered at that time the best prize poem ever written at Oxford. He was elected a fellow of All Soul's College in 1804 and admitted to holy orders in 1807. In 1809, he married Amelia Shipley, daughter of the dean of St. Asaph, the town near where Hemans lived. Heber was appointed prebendary of St. Asaph in 1812 and not long afterward became Hemans's close friend and mentor. Harriet Hughes recalls, "Mr. Reginald Heber was the first eminent literary character with whom she [Hemans] had ever familiarly associated; and she therefore entered with a peculiar freshness of feeling into the delight inspired by his conversational powers." Hemans told a friend, "I am more delighted with Mr. Heber than I can possibly tell you; his conversation is quite rich with anecdote, and every subject on which he speaks had been, you would imagine, the sole study of his life. In short, his society has made much the same sort of impression on my mind, that the first perusal of *Ivanhoe* did; and was something so perfectly new to me, that I can hardly talk of anything else" (Hughes, "Memoir," 39). Heber advised Hemans on literary matters, including suggestions for revisions of individual poems, encouraged her to complete her five-act tragedy, *The Vespers of Palermo,* and helped her get it produced at Covent Garden in December 1823. Heber was appointed bishop of Calcutta (a diocese that included all of British India) in 1823, and worked actively as a missionary until his death in Trichinopoly on 3 April 1826. He was the author of *A Life of Bishop Jeremy Taylor* (1822) and *Narrative of a Journey Through the Upper Provinces of India* (1828) but is best remembered for his hymns, including "Holy, Holy, Holy!"

Petrarch] "Humble in so much glory" from the *Canzoniere* (126, l. 81) of Francesco Petrarca (1304–74), the Italian lyric poet and humanist, known today especially for the Petrarchan sonnet form, which Hemans admired and practiced. Her *Translations from Camoëns, and Other Poets* (1818) includes translations of two of Petrarch's sonnets.

l. 10 Hermon] the highest mountain in Syria, now called "Jebel-esh-Sheikh," rising 9,232 feet above the Mediterranean Sea. From biblical times it has been considered a sacred, inspirational place and was the site of several temples.

THE ADOPTED CHILD

First published among the "Miscellaneous Poems" in *The League of the Alps* (Boston, 1826): 132-34.

l. 19 "Oh! my] "My [LA].
l. 16 heath] turf [LA].

INVOCATION

First published under the title of "The Invocation" in the *New Monthly Magazine* 16 (June 1826): 573. T. K. Hervey asks, "What can exceed the deep, and religious, and hymn-like beauty" of "Invocation"? (*Dublin Review* 2 [December 1836]: 265).

epigraph]

Wordsworth] William Wordsworth, *The Excursion*, bk. 3, ll. 688–91 or 686–89. This epigraph, spoken by the Solitary immediately after his account of the deaths of his wife and children, did not appear in the *New Monthly Magazine* text.

l. 4 As a swift] Even as a [NMM].
l. 8 Ask that which] Ask things that [NMM].
l. 19 ye] *ye* [NMM].
l. 20 is run?] has run? [NMM].
l. 31 part] task [NMM].

KÖRNER AND HIS SISTER

Carl Theodor Körner (1791–1813) fought in the German war of liberation. In 1813, on his way through Dresden to Leipzig, he called upon the populace in his *Aufruf an die Sachsen* (Summons to the Saxons) to rise against the French. Although seriously wounded at Kitzen, he rejoined the war and was killed in a battle near Badebusch in Mecklenburg on 26 August 1813. (The date Hemans gives is incorrect.) In 1814, under the

title *Leier und Schwert* (Lyre and Sword), Körner's father, the distinguished jurist Christian Gottfried Körner (1756–1831) published his son's patriotic lyrics, for which he is best known. Hemans said that "Körner has ever been an object of peculiar enthusiasm to me; his character is one of which it is impossible to read without a feeling almost of *pain* that such a spirit has passed away, with all its high and holy thoughts, and is never to be known to us on this side [of] the grave. How mournful it seems to think of his aged father and mother surviving both their gifted children!" (Chorley, *Memorials* 1:118–19). Hemans's biographer, H. F. Chorley, considered "Körner and his Sister" "the most touching" of all her shorter lyrics and the first to show the influence of her study of German (*Memorials* 1:115–16).
headnote]

Richardson's translation of Körner's *Life and Works*] George Fleming Richardson (1796?–1848), geologist and writer, presented Hemans with an inscribed copy of his translation of *The Life of Carl Theodor Körner . . . with Selections from His Poems, Tales and Dramas* (2 vols. [London, 1827]) with a dedicatory sonnet to Hemans. As a result of this gesture, the two began a correspondence. Three of Hemans's letters to Richardson are printed in Chorley, *Memorials* 1:117–22.

Downes's *Letters from Mecklenburgh*] George Downes, *Letters from Mecklenburgh and Holstein; Comprising an Account of Hamburg and Lubeck* (London, 1822).

l. 16 vail'd] lowered (archaic); also a pun.

l. 54 farewell!] The following lines recently addressed to the author of the above, by the venerable father of Körner, who, with the mother, still survives the "Lyre, Sword, and Flower" here commemorated, may not be uninteresting to the German reader.

Wohllaut tönt aus der Ferne von freundlichen Lüften getragen,
Schmeichelt mit lindernder Kraft sich in der Trauernden Ohr,
Stärkt den erhebenden Glauben an solcher Seelen Verwandschaft,
Die zum Tempel die Brust nur für das Würdige weihn.
Aus dem Lande zu dem sich stets der gefeyerte Jüngling
Hingezogen gefühlt, wird ihm ein glänzender Lohn.
Heil dem Britischen Volke, wenn ihm das Deutsche nicht fremd ist!
Über Länder und Meer reichen sich beyde die Hand.
                    Theodor Körner's Vater. (Hemans's note.)

W. B. Chorley, in *The Lyre and Sword* (1834), translates these lines as follows:

Gently a voice from afar is borne to the ear of the mourner;
Mildly it soundeth, yet strong, grief in his bosom to soothe;

Strong in the soul-cheering faith, that hearts have a share in
  his sorrow,
In whose depths all things holy and noble are shrined.
From that land once dearly belov'd by our brave one, the fallen,
Mourning blent with bright fame—cometh a wreath for his urn.
Hail to thee, England the free! thou see'st in the German no stranger,
Over the earth and the seas, join'd be both lands, heart and hand!
                    (Reprinted in Hughes, "Memoir," 57–58)

Hemans had forwarded a copy of "Körner and his Sister" to Christian
Gottfried Körner. The poet's father translated it into German and sent it
back with thanks to Hemans. Using C. F. Richardson as an intermediary,
Hemans then sent a copy of her poem "The Death Day of Körner," in-
spired, as she said, by "reading part of a letter from Körner's father, ad-
dressed to Mr. Richardson . . . in which he speaks of 'the death-day of his
son'" (*Blackwood's Edinburgh Magazine* 22 [December 1827]: 730).
Richardson later transmitted the poem by Christian Gottfried Körner to
Hemans. She told Richardson, "'*Theodor Körner's Vater*'—It is indeed a
title beautifully expressing all the holy pride which the memory of '*Die
treuen Todten*' [the faithful Dead] must inspire, and awakening every good
and high feeling to its sound. I shall prize the lines as a relic. Will you be
kind enough to assure M. Körner, with my grateful respects, of the value
which will be attached to them, a value so greatly enhanced by their being
in his own hand. They are very beautiful, I think, in their somewhat an-
tique and *treuherzig* [true-hearted] simplicity, worthy to have proceeded
from '*Theodor Körner's Vater*'" (reprinted in Chorley, *Memorials* 1:121–
22, and Hughes, "Memoir," 57).
    See also Hemans's poem "The Grave of Körner." "The Death-Day of
Körner" was first published in *Blackwood's Edinburgh Magazine* 22 (De-
cember 1827): 730 and inserted by Hemans in the second edition of *Records
of Woman.*

THE DEATH-DAY OF KÖRNER

A song for the death-day of the brave—
    A song of pride!
The youth went down to a hero's grave,
    With the sword, his bride.

He went, with his noble heart unworn,
    And pure, and high;
An eagle stooping from clouds of morn,
    Only to die!

He went with the lyre, whose lofty tone
  Beneath his hand
Had thrill'd to the name of his God alone,
  And his Father-land.

And with all his glorious feelings yet
  In their first glow,
Like a southern stream that no frost hath met
  To chain its flow.

A song for the death-day of the brave—
  A song of pride!
For him that went to a hero's grave,
  With the sword, his bride.

He hath left a voice in his trumpet-lays
  To turn the flight,
And a guiding spirit for after days,
  Like a watch-fire's light.

And a grief in his father's soul to rest,
  Midst all high thought,
And a memory unto his mother's breast,
  With healing fraught.

And a name and fame above the blight
  Of earthly breath,
Beautiful—beautiful and bright,
  In life and death!

A song for the death-day of the brave—
  A song of pride!
For him that went to a hero's grave,
  With the sword, his bride!

AN HOUR OF ROMANCE

Francis Jeffrey said of "An Hour of Romance" that "though it has no
very distinct object or moral, [it] breathes, we think, the very spirit of
poetry, in its bright and vague picturings" (*Edinburgh Review* 50 [October 1829]: 32–47). Andrews Norton, professor at Harvard University and
editor of Hemans's authorized collected works in America, said of this
piece, "The poetry is here as beautiful as the scene described is quiet and

pleasing. It forms an amiable picture of the occupations of a contemplative mind. The language, versification, and imagery, are of great merit, the beauties of nature described by a careful observer; the English scene is placed in happy contrast with the Eastern, and the dream of romance pleasantly disturbed by the cheerfulness of life." The poem was first published, without the epigraph, in the *New Monthly Magazine* 14 (September 1825): 228–29.

epigraph]

Barry Cornwall] pseudonym of Bryan Waller Procter (1787–1874); "A Haunted Stream," st. 5, ll. 19–23.

l. 9 Of soft green] Of emerald [NMM].

l. 13 Palestine] *The Talisman—Tales of the Crusaders. (Hemans's note.)* Sir Walter Scott, *The Talisman,* in *Tales of the Crusaders,* 4 vols. (Edinburgh, 1825), vols. 3–4. According to Harriet Hughes, Hemans first read *The Talisman* in a retreat her sons called "mamma's sofa—a little grassy mound under her favourite beech-tree" at Rhyllon, a place she describes in "An Hour of Romance" (Hughes, "Memoir," 90–91). According to H. F. Chorley, this poem describes "a small woodland dingle, near Rhyllon, [which] was [Hemans's] favorite retreat: here she would spend long summer mornings to read, and project, and compose, while her children played about her. 'Whenever one of us brought her a new flower,' writes one of them, 'she was sure to introduce it into her next poem.' She has unconsciously described this haunt over and over again with affectionate distinctness; it is the scene referred to in the 'Hour of Romance,' and in a sonnet . . . printed among her 'Poetical Remains' ["To a Distant Scene," beginning "Still are the cowslips from thy bosom springing, / O far-off grassy dell?"]" (*Memorials* 1:130). See Hemans's tragedy *De Chatillon; or, the Crusaders* (1839).

l. 25 wind] breeze [NMM].

l. 35 swell'd] rang [NMM].

l. 40 faded.] vanish'd! [NMM].

l. 41 flood] world [NMM].

A VOYAGER'S DREAM OF LAND

First published in the *New Monthly Magazine* 14 (July 1825): 77–78.

epigraph]

Cowper] William Cowper (1731–1800), *The Task* (1785), bk. 1, "The Sofa," ll. 448–54.

l. 8 the olive boughs,] the wild olive-boughs, [NMM].

l. 14 roe] a species of small deer, *Capreolus capreolus,* found in parts of Europe and Asia.

l. 22 clustering vines,] wreathing vines, [NMM].

l. 23 summer-breath of the myrtle] breath of the fainting myrtle [NMM].

l. 32 cicala] cicada; a winged insect known for the shrill, chirping sound made by the male.
l. 40 call back] claim back [NMM].
l. 47 that they bear,] they wear, [NMM].

THE EFFIGIES

First published in the *New Monthly Magazine* 16 (February 1826): 192–93.
epigraph]
Goethe] Johann Wolfgang von Goethe (1749–1832), *Iphigenie auf Tauris* (1787), ll. 2067–70. Max Winkler (New York: H. Holt, 1905) translates these lines as follows:

The quick battle immortalizes a man;
If he falls, then may this song praise him.
Only the infinite tears of those who remain,
Of the dependable woman,
Are not counted in this world.

(ll. 2067–70)

Hemans told a friend, "I send my copy of *Iphigenia,* because I shall like to know whether you are as much struck with all that I have marked in it as I have been. Do you remember all we were saying on the obscurity of *female* suffering in such stormy days of the lance and spear, as the good Fray Agapida describes so vividly? Has not Goethe beautifully developed the idea in the lines which I inclose? They occur in Iphigenia's supplication to Thoas for her brother" (quoted in Hughes, "Memoir," 161). This epigraph by Goethe replaced one by James Sheridan Knowles (1784–1862) which appeared when the poem was first published in the *New Monthly Magazine:*

————Women act their parts
When they do make their ordered houses know them.
Men must be busy out of doors, must stir
The city;—yea, make the great world aware
That they are in it; for the mastery
Of which they race and wrestle.
(*Caius Gracchus: A Tragedy* (1823), 1.3.122–27)

l. 34 *Thine*] Thine [NMM].
l. 36 fast] oft [NMM].
l. 39 *Fame*] Fame [NMM].

l. 43 broider'd] embroidered.
l. 50 unguerdon'd] unrewarded.

THE LANDING OF THE PILGRIM FATHERS IN NEW ENGLAND

First published in the *New Monthly Magazine* 14 (November 1825): 402. With the same title as Daniel Webster's 1820 oration, this poem enjoyed widespread popularly in America through the end of the nineteenth century. One often-reprinted edition, illustrated by L. B. Humphrey and entitled *The Breaking Waves Dashed High,* was published by the Boston firm of Lee and Shepard beginning in 1879 and continuing throughout the 1880s.
epigraph]
   Bryant] William Cullen Bryant (1794–1878), American poet, from "The Ages" (1822), st. 32, ll. 1–4. This epigraph replaces the earlier one of the *New Monthly Magazine* text, identified only as by "An American Poet" but actually lines 11-14 of Robert Treat Paine's (1773-1811) "Ode" (1812) beginning "Wide o'er the wilderness of waves" about the founding of America.

> Their dauntless hearts no meteor led
>   In terror o'er the ocean;
> From fortune and from fame they fled
>   To Heaven and its devotion.

l. 19 sounding] surrounding [NMM].
l. 25 hoary] gray or white from age.
l. 27 there,] *there,* [NMM].
l. 39 unstain'd] undimm'd [NMM].

THE SPIRIT'S MYSTERIES

The British Library owns a fair copy manuscript of this poem in Hemans's hand, which differs slightly from the printed text.
   Childe Harold] George Gordon, Lord Byron, *Childe Harold's Pilgrimage,* canto 4 (1818), st. 23, ll. 4–9. Judging from the minor differences between the original passage and epigraph, Hemans probably recalled Byron's lines from memory.

THE DEPARTED

First published under the title "The Departure" in the *New Monthly Magazine* 17 (September 1826): 283.

epigraph]

    Bryant] William Cullen Bryant, "Thanatopsis" (1817), st. 2, ll. 3–7.

    l. 15 reck] take heed of.

    l. 21 And the beautiful, whose record] And the lovely, whose memorial [NMM].

    l. 24 love] gaze [NMM].

    l. 35 light] gleam [NMM].

    l. 45 we fear not!] we fear not now! [NMM].

THE PALM-TREE

    This incident is, I think, recorded by De Lille, in his poem of "Les Jardins." (*Hemans's note.*) The story appears in the last stanza of the second section (song 2) of Jacques J. De Lille's (1738–1813) popular *Les Jardins, ou l'Art d'embellir le paysage* (Gardens, or the art of making the landscape more attractive) (Paris, 1782).

    Francis Jeffrey called particular attention to the opening lines of *The Palm-Tree* to illustrate "the great charm and excellence in [Hemans's] imagery. . . . All her pomps have a meaning; and her flowers and her gems are arranged, as they are said to be among Eastern lovers, so as to speak the language of truth and of passion. This is peculiarly remarkable in some little pieces, which seem at first sight to be purely descriptive, but are soon found to tell upon the heart, with a deep moral and pathetic impression. . . . We scarcely meet with any striking sentiment that is not ushered in by some such symphony of external nature, and scarcely a lovely picture that does not serve as a foreground to some deep or lofty emotion" (*Edinburgh Review* 50 [October 1829]: 32–47).

    l. 9 laburnum] a small tree of the family *Leguminosae* with bright, pendulous yellow flowers in long racemes. The seeds are poisonous. On first moving to Wavertree, just outside Liverpool, shortly after the publication of *Records of Woman*, Hemans told a friend, "Do you know that I have really succeeded in giving something of beauty to the *suburban* court of my dwelling by the aid of the laburnums and rhododendrons, which I planted myself, and which I want you to see while they are so amiably flowering" (Chorley, *Memorials* 2:14–15).

THE CHILD'S LAST SLEEP

    First published in *Friendship's Offering* (1826) pp. 181–82 with the following epigraph by John Wilson:

The lovely child is dead!
All, all his innocent thoughts, like rose-leaves, scattered,
And his glad childhood nothing but a dream!

Chantrey] noted British sculptor, Sir Francis Chantrey (1781–1841). Hemans was probably asked to "illustrate" with a poem the engraving of Chantrey's "Sleeping CHild," depicting the infant daughter of Sir Thomas Ackland. "The Child and Dove" by Hemans was inspired by a Chantrey statue of Lady Louisa Russell (1818).

l. 12 from thy pale brow] o'er thy pale brow [FO].

l. 18 butterfly!] A butterfly, as if resting on a flower, is sculptured on the monument. (*Hemans's note.*)

The Sunbeam

First published in the *New Monthly Magazine* 16 (May 1826): 518.

l. 15 brakest] brokest [NMM]. "Brake" is the archaic past tense of Break."

l. 19 lattice] casement [NMM].

l. 24 smile] light [NMM].

l. 28 molten] burning [NMM].

Breathings of Spring

First published, without the epigraph, in the *New Monthly Magazine* 19 (May 1827): 457–58.

The Illuminated City

First published in the *Monthly Magazine* NS 2 (Nov. 1826): 515.

l. 37 mantle] cloak.

The Spells of Home

Bernard Barton] (1784–1849); from "Home," in *Poetic Vigils* (London, 1824), ll. 13–16. Hemans and Barton were correspondents. See Hemans's "To the Daughter of Bernard Barton, the Quaker Poet" (1839).

Roman Girl's Song

First published in the *New Monthly Magazine* 17 (October 1826): 357. Hemans's interest in what Rome had been came to be shared by her youngest son, Charles Isidore, who would later publish several books about the history, art, and architecture of Rome.

epigraph]

Roma . . . prima] Rome, Rome, Rome! / No longer as it was before.

l. 7 sceptred] invested with regal authority.

l. 23 tall] dark [NMM].
l. 43 proud] rich [NMM].
l. 45 Tiber] river in central Italy flowing through Rome to the Tyrrhenian Sea.

THE DISTANT SHIP

l. 28 weal] happiness.

THE BIRDS OF PASSAGE

First published in the *New Monthly Magazine* 16 (March 1826): 328.
l. 36 may] shall [NMM].

THE GRAVES OF A HOUSEHOLD

First published in the *New Monthly Magazine* 14 (December 1825): 534. Francis Jeffrey said of this poem that it shows "how well the graphic and pathetic may be made to set off each other" (*Edinburgh Review* 50 [October 1829]: 32–47). "The Graves of a Household" became a standard nineteenth-century anthology piece.
l. 11 his place of rest] Hemans's younger brother, Claude Scott Browne, had died in Kingston, Ontario, Canada, in 1821.
l. 15 *He*] He [NMM].
l. 20 Spain] Hemans's second published book was *England and Spain, or Valour and Patriotism* (1808), concerning the Peninsular Campaign of the Napoleonic War in which her husband and two brothers had served.
l. 25 thus they] thus, *they* [NMM].

MOZART'S REQUIEM

The Austrian composer Wolfgang Amadeus Mozart (1756–91) did not finish his famous requiem (numbered K.626), a solemn fugue which he imagined was for himself, before he died of typhoid. The mysterious stranger, whom Mozart took for a supernatural messenger of death, was an emissary of a Count Walsegg, who planned to claim the composition as his own. H. F. Chorley recalled that Hemans was "so perilously . . . excited by the composition of Mozart's Requiem, that she was prohibited by her physician from any further exercise of her art, for some weeks after it was written" (*Memorials* 1:128–29). Hemans once remarked, "I think that those who have felt and suffered much, will seek for a deeper tone in music than they can find in [Rossini]; something more spiritual and more profound, such as the soul which breathes through the strains of Mozart and Beethoven" (Chorley, *Memorials* 1:199–200).

Prophecy of Dante] (1821), by George Gordon, Lord Byron, canto 3, ll. 169–70. "Birds of Paradise" is a trope here for "great poets." The full passage reads:

For, form'd of far too penetrable stuff,
These birds of Pardise but long to flee
Back to their native mansion, soon they find
Earth's mist with their pure pinions not agree,
And die or are degraded, for the mind
Succumbs to long infection, and despair,
And vulture passions flying close behind,
Await the moment to assail and tear:
(11.168–75)

"Mozart's Requiem" was first published in the *New Monthly Magazine* 22 (April 1828): 325–26, with an epigraph from canto 4 of Byron's *Childe Harold's Pilgrimage* (1818): "Of its own beauty is the mind diseased, / And fevers into false creation" (canto 122, ll. 1–2), which this present epigraph replaced.

l. 2 its] her [NMM].
l. 38 secret] hidden [NMM].
l. 39 founts] springs [NMM].
l. 46 Shall] Will [NMM].
l. 52 fervent] solemn [NMM].

THE IMAGE IN LAVA

The impression of a woman's form, with an infant clasped to the bosom, found at the uncovering of Herculaneum. (*Hemans's note.*) Hemans substituted "Herculaneum" for "Pompeii," which appeared in this note when "The Image in Lava" was first published in the *New Monthly Magazine* 20 (September 1827): 255–56. Herculaneum, an ancient city of about five thousand inhabitants in Italy near Naples, was destroyed in 79 A.D., along with Stabiae and Pompeii, when Mount Vesuvius erupted. Excavation of Herculaneum began in the eighteenth century, and much was found perfectly preserved under more than fifty feet of ash and lava. Plaster casts were made of some of the human forms whose images the lava preserved.

l. 13 brightly] calmly [NMM].
l. 28 on which] whereon [NMM].

THE LAST WISH

Lights and Shadows] John Wilson, *Lights and Shadows of Scottish Life: A Selection from the Papers of the Late Arthur Austin* (Edinburgh:

William Blackwood, 1822), from the fifth tale, "Sunset and Sunrise." These lines are spoken by Anna, an Englishwoman, to her Scottish husband as they watch the sunset. Anna dies later that night in childbirth. The full passage reads, "Well may I weep to leave this world—thee—my parents—the rooms in which, for a year of perfect bliss, I have walked, sat, or slept in thy bosom—all these beautiful woods, and plains, and hills, which I have begun to feel every day more and more as belonging unto me, because I am thy wife" (pp. 56–57).

FAIRY FAVOURS

Hemans told a correspondent, "I am so glad you liked 'Fairy Favours.' It is, indeed, filled with my own true and ever yearning feeling; that longing for more affection, more confidence, more entire interchange of thought, than I am ever likely to meet with" (Hughes, "Memoir," 134–35). "Fairy Favours" was first published in the *New Monthly Magazine* 20 (December 1827): 544, with the following epigraph from Bryan Waller Procter, pseud. "Barry Cornwall" (1787–1874): "————Let there be / A something on this visible Globe that may / Have leave to love me; something I may love" (*Werner,* sc. 2, ll. 116–18).
    l. 5 spoiler] robber; ravager.
    l. 11 should] could [NMM].
    l. 15 shore] cave [NMM].
    l. 16 fetch] bring [NMM].
    l. 22 turn] grow [NMM].
    l. 37 boon] gift [NMM].
    ll. 39–40 Thou scornest the treasures of wave and mine, / Thou wilt not drink of the cup divine,] Thou wilt not drink of the cup divine, / Thou scornest the treasures of wave or mine; [NMM].
    l. 43 Oh! give] Give [NMM].
    l. 48 Bid the bright calm] Oh! bid the calm [NMM].

A PARTING SONG

"A Parting Song" should not be confused with Hemans's similarly titled poem "The Parting Song," first published in the *New Monthly Magazine* 13 (April 1825): 395–96, later retitled "Greek Parting Song" and beginning "A youth went forth to exile."
epigraph]
    Corinne] "Oh! my friends, remember my verse sometimes; my soul is imprinted there." "Oh! mes Amis" does not appear in the original French text of de Staël's *Corinne ou L'Italie* (1807), bk. 20, chap. 5, "Dernier chant de Corinne" (Corrine's last song). Hemans told a friend, "Do you know the *Dernier chant de Corinne?* I sent it, marked in the third volume

of the book, and you shall have the others if you wish. If the soul, without the form, be enough to constitute poetry, then it surely is poetry of the very highest order" (Hughes, "Memoir," 160). On another occasion, Hemans said of *Corinne*, "That book, in particular towards its close, has a power over me which is quite indescribable. Some passages seem to give me back my own thoughts and feelings, my whole inner being, with a mirror more true than ever friend could hold up" (Hughes, "Memoir," 160). Hemans wrote "*C'est moi*" in her own copy of this novel after the following passage: "De toutes mes facultés la plus puissante est la faculté de souffrir. Je suis née pour le bonheur, mon caractère est confiant, mon imagination est animée; mais la peine excite en moi je ne sais quelle impétuosité qui peut troubler ma raison, ou me donner de la mort. Je vous le répète encore, ménagez-moi; la gaieté, la mobilité ne me servent qu'en apparence: mais il y a dans mon âme des abîmes de tristesse dont je ne pouvais me défendre qu'en me préservant de l'amour." (Of all my faculties, the most powerful is the faculty of suffering. I was born for happiness, my character is confidant, my imagination is animated; but sorrow excites in me impetuosity that troubles my mind or drives me to death. I repeat, take care of me; gaiety, animation is only a facade; but in my soul are abysses of sadness from which I am only able to protect myself by preserving love.) (Chorley, *Memorials* 1:304). See also Hemans's poem "Corinne at the Capitol."

Index of First Lines